BIG SKIES & COW PIES

Building a Home and Family in Montana

© 2005 Pennie Wise
All Rights Reserved.

No part of this publication may be reproduced, stored in a retrieval system, or transmitted, in any form or by any means, electronic, mechanical, photocopying, recording, or otherwise, without the written permission of the author.

First published by Dog Ear Publishing
4010 W. 86th Street, Ste H
Indianapolis, IN 46268
www.dogearpublishing.net

ISBN:0-9762173-5-X

This book is printed on acid-free paper.

Printed in the United States of America

BIG SKIES & COW PIES

Building a Home and Family in Montana

Written from the journals of
Pennie Wise
Artwork by Nathan Wise

Forward & Dedication

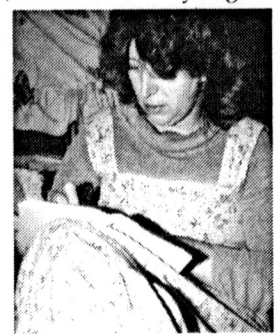

I've never been accused of speaking perfect English, and I'm sure any English teacher will cringe at my grammar and usage in this book; but in my defense, the pages you will read have been directly transcribed from my journals wherein I freely expressed my thoughts, feelings, and the days events with little regard for English rules of grammar and usage.

So please enjoy reading the book as it is, and know it's written as it was lived. I thank the Lord that He's blessed me to be able to have preserved some of my experiences for my family and my posterity.

I dedicate this book:
To my Family who went through this whole mess with me; Especially Bill, for always being there for me. And the closeness we developed through hard times.

To my kids for keeping me on the straight and narrow, for giving me so much love, encouraging me, and for always thinking that things weren't that bad and always looking for the good.

All the People in our little community Drummond, for encouraging me to write this book and helping me get it to the publisher (Kathleen) and my son Nate for helping with the Technology end of this.

Especially all my Friends... I couldn't have done it without your love, friendship, and assistance when we really needed it.

To Luckie and Terrie for helping us when things seemed like we would never make it, they were always there to give us encouragement and love.

To my Grand kids, who I love so much, all eleven of them, what a joy they are to our life; in all the trials that are facing me and things that depress me, my grandkids are the best; No one makes me feel better or smile more.

Table of Contents

Chapter 1	Craziness Begins.	4
Chapter 2	Dumb Dora & Building the house.	17
Chapter 3	Frozen Limbo& I Hate mices to Pieces	33
Chapter 4	Stepping back in time	47
Chapter 5	Blessings and Animals	58
Chapter 6	Brrr it's Cold	69
Chapter 7	Don't open the door! Crawl	83
Chapter 8	My Dream House?	88
Chapter 9	Insanity sets in	94
Chapter 10	Is This Everyday Life?	109
Chapter 11	Logging	121
Chapter 12	Living with Poverty	126
Chapter 13	Cool Clear Water	136
Chapter 14	Life in the Country	145
Chapter 15	Cats and Bad Luck	162
Chapter 16	Trials and Survival	174
Chapter 17	Poverty and Pain	199
Chapter 18	Something New	210
Chapter 19	Ranching Moo Moo & Manure	217
Chapter 20	Adversity and Blessings	221
Chapter 21	Trip to hell and Back Scouts	227
Chapter 22	Yellowstone on 100 bucks	237
Chapter 23	Hard times and Good Fairies	243
Chapter 24	Chimney Fire and Bats	252
Chapter 25	Chubby and Wrecker Bait	258
Chapter 26	Rattle Rattle Crash Beep Beep	265
Chapter 27	Bad Smells	271
Chapter 28	Cover your eyes.	276
Chapter 29	Is this the End?	279
Afterward		285

© Copyright 2004, Pennie Wise
All rights reserved.
No part of this book may be reproduced, stored in a retrieval system, or transmitted by any means, electronic, mechanical, photocopying, recording, or otherwise, without written permission from the author

Chapter 1
Craziness Begins

What are we doing here? I ask myself, Montana is such a pretty place. But it's not for everyone. Montana seems to not welcome everyone with a smile; yes the place is beautiful, beyond comprehension. It is like some of the obstacles in Sinbad, or the Odyssey. You never quite know what is waiting around the next corner. I grew up in Montana, but when you're a child nothing seems to bother you, if the snow is above your head, just make snow forts. If there are rattlers on the doorstep, go out the other door.

Montana seems to get in your blood, and you have this desire to return. The Big Sky, wooded mountains, and people, not many of them, but the ones that are here, are unusually nice. They will do anything for you, if you're a hard worker and add to the community spirit. Bill and I moved to Montana on June 2, 1978 this is when our life changed forever...

We lived in Utah, both of us had government jobs, Bill at Hill Air force Base, and I worked at IRS full-time, making really good money compared to others. We had a sports car, a custom van, went out every weekend, life seemed to be great. But we weren't happy. I don't know what really triggered the escape to the mountains, but we both agreed our lives needed something different. Our marriage was struggling and the stress of the city and government jobs was more than both of us needed at the time.

I guess I really do know what started all this: selfishness, drinking, and parties. Not living the way we should, not communicating. Our Marriage was on the rocks. I knew that we had to do something to get away from the friends and drinking buddies Bill had if we had any chance at all.

I had grown up in Montana when I was a little girl. I loved the place, even though I had a lot of heartache there, my mother dying from a drunk driver, living with only one parent. But there was still something that was calling me back to the big skies of Montana. I know that we were being guided there, to help Bill and me and our little family to start a new life. I just never dreamed it would be so hard...

We made a trip to Missoula, Montana to visit my brother, Luckie, who had moved up near my Aunt Elaine a year earlier. That did it. The country was beautiful. We went around to log house companies and decided that we could build a log house. After all Bill had built one of those tree house swing sets, we could surely handle a Lincoln log set in large size. We must have had some of that wacky weed left over from the early 70's, because how could we think like that? We could live in pure simplicity forever after. We had savings that we could use for building the house; we had all the answers.

We bought 8 acres from an old rancher, a relative of sorts, 2 acres of plush bottomland and 6 acres of mountain. The view was fantastic as we hiked up to the knoll where we planned to change our lives. I was huffing and puffing part way up as I maneuvered step by step up the steep grade, winding up the mountain to the knoll at the top. I looked over the valley, so quiet and serene. Beautiful fields of hay lay before us, the Clark Fork River winding around the small valley, cottonwood trees, pine trees, and willows added to the beauty. Where I was standing was treeless, but this would be a great place for a house, and we could sit out on our porch and enjoy the Montana Big Skies... Oh just think of it.

This was early fall. A skiff of snow lay on the ground. It was beautiful. We were so excited; our dream was going to come true.

Now to return home, quit our jobs, sell our home, Bill will graduate from college in June and make a new life, we are set. If we had only known what lay ahead, we would have firmly planted our feet and been fat and happy in Utah, as boring little government workers, 7 to 4 jobs, weekends off, paid holidays and sick leave.

Oh what foolish people we can be, or how lucky we are that we made this choice to bring kids, our marriage and ourselves together forever. I sit on the floor of my home in Utah and think back of when I first entered in this little dollhouse.

MY FIRST HOME....

Have you ever thought what your first house would look like? A Doll House, just so, everything new. But it seems, your first house can never be that way, because you're young and flat broke; you have to make a can of Campbell's soup into a 7 coarse meal. Well my first house on first impression wasn't what I would call a dollhouse.

FIRST LOOK...
"Come on Honey," Bill said; "Ken, my dad's friend, wants to show us a house."

"A house what do you mean? Look at my hair!"

"Oh, come on, the house won't care". So we met Ken and jumped into his car.

"I'm real excited for you kids this house is a real steal."

We drove up onto the foothills. "Gee," I thought to myself, "my old girlfriend lived up here.
I always thought these houses were duds, oh well maybe, it's nice."

We then turned on Taylor. I looked at the houses. As we passed, I saw a yellow brick one that stood out like a sore thumb. "Boy, I hope that's not it," I said to myself just as the car pulled up in front of it and stopped.

"Well, here it is," says Ken. Oh my, what a disappointment. Oh well we can look at it but this isn't going to be ours...

We walked up a cracked driveway and stepped over garbage piled out of the back door. "Excuse, the mess kids," Ken said, "They've been fixing up the place."

I walked into a blue turquoise kitchen. "Fixing up" I thought, the whole house looked like they had a sale on cheap paint. Old brown rugs and red and white stripped curtains helped everything to convince me more and more that it had to get better down stairs. But as we walked down so did the looks of the place. If you've never seen fake knotty pine wall board, you're not missing anything...

Bill wasn't saying much. I could hardly wait to get out of the place.

"How much did you say they wanted?" Bill asked.

"15,300 dollars."

"Huh well, we'll take it."

My mouth dropped open. "What do you mean take it, this house?"

Bill just gave me the look of, hush woman; I know what I'm doing. I was crushed as we drove away, the proud new owners of a house I Hated...

MOVING...

"The memories in this little house are so many," I thought to myself as I packed our last box to move... Sitting down to think back and looking around, the blue turquoise paint was covered with 4 gallons of white paint. And the red and white curtains were used for rags. "Gee, I hate to leave you," as I sat on the floor in my cozy kitchen. Everyone always commented on how cute our house was and how ever did we find it? (Little did they know.)

But I love this little house. It's lived our lives with us, for almost 8 years, been through three rug rats and 2 dogs, wild parties, and visiting teachers. Boy if these walls could talk... A beginning life of a little family – Dustin walking, Nathan sticking his head into the frosting bowl, Tiffany coloring on every wall in the house. I think old 716 Taylor will miss this little family, as much as we'll miss it. But there will always be that special spot in my heart for our first house, that I hated the first time I walked in, and loved and cried as I closed the doors for the last time behind me, never to enter back into the history of our lives. Take good care, we love you...

PACKING THE U-HAUL...

The normal routine for all U-Haul idiots – First you go to the Company and sign away your life. They put you in some huge truck, as big as some semi's that you are supposed to maneuver down some back street and up a steep driveway so you can load it. Okay, after a few attempts, and yelling at the wife, a few flattened garbage cans, tree limbs now missing or hanging from the top of the truck, if we're lucky they are not sticking through the truck, but we are finally here.

What an adventure! They named the company right. If you haven't packed a U-haul you haven't had the ultimate adventure, in stress, management, marriage survival, and the list goes on. You start by pulling everything you have ever collected in your life and stuff it in any sort of container you can find, preferably liquor boxes, they are heavy and hold a variety of things. Things that soon you will learn to live without and wonder why you packed this stuff. Yes, Stuff. What a name for the stuff. You stuff it here and you stuff it there. Shall I put this stuff on the counter, or where? How we can collect so much stuff. It stuffs our home; it makes our life miserable if we don't have enough stuff, we can't live without the stuff. If you find a box you are carrying out and one says misc. just throw it in the trash, if it isn't important enough to have a name or place, chuck the whole thing because you probably won't miss the stuff anyway.

Now get all your friends, relatives and whomever else you can con to break their backs and ruin their Saturday to help you pack everything out in the yard, and up into a huge truck that you know you will never fill. As you load furniture, beds, fridge, stove, tables and boxes, blankets, more boxes, the truck gets smaller. The door is coming closer and the stuff on the lawn seems to be growing not shrinking.

We have to pull half the furniture out and repack, turning tables sideways or upside-down, shoving trikes and whatever in every cubbyhole we can find. How did we ever gather this much junk?

This is when you start gleaning, and deciding that maybe the Salvation Army needs this stuff more than you... This is when you learn that you don't need the old exercise bike, the abs buster that still has plastic on it, the glamour stretcher still hooked to the doorknob, the exercise blow up pants and the old size 9 pants that you haven't fit your chubby butt in for the past 5 years. Toys, trikes and bikes. Let's see, here is a GI Joe tower and Barbie town house that is almost as big as I am. Okay no room. Some lucky kid and poor mom will have a great find. We can't get another thing in. People are tired, the liquid refreshment is now empty cans on the lawn, and the night is approaching. Finally the U-haul is packed tight to the doors and two cars with all our worldly possessions; we are ready to start a new and exciting life.

OUT OF GAS...

The road seemed to go forever. I drift into thinking about different things in our life when the kids say, "Mom, you just passed Dad, and he's broke down."

I pull over and get out. The gas hog truck wouldn't make it from one city to the next. I think everyone that has ever rented a U-haul, Ryder, or any other moving truck has a break down story. I think it is in the contract. And you have to sign it, and only guess what is in store for you!
It's not like there is a gas station on every corner.

I have to go ahead and go finagle a gas can from the first station I found. You ask how do you do that? Well, you drag out your three kids, bring them in the station, and have them stand there with a pitiful look on their face. One cries that she wants her dad who is left out on the highway, what are we going to do? The man can hardly wait to get rid of you and send you down the road with a gas can and his blessings.

Back on the road again, the kids asleep, the hours seem to creep by. Once more the ole gas gauge is leaning on the E. but this time we are in the middle of "nowhere pass". It is dark and late, everything is closed down. I pull over and say to Bill, "What are we going to do now?" He looks at me and says, "We are going to pull into the next gas station that we see, closed or open and get some gas."

I thought, "sure thing buddy, are we going to turn into Bonnie and Clyde or what?" Then I think, "Okay, go ahead and try."

A few miles down the road was an old roadside grocery/gas station with an old house in the back. Bill pulls to a stop, and says, "Go back to that house back there and knock on the door and ask the people if they could open and get us some gas?"

"You have to be crazy. Why do I have to do it, and not you?"

"Because, you look more wholesome then I do, and the people will talk to you or at least not shoot you!"

I crawled out of the car; the kids all sleeping or I would have made them make the trek with me, safety in numbers you know.

A huge dog was barking as I entered the gate, and quietly closed it behind me. The house seemed forever down a long sidewalk. I knew any moment I would hear a voice that said: Sick her Killer! Or a barrel of a Shotgun comes out of the screen at me. I could see the flickering of a TV through the window.

I knocked on the wooden screen door. A gruff voice said, "Go away!"

"Excuse me sir," I said, "but I'm in a world of hurt here."

A chubby ole guy comes to the door, pants and an ole T-shirt that doesn't cover all his stomach. I start to stutter as he approaches. He has a mean look on his face, and you could tell that he had been through this before.

"When I'm closed, I'm closed!"

"Well, sir I know, but see I have 3 little kids in the car asleep, and trying to get to my sister's," and before I could finish out the door he came.

"How many little ones?" He had his shirt on and slippers and was walking down the sidewalk with me.

"Just have to screen the tough ones you know honey, if you're brave enough to walk back here with that dog of mine, you must need gas awful bad, and if he didn't rip you apart by now, he's a good judge of character."

My heart fell to my knees. "I thought the dog was chained up not running loose."

"Oh no, what good is a dog if you chain him up?"

I swallow hard; there standing by him was a huge ugly dog, mangy and showing yellow unbrushed teeth. The guy pats his dog's nose and tells him to go lay down and the dog wanders off. He gets to the station turns on the pump and starts to fill our truck with gas, without any lights on. "Can't turn lights on, don't need riff raff you know."

We explain that we were from Utah and gas stations are around every corner and open at all hours of the night.

"Well get a clue," he says, "you're not in Kansas anymore girlie, Montanans do what they want and if I want to go to bed early I shut her down."

We pay for the gas, and he gives us his blessings and a cussing out for letting our truck get empty with 3 little kids.

I smiled and thanked him once more and said to Bill, "next time you're going to get eaten by killer! Because I'm not going."

He just laughed and thanked me for going. "We would have never gotten any gas if I would have gone and you know it!" We laughed and went on down the road to our new home.

Drummond Exit, finally! As we pull into this small town we were wondering what are we doing here?

Three streets made up the town, The Main street had buildings just down one side, and it seemed like it hadn't changed with time. The buildings were old, and run down, 3 bars lined one side of the town, 3 gas stations, 3 motels, and 1 ½ grocery stores. We were in booming metropolis now. An old railroad station sat in the middle of town along with a old water tower for the trains that were now long gone. The fast freight trains now don't even slow down for the big tower that stands ominous in the middle of town. At one end is a Bull shipping yard so as you enter you are reminded of where you are by the aroma that fills the air

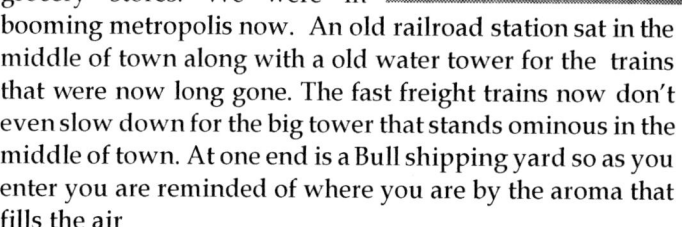

8 more miles and we pull into what we call our new home.

Wise Acres

The mountain seemed different, than when we saw it in the winter, all covered with snow. Now we could see exactly what we bought, A mountain of rocks. Now to make the best of the situation, okay let's look at this objectively. We can plant trees and make a beautiful yard; the view from our mountain is breathtaking, as we look over the Clark Fork River, and the valley that spreads for

miles before us. Trees cover the mountains all around us just not where we decided to build our home No wonder we got a good deal. I think it could be a rock quarry. No road up to where we were going to build the house. So this little fat body has to hike, a new word for my vocabulary. And one I will learn to hate, and know if I don't I WILL DIE. As we walk up to our new home, which is a tent later in the evening or early in the morning, deer scatter as they have bedded down where we are going to put our home. They don't make a sound we can just hear the shuffle of the rocks moving as they bound up the mountain away from us.

Bill is excited, he pitches our family tent and says, "Well kids, this is where we're going to live until the house is built."

"Just for the summer!" I said. "Wait a minute Bill, What is the gulch next to us called? Rattler. There has to be a reason for that, wouldn't you say?" I lived here most of my young life and I know about Rattlers, they cozy up to anything warm on a cool summer night, and in Montana there are always cool summer nights, so this idea didn't sound too good to this citified mom. This little fat body is not living in a tent on this snake-infested mountain.

Oh yes, we have rattlers too. Rocks and Rattlers, Each time I entered the tent, I would do a dance on any humps that I saw on the floor, knowing it was one of those little hummers waiting to bite my kids and me. They would pay dearly first, being smashed by my snake dance. I don't know what I would have done if one of those humps would have slithered off. I probably would have had a heart attack. Then the volunteer ambulance would have to hike this mountain to get me. Oh I'm doomed.

RATTLE RATTLE

The first little while on the mountain, we would be working and we would hear the familiar rattle. Stop and look and then move back for there was the snake curled up and defending his territory. When you have 3 kids 7, 6, and 4 running around, rattlers are the last thing you want. I grew up in Montana but snakes I hate. These babies were poisonous and could hurt my kids. So if they wanted to live, they had better move out of my territory, because I just took over with a shovel and .357 mag. Now it's easy to shoot a rattler. First you get out the rifle, I had both pistol and rifle but a rifle was a little safer when I had to start waving the thing in front of a nose of a poisonous snake, like yuk!! And start moving it back and forth; the snake will keep its eye on that barrel then you fire. They die.

Sure this all sounds good until the fateful day comes that you really have to face a rattler, just you and him as he coils up 8 to 10 ft from you. You're going about your business, carrying in boxes when you hear that rattle, the rattle that sounds like nothing else. It sends a cold chill up your spine. As you spin around to see where the warning is coming from, there on the rocks is a rattler 3 to 4 ft long with 8 buttons, and rising up coiled and ready to strike. His eyes watch every move you make.

Now I don't want any part of this varmint, but dang it he's in my territory now, and I have little kids, so the battle begins. Of course I don't have a .357 when I need it, just a trusty BB gun, to ward off cats (in the mood let's say). Anyway, grab the one step up from Red Ryder BB gun and pump her up, one, two three, pumps. As I stand there, the snake senses this isn't going to be pretty, so he raises high in striking position, his tongue flickering and his tail moving so fast that you can't see it move, just the rattle that is deafening. I'm shaking as I lower the gun point it to its head, and fire, the snake drops for an instant, and then rises again this time with its mouth open and trying to bite anything close, blood is dripping from the snake's head. He follows closely each movement I make. Once more I shoot the gun, but it won't work the BB is caught in the chamber. I go and get a shovel.

The real country girl has to come out sooner or later. Now if you know me, I can't even have a rubber snake any where near me. I won't even pick one up in the store, I freak. So here I sit face to face with a deadly enemy, He had just eaten a mouse or something so he couldn't move to crawl off so he stood his ground. He followed my every movement. If I circled behind him his eyes never left me, every move I made he followed, back and forth he moved. I was almost amazed at the way he moved, and studied my every move.

I took the shovel and stood as far back as the shovel handle would allow and he struck the blade. He had way too much life for me to come any closer. I have to even the score a little bit more than it was so I hit him on the head. That didn't do him any good. As he lay down away from striking position, I went in for the kill. I took the tool and placed it just behind the head, and it took all my might to push and cut at his neck and body. He squirmed and tried to bite, turning and flaying every which way but I wouldn't let up, not until the head was destroyed, but the body kept moving. I would touch it and it would coil and move and roll as if it didn't want to give up, but his head was gone.

I left it so Bill could see, strong wife, big Snake killer, defender of children, besides I was sick to my stomach. I had enough of the snake. I sure didn't want to give him burial rights. You have to bury the head so the hornets don't eat the poison part of the head; then they become more infectious when they sting. I don't know if that is true, but as many times as I get stung with hornets and yellow jackets around here I don't want to chance it, if it's a wife's tale or not. I told Bill that the snake was moving for almost an hour later and he said don't you know that a snake won't die until sun down. I cringed and hoped that he was pulling my leg.

It takes a while for rattlers to get the message that we are taking over their territory. The kids learned to carry a stick with them as they hiked over the mountains and gulches. Tiffany was running over to the river, and felt a sharp jab; she thought it was a stick or sharp weed that hit her on the side of the foot. She heard the rattle, but in the summer the clapping of the hundreds of grasshopper' wings make that crazy buzz, and when you're young you know it's just another bug. No big deal.

But as evening drew near and she wasn't feeling well and her leg swelled twice its size to her thigh, we decided to look at her foot, sure enough there were 2 small puncture wounds. We took her to the doctor and they said that she had been bitten but it was a dry bite and had just grazed her. Just telling her to beware, and I don't want to hurt you. The doctor cleaned the area well and told her to be more careful and she was very lucky.

Once more Tiffany comes in contact with the dreaded Rattler. She is playing outside and is chasing her cat around, when her cat stops and rares back. Tiffany bends over to pick it up and there coiled up and rattling is a 3 ft rattler. Tiffany is face to face with a rattler ready to strike. What a blessing that the cat had its attention so that she could back up slowly and leave the cat standing his ground. She then runs up stairs and hides in her room, after a while she calls down to Uncle Luckie to come up and kill the rattler under the porch. He comes up to find this huge snake, takes the gun and one less rattler on our mountain. You know we really don't want to kill them but when they come into my territory, I say, "do not tread on my land or you will end up a hatband sneaky snake."

BUILDING A ROAD SO I DON'T HAVE TO HIKE

We had to get a cat (to those of you that don't know, its not the meow kind, but the caterpillar kind) to plow our road. Or at least make a trail up the mountain, to where our house was one day going to sit.

Our Uncle George worked for a logging company, so he asked them if he could bring the cat over to make us a road.

When they moved it past our house to log the mountain behind us, the big yellow beast showed up early on a Saturday morning. No one can sleep when one of those D8's fire up and start to rip at the mountain. Smoke bellowed out of the stack, as the big tracks turned and rattled up a steep grade. He makes a turn, and climbs again. There is no way that we can get up this mountain without having a few turns in the road, to mellow out the grade. Back and forth he worked. After a few hours, we could see a road that lead to the top of our Wiseacres and the little knoll that we were going to call home.

Now the road was there, Bill says that we have to go and pick rocks. If you could see this road and the rocks that covered it, there is no way that we can pick up these puppies to make a difference. But the Wise family is doing it; Dustin 7, Nathan 6 and Tiffany 4, me a city girl, and Bill. (Who knows if he stays on us, this house and mountain will one day be Wiseacres.) Back and forth we go up and down the mountain. The June sun is hot and the mountain steep, It's hard to bend and throw, bend and throw. Some rocks are so heavy that you can hardly move them and the ones that look small, the other two thirds, are buried just beneath the surface.

The kids are hot and tired, and Mom has been complaining for a long time. This is not fun. I.R.S. beats this any day, a nice desk, coffee breaks, and air conditioning. What have we done???

Tent life was wearing thin, if it wasn't hot, it was down right cold, and rainy. Here in Montana they have a saying: "If you don't like the weather wait 5 minutes, it will change." It is true, everywhere you go, you better be prepared for change. The nights are cold, you have to wear layers in your sleeping bags, and the ground is harder than I want to tell you. NO I want you to know how miserable I was. I lay in the double sleeping bag so tired, from the day's hard work, but I can't get comfortable. The kids are sleeping around us, except our daughter, she always needed to be right between us, so that put me on the outside tugging for more covers, and just winding up in a ball with the zipper stuck in my night clothes. My nose freezing, my ears ready to fall off, and then not to mention the mosquitoes!! Those buggers will carry you off, let alone the constant buzzing as they dive bomb for you. You can hear them zero in on you, as the high-pitched hmmm gets closer and closer, and then you slap yourself, Whap! Only to hear the buzz again. So you have to bury your head in the sleeping bag. We have had no water, so showering is not as frequent as we're used to. Putting your head under the covers is not a pleasant experience.

At times we would raid my brother's house and use a real bathroom, but most times the river was our family bath place. No running Hot water here. Cold, let's say frigid water, so cold that when you get your head wet, it makes your head ache. The river is right next to a road where we bathe. There is a brief hole in the trees that those passing by could get a glimpse of what was going on but by the time they noticed they had to shake their head and deny they even thought they saw anything. There is a warm springs down the road but its right by the freeway and too deep for little kids. It has a cave you swim to underwater and a real hit with the young crowd. But we stick to the river. Our kids love it and another good thing, it closes your pores.

Chapter 2
Dumb Dora...
And Building the House

I finally put my foot down. I had enough. I'm going to find us a home. Luckie and Terrie live in comfort; George and Elaine, Jean and Bob, everyone but us. I want something I can go inside and shut the door, not tie a tie, or zip a zipper, and sit or lay somewhat off the ground, something with substance.

I woke up early on a Monday morning, got the *Missoulian*, and decided I was going to find us a home, But one catch, it couldn't cost very much, we hadn't sold our house in Utah yet, and the little retirement that Bill and I had was going fast. We had to have over a thousand dollars to dig a well, have someone witch it, not the flying kind, but....

That is where a guy comes out with a fishing pole and a vile of water. When the pole starts bouncing, it will tell you how deep the water is and how much water is there. Then you mark the spot and hope your water witcher is right, because once they punch a hole and start to drill and they don't hit water you pay anyway, for however many feet they drill at $18.00 a foot.

So we trusted Charlie, a logger from the valley. He said that we had all kinds of water – surface water around 20 to 30 ft and second water around 60 ft. Sixty times 18 is 1,080 dollars, not counting pump, water line, and digging a 5 ft trench straight up a mountain. The water line will freeze in winter unless it's buried in a 5 ft trench. You better do all that it requires, and all the other crazy things that it takes to get you started in this wilderness. I'm so used to walking in and turning on a facet and knowing water is going to be there, but not so in Montana. Wells, everyone has to have one, we have no central water company that you can yell at for not having your water on. How depressing, the money is going fast, and I have to have a place to live, the tent is going to cause more grief than I want. So I'm going to find a deal....

Dumb Dora, Delightful Dora, or get me the Hell out of here...

This is a picture of Bill with Dumb Dora, and our old truck that worked so hard with us on the house. (What a dream home huh?)

I found the *Missoulian* and quickly went to the classified ads, looking under camper trailers, trailers and any other moveable home I could replace a tent for.

The dollar amounts were astounding to me. How can these people ask so much for a 20-ft trailer, nothing under 2,000 dollars? I go much larger but the price just seemed to climb with the length of the home. What are we going to do? I couldn't take the tent much longer. All of a sudden my eyes caught a glimpse of "a cozy trailer home priced right for you $799.00. 35 ft of pure joy, I Phone for directions." I couldn't believe my luck. 8x35 it will seem like a mansion, wood-burning stove, shower, and civilization here we come.

I called the lady that owned the trailer and she gave me directions to my great find. Terrie and I jumped in the van and headed for parts unknown. To the back mountains of Montana, over the river, up a steep mountain then down into a field. Where in the heck is it?

"It's probably that ugly blue thing down there," I say to Terrie.

"Oh, it can't be that bad," says Terrie.

Sure enough it was the ugly duckling, an old 1952 Blue relic. I felt like I was stepping back in time, and we had already done that coming to Montana. My child hood flashed before my eyes, the louvered windows in the door, Oxidized blue, and silver. And an old log slab was the front step.

Terrie looked at me, and said, "You're not thinking of going up to that door, are you?"

"Yes," I said, "it has real possibility."

I was shaking as I approached the door. It looked like a place some criminal would hide out in until he found his next victim to come buy a trailer. Woe is me....

I quietly knocked on the door. A little girl answered.

"Mom, there is someone here."

She was barefoot, and wearing a dress that was way too large for her frail frame, her hair was tangled, and unkempt, but it was clean. She smiled at me with a toothless grin and yelled for her mother once more. All of a sudden a hand grabbed the little girl into the house. And once more I was standing there alone, wondering what to do.

Then a woman appeared holding a little baby. "What can I do for you?"

"I came to look at the trailer you advertised."

"Oh it's you," she replies, "you never know anymore; we don't get much company around here."

"Well dah," I thought. "Why would you? You have to have Bloodhounds to find the place, and when you did, you wonder why the heck you came in the first place."

I reluctantly entered the small doorway. Just adjacent to the door, was a wood stove about 10 inches wide and 2 ft long, it had fake brick behind it, as it was nestled up next to a small closet. The front room was surrounded by 3 windows – side, side and front. The sun blazed in on the dingy floor covered with kitchen carpeting that was so dirty it looked like it had been in the Tide test kitchen and never got its turn in the washer; the walls were covered with a dirty film. Tattered furniture, what you could call furniture was sparely spread around the room. A recliner without legs and a large pillow lay on the floor. A ladder adorned a corner of the front room.

"That's the kid's beds up there," she said as she points to a makeshift bed over the top of a front window. As we turned, not stepped, we were in the kitchen. It had a small propane stove, red cupboard tops, a little fridge and one big sink. A small bench sat over the wheel wells, and a board that was propped up with a 2x4, was the dining room table.

We stepped to the back, not more than 2 steps and there laying in a bed that took up the whole room was a burly guy, snoring.

"Jim," she shakes the bed. "These ladies our here to see the place, do you mind?"

"He's a logger; you know, they have to go to bed early, cause they leave before the sun comes up."

She opened the only closet located in the back, and then I hated to ask, "Does this place have a bathroom?"

"Sure, a nice one."

She opened the door beside me. I couldn't believe my eyes. I didn't think they could shove so much into such small tiny space. A tin shower that I wasn't sure would fit my chunky body, a miniature toilet and sink, and even room for a trusty plunger.

"Well you have seen it all," she says as she ushers us out into the front room and soon out the door.

"How much do you want?"

Terrie is pulling on my sleeve. "Lets leave, and we haven't been vaccinated lately," she says under her breath.

The lady doesn't hesitate, "$800.00"

"Well it's the best I've seen for the money, and I'm too tight to spend more. Bill isn't here, he will just have to trust my judgment. This is a real fixer upper." I paid the lady $800.00 and left.

Terrie shakes her head, "I don't think the guys are going to like this."

"I don't care," I said. "I made a decision, it's better than that snake-infested tent. It's going to be nice." I try to convince myself as we drive off.

GETTING DUMB DORA ...

I was excited that I had made a decision in the wilderness of Montana. I was a proud new owner of a broke down, 1952 United trailer with old dirty paneling and contact paper peeling off the walls, and the smell, I wasn't sure what it was. Won't Bill be thrilled?

I tried to explain to the guys, where this great find was, and that it would be no problem getting it hauled to Drummond a good 70 miles away. I was wrong. The tires were rotten, and the old logging road was a real adventure for the guys. Bill took my brother Lucky, to haul the trailer back. They could find anything anywhere. And if it could be moved, leave it to those two it would be moved, maybe not in one piece. But it would be moved.

I anxiously waited for the blue bomber to round the mountain and come up the hill. Hours started to haunt me. What has happened? Maybe they got in a wreck, for they went to get it in a pick up truck and it's an 8x35 ft piece of workmanship. NOT....

Finally I see this blue and silver blur coming up the mountain, I couldn't believe my eyes. There on top of the trailer was a cinder block.

"Well did you see anyone?"

"NO," the guys said. "We were hoping they weren't inside sleeping cause we didn't even knock or enter, just hooked on and got out of there."

"You mean you guys didn't even check to see if they were gone?"

"Nope," they replied.

Now Bill looks at me and says, "What have you done Pennie? You think this is better than that tent?"

"Yes, I do and you just wait Henry Higgins."

Fixing Dumb Dora

I went to town bought some cream paint for the walls, contact paper for the cupboard tops and black paint for the floors. Some stick on tiles, sheets for curtains. The work began

We worked for days, painting and scraping the floors and walls, cleaning filth out of everything. The little trailer was starting to look like a home, at least one I could live in for a few months,

We had wicker furniture to sit on for the front room, a little love seat and a chair. A stump for the TV that didn't work because of no electricity, no table, so Bill made one that dropped from the wall. We could sit on Nathan's bed while we ate, which was a make shift bench that folded out and rested on two stumps, the board was covered with foam and a vinyl table cloth. All in all it was pretty cute, not that I want to live here forever, but it's better than that mosquito, bugs, spiders and snake infested tent…

I mean how long can it take to build a Lincoln log house, just stack logs, drill, and pound and do it over and over again. If I only knew what a turn around our life would have in the next 20 years. Our life seems to change day by day from the hustle bustle of city life.

Building the House

What a long hard process. I never dreamed a house could take so much work. The first thing we had to do was set up the trailer, bury the power line, when they decide to run it up to us, but before they do the connection has to be out of sight which is a chore since our ground is solid rock. Bill worked for days with a pick and shovel to dig a 12-ft line from the trailer to the pole, not as deep as they wanted it, but Bill said they could dig it up and check it if they wanted to, as he threw boulders over the top.

When I lived in Utah I never even thought of a well for water, you see it on cowboy shows, but reality was hitting me, we are really in the country. Every drop of water we drank we packed from somewhere else and then up that fun hill…

Next we hired a guy to drill our well. He used a big truck with a huge drill on it that almost looked like a oil derrick. It was a constant pounding and they poured water on their bit and kept pounding, then it quit, we found water. Sure enough, at 25 ft we had water, but it caved in and we had to go for second water at 60 ft, $1080.00 later. Our water had lots of oil shale and mud but not a very good flow because it has to trickle down the pipe from the main source at 25 ft, so we have about 5 to 7 gal a minute. Now that is enough to run your house, but don't even think about running the hose for over 5 minutes, digging the trench will take some doing and long hours before we actually get to taste the stuff but we finally had the liquid gold, WATER!

Living in the city before, I was used to running to town in a few minutes, when I need something, not here I have to travel over 50 miles. It seems every time we went to town, we forgot one thing or the other. And if we didn't forget something, another problem would arise and off to the city we would go, once more blowing another day of work. Ordering our septic tank, bricks, sewer pipe, water pipe, well, pump, pressure tank, valves joints, glue cement lime gravel mixer, tools, wheel barrow, you name it, we had to get it for our building project.

When will our new home ever come to be? Into August and the power company still hasn't gotten around to hooking up our lines, The kids really miss not seeing any TV for over 3 months now, if they had only known that their was no reception here, maybe the wait wouldn't have seemed so bad.

No water in the house yet, because we need electricity to push the pump, no cement works done, cause we need the well for the water, summer clicking away, How can the power company be so backward to have people wait almost 4 to 5 months for electricity.

But the phone around here is a real adventure, an 8 party line. Having come from Utah and private lines this is far from what we are used to. First you have to listen for your special ring, our ring is 2 long and 1 short. And the trick is to find the line empty so you can call. Then when it does happen to have a dial tone, then people on the line know all your business, because they listen to your business. The one upside to the 8 party line is all around the community you can answer your phone from any of those 8 houses, just listen for your rings and pick up. Well the end of August, we finally have electricity.

The first thing our kids do is go find a TV antenna since their dad isn't going to pay $50.00 for one that will pick up anything. The kids go on a scavenger hunt. They find 3 junked ones and drag them up the mountain. It was so funny to see them coming up the hill. All dragging these weird mangled antennas, all junk, in hopes that their dad will make a good one out of the menagerie they brought him. Bill sets up the antenna on the hill. To do this he has to hike up a steep incline, because we decided to build on solid rock, a rock slide area is just above the house so that's where the famous pole is placed for the next 2 decades.

The wire runs for at least 100 yards up a rocky mountain and the antenna is secured by rocks piled up at the base, now turn it so the snow is a lighter hue so we can see the station that half way comes in. You have to make your way up the hill through the weeds, rocks, and snakes trying not to fall and roll down the steep mountain.

We yell from the door as the kids move the antenna, "A little to the right, no more to the left"

We try to secure the ugly piece of piping to the tree so the wind doesn't move it or the deer that seem to rub against it. And then it has nothing but snow, and a shadow that happens to look like a person. 2 channels but the kids are in heaven. We call the antenna ole limp Louie. Our family is so close; we laugh and have so much fun together since we moved to Montana and Dumb Dora.

Friends

Well, now we have electricity and all our friends from Utah have left. Yes, you know when you move somewhere, your friend have to visit. Well our friends decided to come visit us, but they all decided to come on the same weekend. Now if you knew Bill and me before, we had 2 groups of friends, his and mine. Bill's were more free spirits, into drinking and marijuana, and illegal fun. Whereas my friends were your regular back yard friends. One weekend all these people ventured to our mountain retreat to see Dumb Dora, a hole in the ground, and cement blocks. Oh well, time for a party. This was a real trick with so many personalities and different life styles but we just managed.

We stopped progress on the house to show them all around; ghost towns, trees, picking thimbleberries, listening to the elk call for their mates, panning gold, hiking and floating the river. We couldn't believe all the visitors we had in such a short time Lynn and Lynda Dunn for 2 days, then Bill's parents for 2 more days. The rain pours and we go to Missoula to entertain relatives. Off they went to Seattle after we convince that we can do the cement work on our own. Who shows up a few days after but Rick and Sheila they do help us lay some forms for the basement... A week later who shows up again but Rick, Sheila, Joe, Brandon, Mike, Georgia Shane, Jason, Ryan, Dave, carol, David, Tony, Launa, Randy, Ranae, Charlie, Kristy, Shane, Shantel, Laurie, Jill. The mountainside looked like a car lot with so many vehicles, tents and motor homes.

"House building, what's that? Let's party!" Bill says, so we go to Missoula, Garnet, raft the river and have a bon fire.

Earlier in the week I was talking to my friends about the prison in Deer lodge, and how neat I thought it would be if they made it into a mall, a few cells could be stores, and restaurants, every one could wear stripes and it would be a riot. Well they weren't listening to me, or only partially cause they stopped at the prison in Deer lodge. Parked their car and walked up to the big Iron doors of the Old Territorial Prison and started to bang on the door, and trying to open it up.

"Look at this place," they said, "it is so real they even have guards on the wall…so cool."

A guard hollers down to them, "What in the heck are you doing?"

"We want to come in," says Launa and Ranae. "How do you get in there?"

The guard shakes his head. "Well if you don't move back, you will find out. Now leave."

"But, But isn't this a mall?"

"A what?"

"A mall?"

"No, "This is a working State Prison, and you are trespassing."

They loaded back into their motor home, and I'm sure cussed me for telling them about the mall. It was a good idea, and it could have been a trip.

Cement

After a crazy weekend we say goodbye, to part of the past, knowing that we probably will not see them again for a long while. More than a week without visitors, we can't believe it, work here we come. The weather has given us a break for a while. We bought 60 bags of cement, 8 bags of lime and 3 loads of gravel and sand. Now we need all the help. Where is it?

The first thing we do is pour the footings, an all day job. Bill knows I don't know anything about finishing, so he jumps in the basement hole and I stay on the top with the shovel, mixer, gravel, cement and water. I throw 12 shovels of gravel and sand into the mixer, 4 bags of cement, a touch of lime and water till it looks like rolling pudding; turn the batch over onto the homemade shoot. And do it all over again. For 8 long hours I shoveled gravel and cement and poured it down the shoot.

Bill was down the hole finishing and spreading the cement, he is trying to work it and keep up with me. The floor was next; it took another 10 hour day.

I was given a break. Luckie came to take over my job so I could go to town with the girls. He swore that my job was the pits and wondered how I could do it. I guess its just desire to have a house without a lot of expense.

Now the cement cinder bricks, 500 at 40 lbs each. The truck that brought them from Missoula couldn't get up our mountain. So they dumped them down on our lower road 3/10 of a mile away. The long process of loading the bricks into our '36 pick up and drive up the hill and unload it. We move about 40 at a time and bring up enough to start bricking our basement. We slide them down the same shoot we made for the cement to slide down. I start them from the top; Bill down below catches them before they hit the bottom. The weather in Montana is so unpredictable wait 5 minutes and it will change, if it's not raining it's hotter than hell. But you never know what it's going to be. So we work like hell while we can. I think I hate the cement brick part of the house the most. So after days of laying brick and mixing mortar, being sunburned, rained on, eaten by bugs, stung by bees, and just plain tired, I talked Bill into only going two high on the foundation for the bricks.

Lesson one:

Do what you're supposed to, because you will pay for it later; as Bill crawls on his stomach under beams to fix waterlines, or fix cracks and holes that have let varmints, cats, and anything else in. He cusses me each time he slithers on his stomach, having a hard time getting out of the mouse droppings, old frozen cat carcasses. He says there is a limit to what he will go under there for, and it has to be life or death…

We hired Bob McMahan to dig our water line and sewer lines. 1,500 dollars later, we decide to cover the line ourselves. We can't afford that.

I wonder where our brain was sometimes, our little kids out there in the cold rain, or it was so hot you could hardly stand it. The water line was too deep and long to cover by hand, but the septic system the 5 lines and the main line from the tank, we took on. Our little kids out there working for hours, shoveling a half a shovel at a time, but as much as a 6 and 7-year-old can lift. The task now seems overwhelming for small little kids, but Dad and Mom took over when we finished the other work we were doing. Bill would soften and tell them to go and play, and he didn't have to say it twice. There lay empty shovels and kids, well they were nowhere to be found.

But we knew money was short, so we cut corners where and when we could. Back to the basement I even dread writing about it, let alone doing that blasted lifting, leveling, tapping down slapping on mortar,

Up the ladder, mix the motor, and start the whole process again. Each batch would cover one row of bricks on one side. What a pain. The heat was unbearable in the hole. The cement we worked with dried on our hands and sucked all the moisture from them. Our lips became cracked and bleeding from being out in the wind, and heat, and then the next day, it would rain, and be cold. Montana never has a warm rain; it's always cold and bone chilling even in the summer. The winds come up and you know there is a front coming in, and button down the hatches. From the west typical storm, from the east put on another layer of clothes.

We finally finished the basement room after 10 days of hard work. Everyone always razed us because we didn't have more done but no one seemed to be coming up to help us. I really thought we would have more help but it never seems to work out that way. Our house was finally coming together.

It's well into September and getting cold. Our nice days were numbered, and still we didn't have one log. We weren't used to the cold brisk nights that come blasting in the fall, and waking to frost on everything. We are from Utah where peaches and tomatoes are still being picked from the garden and orchard. Now we have to throw another log on the fire, at least one, cause that's all that will fit in the stove. The stove cooks all night, and we barely notice the wave of heat unless you happen to get to close with your fanny and then a quick appreciation of molten hot metal is pierced into your mind or was that the other end?

Here comes the Log's

Swede, the ole guy we bought our house logs from, calls us and says be ready the first load of logs would be there today. We need to find someone who can unload them for us. Bill looks all over for a forklift, with no luck. The truck arrives with our floor joists, and beams, over 100 logs and we unload each one by hand. The driver Leo Taylor helps us. He was really nice I invited him in for spaghetti and he talked to us about building our house cause he had just finished his log house. Then we paid him $125.00 for trucking them to us and he went on his way I was so excited, finally we had our logs. Now my home would soon be done. I know before Thanksgiving. Little did I know. I found out this was only 1/4 of the logs we needed, oh no, sweat. We still have money to have Leo bring us 2 more semi's full and then we will figure how to get the rest.

The days rolled by. Bill and I worked and worked trying to get those beams over to the house site. We had to go get Dad's wrecker and lift 4 logs at a time and I drove, big mistake.

Going for a Ride.

"Okay Pennie, you just back up the wrecker till I say stop. I'll hook up the logs, and then I'll balance them while you drive 'slowly' over to the house."

"Sounds easy enough," I replied."

"Well then get in and do it!" says Bill.

I jump in the ole International and put it in reverse, let out the clutch and push on the gas. That ole wrecker must have had jet fuel in the tank, cause I almost run over Bill! "STOP! You fool!

What are you trying to do?" I shrug my shoulders, "Drive," I say under my breath.

He hooks up the logs and sits on one end. These logs are massive beams 20 and 30 ft long wrapped in chains and cables, and me, as one of the three stooges maneuvering these things into place.

"Okay take off!"

Bill should know by now that I usually do what he tells me to do, that is just what I did. I shoved it in gear and stepped on the gas.

You should have seen Bill holding on for dear life, with those massive beams looking like teeter totters, him trying to duck them as he flew down and they flew up, him trying to stutter, S_T_O_P_!"

I slam on the brakes; he flies forward, getting a crotch full of slivers. A few choice words that I am not going to relate to you streamed out of his lips. And then I understand the part, "just drive without touching the gas. Can you do that?"

I stick my tongue out at him when he's not looking, as his patience is wearing thin, but not as thin as his pants were where the log had rubbed them to a high shine.

His teeth clinching he says, "let's try it one more time."

Gee it goes pretty good. Bill survived a little sore and battered but he is lucky I'm a fast learner....

The majority of the logs are up the hill now. Now the problem is moving them onto the house, making the cap logs fit. The mill cut some wrong wouldn't you know it, that's all we need when we don't know what we're doing anyway. I don't know how we ever thought we could build a house after just building a swing set in Utah. I know the Lord had his hand in this one, but sometimes I wonder if I'm going to be strong enough for this frontier life.

Bill and I found out that to make the cap log fit, we have to chisel off what they milled wrong. 44 ft of chiseling 2 inches thick, first you make cross cuts in the log probably 2 to 3 inches wide, 44 ft long this amounts up to 192 cuts with the saw.

We stand for hours in the sun, working bit by bit. The wood pieces fly off the log, so it will lay flat on the structure. The sun beats down on us, it seems unmerciful, and the horse flies, and hornets add to the confusion and misery, as sweat rolls down my back, and between my boobs. I don't know if men know how miserable that trickle is, but having to wear an over the shoulder boulder holder anyway and then in this intense heat, I want to scream. This mountain has no shade, so the sun just keeps beating down on us as we hammer and chisel away at our new home. I'm flat miserable, and I at times don't handle it very well, my mood swings, and anything can set me off.

I start to cry. Bill saw many of those days and he would ask me what was wrong. I would say, "nothing," so he would ask me to make dinner for the family then. Well that's when pans went a flying. Can't he see I'm upset, can't he read my mind? As I bang pans and cupboard doors, the kids know enough to stay away, or just say the right things to get mom smiling again. And most times they could.

The chiseling now done, it is time to place the 44 ft beam in to its place in the middle of the house. This beam will be the stabilizing beam for the rest of the house, it is massive. We lift the beam with chains and I guide Bill to the exact spot.

This middle beam; I don't think anyone can realize how heavy that baby is especially when Bill set it on my hand and found super strength to get it off of it quickly, only turning a few fingers black and blue. Next we put each floor joist on, leveling each one, drilling it, and doing the whole process over and over; long tedious hours of work, and no soft furniture to sit on when we are done.

No fast food place for a quick easy dinner. When the sun goes down, I go into the trailer to cook and get the kids ready for the next day, then fall into bed.

Each log has to be never rotted, that is a liquid that we brush on to keep the logs from rotting over time. Then we turn them over and roll out pipe insulation in the groove that was made by the mill so the logs set on each other tight, and don't let air through, this is called Swedish coped and suppose to be warmer than the chink style logs, the kids stapled on the insulation and helped turn logs and paint on goop, Let it dry and move on to another task of heavy lifting, nailing, sweeping. What ever needed to be done, and the kids we are best helpers.

We then have to cut each log to the correct length, as so the ends don't all fall together. So Bill would cut them in 4, 8 12 and 16 ft lengths and stager each layer. When we started stacking the logs we would secure them with 8 inch spikes that we hammered in each log, marking with a crayon where each spike was, and try to plan for door ways and windows, so when you use the chainsaw you don't hit a huge spike that dulls your chain or completely destroy it.

We then had to drill where the logs met and then fill with chalking and then pound a wooden peg down inside each seam. This was long tedious work, while Bill was cutting and lifting I got to drill with a long bit probably 10 to 12 inches long. Then the kids would help with the chalking and pounding the peg into the hole that I had drilled. It was teamwork, and we all had our hand in it. We were usually exhausted by the end of the day.

If it wasn't hot, it was raining, or we were being blown over by the afternoon breeze, no, let's say gale. We even thought about a windmill up here to get electricity, but of course that didn't happen, because everything takes money, and we had barely enough to get by.

Chapter 3
Frozen Limbo &
I   Hate Mices to Pieces

We're at a stand still again no logs. The months rolled by and on November 1st we got enough logs to get four high on our house. Then the winter really set in, below zero for a solid 4 ½ months. So the house sits unfinished. Our dreams sit in frozen limbo...

Jim, Bill's brother, lives in a teepee up the gulch from us. He snow shoes, or cross country skies everywhere he goes. He lives in his teepee year round, with his dog Bronze. Now Jim is a mountain man sort, not too keen on kids getting into his space. He has moved up by us; let's see to bug me I think. But the truth is, he really doesn't like city life and Montana is a great change. Most days Jim comes flying in on his skis, his mustache frozen and his clothes are also frozen stiff. He plunders into the house, dog, ski shoes, snow you name it. In this 8 X 35 ft trailer, with 2 dogs and 5 people it is rather tight, now we add Jim and his dog and ski attire stretched around the room.

When I could get the strength and gumption up I would hike up the mountain to Jim's house. I see the smoke coming from the teepee, a huge sort of place, much larger than I imagined a teepee being. It is made out of poles and layers of canvas and skins. He puts heavy coverings on the ground and has a fire pit in the middle of the teepee.

As you enter you crawl into an opening that is like a front door, then into another section, and then he has an inner layer wrapped for warmth. I was amazed at the warmth of the home, even with a gapping hole out the top to let the smoke escape. He has a flap that he can close at the top and or direct the smoke to the change in the weather. I have to admit I was amazed at the creativity around and in his place. It made me feel like I had stepped back even more in time, as I sat like an Indian in his teepee while he explained how things worked, etc.

I really don't need to go back in time anymore. I need to move FORWARD.... What a difference my trailer was to his warm teepee. The trailer seems like a refrigerator, the floor so cold your feet burn when they hit the floor. It was so cold the other morning that when I went to get the milk out of the fridge I thought it was broke because it was warmer in the fridge then out of it. If you didn't want it to freeze you put it in the refrigerator.

The snow blows through the window and doors. We wake up with 2 inches of snow on our covers of our bed. We get some wool blankets and staple them to the walls and over the back door. Plastic was on the inside of the windows. We still lay in bed in the morning and practice-blowing smoke rings in the cold frost from our breath. It is so cold, you hate to crawl out of bed to face another day, and the kids are great. They take everything in stride. Me, well I'm having a nervous breakdown. Hives all over, uptight.

We lie in bed and listen to the mice, make nests in the walls and under our bed. While we're sleeping at night the mice would run over the top of the headboard. How did we found this out? We were sleeping and Bill put his hand over his head, one crawled onto his arm and ran down it to his shoulder. That did it for Bill, he grabbed one of the many cats we had to keep down the mice outside, threw him under the bed. Our bed had a box around it on the bottom so it was completely closed in, the mattress sat on a board and old wire springs. Now this cat had a hay day. We laid as the bed swayed from the cat howling and growling at mice. Everywhere you look those little beady eyes are looking back at you.

I'm going Crazy!!! As you walk in the trailer you can smell that famous sickening odor of mice, no matter how much Purex or Ajax I use the odor still permeates the air.

Yes Doctor, It's my Pants....

"I can't stand it Bill! I itch all over," I say as I lay scratching my belly and legs. "It has to be hives or something like that!"

"Nope," Bill says, "its bed bugs, from this flea ridden ole mattress on this bed. Who knows how many varmints have slept in this bed. Makes me crawl."

"Oh, quit it Bill, it's not bed bugs or you would be itching too."

Morning only brought more welts on my legs and torso. Terrie talks me into going to her doctor, "This isn't good," she says, "you need serious help."

I pull out the only decent pants that I own anymore, some cute bib overalls with little pockets and a zipper that zips up the front. I tug and pull, but my belly is hanging out the front.

"Something is wrong here," I say to myself. "I never looked this way when I bought these things. They must have shrunk since I wore them last." I lay myself in the prone position on the bed and find my trusty pliers. With one hand I grip tightly to the pliers and with the other I delicately tuck and roll my belly. I roll around the bed, but finally the zipper goes up only catching my skin in a few places.

Man do I look good. I'm tucked in these pants like you can't believe. The only thing different is I have a extra roll around my chest where all the fat has moved up. Oh well, just move the bra down and tuck some more.

Now to get off the bed cause I can't bend in either direction. I start to roll like a beached whale. Finally off the bed, I grab the pliers and stuff them in my purse. If I have to remove these puppies I want to be able to have something to stuff me back in...

Off we go to Missoula. I sit in the doctor's office waiting for my turn. I hear my name and slither out of the chair like some pregnant girl 9 ½ months along. Pushing myself from the back and using my legs to lift this pudgy body up. I walk to the desk and they ask me what I'm seeing the doctor for?

I say, "I think I have hives or something like that, I have a heck of a rash."

They escort me into a room and tell me to sit down; the doctor would probably just want to talk to me. So once more I try to bend the unbendable pants to sit in the chair, but believe me, if they were miserable it was worth it, cause I looked good. I bet I squished in a good 20 lbs. under compression. The doctor walks in introduces himself and sits down.

"Now tell me about your problem miss."

I proceed to tell him how I've been itching terrible especially at night. I feel like I'm going to go insane, the more I itch the bigger the welts become.

"Well go behind that curtain over there and take off your pants, I would like to see this rash."

"Oh hell," I thought. "How am I ever going to pull this one off?"

Behind the curtain I unzip my pants, my body seems to explode and flow out of every opening, now I peel off one leg at a time. I have to roll my pants down each leg as they are about painted on. But don't get me wrong I looked pretty dang good. The word is looked, cause now the amazing pants were in a slump in the corner and my skin was dented and wrinkled in different designs.

I walk out to the doctor and he has me stand on the scale, and then says, "Get off. Now get back on. Holy cow you pack a lot in a little package. I can't believe you weigh that much. Now what is this on your legs?" He points to seams and wrinkles in my skin.

"Oh, those are my pants, they are a little tight." He looks at my belly and legs, and says, "go back behind the curtain while I write you a prescription I think I know what is causing this rash".

Now the fun begins, I enter the curtain area, and get in my purse pull out the pliers, start to pull my pants on, but its impossible to do, no matter how I tuck and roll I can't push all my belly back into those pants. I am going to have to get in a prone position so all the fat rather slides to the back. I sit down on the chair and start to struggle with my feet sticking out of the curtain. I must look like I'm in convulsions or something, still no luck.

I have to get on the floor and then I can stuff the excess of three kids and whatnot into those tight jeans. So I stick my feet out from under the curtain and lay in the prone position again and gently zip with the pliers as the other hand tucks and rolls the extra 20 lbs neatly into its little package. In the mean time the doctor sat watching me. I roll around the floor like an overturned turtle, until I can get a hold of something to pull me up. Then I crawl over to the chair to help me get up, he was sitting there in amazement.

"I can't believe it," he says. "I'll tell you what's wrong with you. Your body is so nervous about being shoved in those pants that it has hives. I'll tell you what I'm going to do. I won't charge you for this visit if you take the money and go buy you a new pair of pants."

I agreed. He gave me some kind of steroid or something and told me to drink a glass of wine each night, and I would be fine.

I said, "Thanks," went to buy some polyester big girl pants and went home smiling. The hives seemed to leave. I guess the wine and just knowing that life was a changing seemed to work.

Watch where you walk

The little stove by the door, no matter how much wood we put in can't keep the trailer warm enough to keep the water from freezing, so we have no running water or toilet. Everything is frozen solid. Going outside isn't much fun either, especially to drop your drawers. Guys have it easier than girls who have to bare everything. Tiffany only being 4 yrs old is really good about not complaining as she trudges outside and up to the only tree on our property to our makeshift outhouse, to go to the bathroom.

We have to be careful to stay on the beaten path, because if you don't you'll sink to your waist. I know this cause I was sledding with the kids and I fell off the trail and thought I would be buried alive. I couldn't get out. I finally got horizontal in the snow and rolled over to the path. Pretty bad when you think you're going to die in front of your front door. Now this would be really bad when your pants are around your knees, to have someone find you in the spring, frozen.

Thanksgiving and then Christmas, still no progress on the house, we never thought winter could be so long and ugly. Snow just kept piling up, and up. We can't drive up to the house because of the snow, even in a 4-wheel drive. We park at the bottom and walk. For groceries we put them on a sled and pull it up the hill. The kids know to bundle up; just keep walking no matter how tired and cold they are Bill says we will die out here if we give up.

At times the wind is blowing the snow so hard that it is drifting to waist high, Bill holds on to Tiffany's hand and breaks the trail for the boys and me. My lungs feel like they're going to explode. They hurt so bad, my throat is burning. The house seems so far off, when you're hiking up a steep mountain in a snowstorm.

"I just can't go any farther," I say to Bill.

He comes back and gives me a swift kick in the butt. I was so mad at him I could feel my temperature raise, and I almost ran to the house. But his method did work; he got me up the hill. The storm was terrible. When we reached the house we had to start the fire, and try to take the bitter cold out of the house. Our wood is just outside the door, but it is also covered by a couple of feet of snow. The kid's sleep close to the stove, well at least the boys do. Dustin has his bed over the front window next to the ceiling so the heat rises and seems to warm him first. Nathan has his bed in the kitchen, moving the 2x4 and sliding 2 logs over so he can lay his sleeping bag on a foam-covered board. Bill, Tiffany and I sleep in the back room.

THE OLE SACK

I dread it, yes, dread bed. I'm sure you would too if your bed was 4 ½ ft wide and 3 people sleep there. Oh my aching back. It wouldn't be so bad if I didn't have to try to shrink my body before I get in bed. Tiffany wants more room. She just kicks and gives you an elbow or a nice knee in the middle of the night. Bill, well it doesn't matter where you are in the bed. Bill is a snuggler and he has to be right next to me. Tiffany has to have body contact also. So here I am in the middle being squeezed like a sardine I measured how much room I have to sleep: 10 inches; 12 if I overeat before retiring. When I turn over on my back it takes 5 minutes to maneuver around the bodies. When I'm finally there my two arms are like a v on top of my chest. I just accidentally elbow two loved ones who happen to be snuggling with me and they groan and move over. I think my sleeping situation is making me restless, have hives and down right irritable. I wonder what it will be like to be able to turn over in a real bed, lay in any position without trying to figure out which arm and legs are mine. They all feel the same cause they have been asleep long before me.

Christmas

What a change from Utah, we used to buy 2 trees, one already flocked and then one for the kids down stairs. Tree shopping here is a whole new concept. Lets see get in the ole Tessie Truck, bring a chain saw, hand saw, boots, gloves, and some food in case we get stuck. Up the mountains we go, looking for the perfect tree. You have to admit it is fun and the choices are countless too big, too small, too fat, too thin, I like more branches. Trees look a lot smaller from the road than they do after you hike up a mountain for that perfect tree only to find it is over 10 feet tall. Hike around in knee-deep snow, stumble on snags lying under the snow, and then get plastered by your family bombarding you with snowballs. Finally the perfect tree, now to get it home, and hope it fits through the door.

Decorating the tree was also a change. In Utah we had a tree upstairs all flocked and each light and ball placed just so, no one was to touch it. The tree in the family room was for the kids. In Dumb Dora there was just room for a little tree to go on a stump that wouldn't fit in our small stove. Ornaments were paper chains, and salt dough snowmen ornaments.

Before, the kids got everything, they wanted. But a new life and circumstances seem to bring a new attitude with the kids.

"Just bring us a surprise, okay mom? Whatever you and Santa can afford, cause we know that you have to pay Santa."

I would go into town with Terrie and Jean and we would bargain hunt. I always seemed to find the clearance isle. Great toys too, Shaun Cassidy record player, a ballerina doll, for Tiff, and walkie-talkies for the boys. Christmas morning the kids are all in the back room of the trailer to keep warm as we tell them they can see what Santa brought. Screams of delight as they open the few presents they receive. But to my dismay the record player would only play in extra slow speed so Shaun Cassidy sounded like a sick old man. The ballerina doll spun so fast her head came off. You couldn't hear the walkie-talkies across the trailer and we could whisper louder than that. I told them that we would all go to town the next day and see what we could do with the mess they got. We took everything back. Everything was on sale for 75% off so the kids went crazy and bought to their hearts content, headed home happy and tired in our little red beetle.

The kids amaze me, how they just adjust. Going from having a nice van, sports car, nice home and every convenience you could have, to nothing! Everything you do is work.

The kids all have cross-country skis from when we were the jet set in Utah. We used to go out on the golf course in Utah, stop at McDonalds and get breakfast before weathering the elements of at least 30 degrees. To go party for the day, thinking we knew what cold and winter was all about.

Our house is that temperature inside as you start the morning. Dustin being the oldest helps Tiffany get her skis on and then razzes Nathan till he gets his. Then down the mountain they go. They ask me to go with them, but I usually refuse cause I'm horrid at skiing and only slow them down as they have to keep stopping an waiting for me, or hiking back up to pull me out of the snow.

Toboggan Washday

When it comes to wash day, we load the clothes in pillow cases, and put them on the toboggan then down the hill we go, Tiffany on the top of the clothes, me trying to keep up with the sled as it careens down the mountain at light speed. Once at the bottom I pull her and the clothes for over a mile, all you can hear is the river next to the road and the runners on the sled and the squeaking of the snow under my feet. This place is beautiful, the trees, fencepost, and weeds, are covered with the frost that just comes with Montana winters. Everything glistens as the sun beats down on me. What a great place to live, if only I had running water, a washer, heat, you name it.

It is awesome how quiet it can be in the middle of the day. Every sound magnified as I walk with my daughter, our cheeks are numb, and nose red as I pull the heaping load of laundry and the little girl over to people who have a normal life. We go to my aunt's house where she lets me wash and dry the clothes, we have a good visit and she always fixes us something good to snack on and a warm cup of Herb tea. If I'm lucky, someone gives us a ride to the bottom of the hill, and the whole process starts over.

I Hate Mices to Pieces

The mice are horrible; all those field mice decided that dumb Dora would be better than the frozen fields, so they moved in with us. Mice are everywhere I open the kitchen drawer and they scramble. As you walk in you can smell a mouse. They have this disgusting penetrating smell, mouse urine, it is horrible and it emanates from every room in the hellhole.

When I get up in the morning, I haven't figured it out yet, but I found them hanging on the screens of the windows. I don't know if they were frozen or saw the light and wanted out of that hole. But I took the broom and smacked what I could. They almost became friendly. You would be watching TV and one would crawl on top of the TV and stare at you. When you opened the silverware drawer, they would just move to the back of it. This would make me sick having these things running over everything, especially our silverware that we ate off of, so I got in the habit of washing everything. The mice seem to take over everything; everywhere I look they have left droppings or piddled on something. I open a cupboard or door and a dark streak will sleek past. Other times the whole closet will move with the varmints, it's like they are like maggots in a container rolling and squirming to get position over another.

I find nests of baby mice everywhere I turn, and put them out for the cats. It's like caviar to them. I don't know how much more I can take, if I put my feet on the floor at night they will crawl over them. I place traps to catch them only for them somehow to empty the food out of it, or sacrifice one of their own and they go in and eat the food he left behind. I've watched them swarm over a trap that has a dead mouse in it, like no big thing. I can't stand it, but we have no choice. I guess we live with them and pray that my kids don't get sick. I get so tired of washing everything when I take it out of the cupboard, try it when you have to haul water and boil it. Pretty soon we would just brush it off, or we put water in the fridge that we can use just for washing mouse crap, cause it was too difficult to get the water out of the jugs if it had sat one night in the trailer, the ole dreaded frozen limbo had set.

Today we worked our seats off, got the pantry tongue and groove on. Cleaned the bottom floor, I'm really tired. Been so depressed I cry at the drop of a hat, when will we ever be in the house and rid of the mice and bugs? My kids need sleep at night. Bill tries to be cheerful, but he says he can't if I don't get a hold of myself. I really try, but it's so hard. I'm falling apart at the seams. God please help me!! I need you to hold me together. I keep my feet off the floor because I'm so scared of those dirty mice. I've put traps, poison and you name it. But this ole trailer has so many hiding places in cracks and corners. It seems we've seen 5 generations of mice come and go. And at night they all come back for a family reunion.

I don't get hives any more because I let it all hang out and I'm just going crazy. I watch on TV about severely depressed people and their lives look like a piece of cake. Maybe I have a nervous breakdown and I'm coping with it myself. I know I yell more than I ever have. Cry more and smile less. And a simple task seems like a mountain to me at times. I almost hate myself right now. I have no nice clothes I don't like my hair and my body, well that's beyond help.

I dream at night what it would be like to be a size 5, 8, 10, ok I'll take a 16 I'm not picky. I've asked God so many times why I wasn't given a small body to make my life better. It seems that's one of my life ambitions to be a small girl. Wrong ambition cause it is not going to happen. I'm, let's say, walking food storage.

My attitude needs to get better, I need to get out of this depression and not let it devour all that I have. And don't let that terrible feeling come over my family and me. But a family's love for you can swell your heart. When I'm with my kids and Bill, I forget trying to be a girl I'm not.

Our water froze up just before Christmas and never thawed out till April. The toilet froze solid and broke a huge piece out of it. One plus to everything being frozen, we just chipped the water off the floor, no wet mess here. Throw it in a bucket and throw it outside with the rest of the unbearable stuff.

The cupboard doors in Dumb Dora drove me crazy, they sat on a slant and when you shut one, then another would come crashing down on your head, and when something hits me in the head, I go crazy, and I start hitting every door I could see, the kitchen was a war zone. Arms flying and mom yelling Rackle Fritz fiddle looper or some strange words like that. Those doors would have it out for me and wait till my patience was at its end, and then open they would come smacking me on each side of the head.

"I hate this place!" I would say with my teeth clinched. I just wanted out of here. As I reared back to give the doors another smack, when the back cupboards would sneak up on me and hit me from behind. The only comfort is that I was not the only person they bugged. Jim hated those cupboards as bad as I did, and would cuss with the best of them, but I would carefully latch them, and go on with cooking.

We had a little gas range, big enough oven to cook a cake maybe an 8x8 not a 9x13 or you couldn't shut the door. I would have to watch the light as it would be warm, and the mice would crawl up in there and then die, and bloat, "Not a good thing," as Martha Stewart would say.

99 Bottles of Beer on the wall

Jim is helping us all he can, but the weather is too cold and the snow too deep to do much. Jim did get us 6 cords of wood. I think we would have frozen without his help, and it gave me someone else to get mad at besides Bill.

Oh yes, I would be so angry at Bill. We weren't in the church at the time. And Bill loved to drink. You have to know Drummond and bars, you go in to get one drink and then you're offered another and another, and Bill well, he will drink anyone under the table.

Many a time he would call me when we lived in Utah; he went out for a drink before coming home and was so drunk he couldn't remember where he left the car. This trend seemed to follow him to our new home in Montana. But having to hike a steep mountain in a snowstorm when you're falling down drunk is life threatening. If not the storm and cold, it's me, because I'm going to kill him. Bill is a trial with his brother here. Jim is an influence I don't need right now and he makes life miserable at times. Bill is a great guy, but he has not quite conquered the drinking. It seems you can always find those drinking buddies no matter where you move, and Drummond is no different. Jim, his brother moved close by. I think it was to make me miserable, and test my patience. He encourages Bill to not stress about the house. If there is snow in the mountains, then ski it. They head off with their cross-country skis, and ski down the mountain behind our house, and then drink in the hay stack after feeding the cows, but my house sits, and waits. They come home drunk crawling up the driveway, and into the house. Having to drag him out of another bar is way more than I bargained for. But he swears he will change, and I pray he will, but I guess, we need to change together and find the gospel in our life again.

One night Jim and Bill went to get me hamburger for making our dinner and 4 hrs later they came through the door. They didn't know how they drove home. The last thing they could remember they were both setting in the back seat of our Bronco. Needless to say the hamburger never made it home. My temper would get the best of me. I painted a frying pan with the cartoon character Flow on it and met Bill with it at the door. Now it hangs on the wall as a strong reminder of the school of hard knocks.

Jim's dog died today, He killed one of the mice around the area, and it carried a deadly disease. We could have gotten the same thing. We are so thankful and we were spared that heartache. I guess we became immune from all the varmints crawling over everything we own. Jim was adjusting too; he had just moved from Colorado and hadn't been around 3 little kids before. He would make popcorn, and the kids would come over to him to get some, and he said, "don't breathe on me kid," then he would offer them popcorn, and they would go screaming to the sink, as it was peppered with cayenne. Just another trial, but one I needed for all our sanity, we needed Jim. He helped us survive and not freeze.

Chapter 4
Stepping Back in Time

Old School

Winter seems to last forever with no money and little food. We're trying to save as much as we can for building the house. The kids catch the school bus at the bottom of the mountain. They go into Drummond to an old school house with the 8 grades in it, the first 4 grades on the lower floor and the last four upstairs. It was like everything else that we experienced in Montana, a step back in time. The halls were hardwoods that creaked as you  walked and the halls seemed to echo every sound that was made. The old school had a special smell, years of hard learning and personalities that seemed to help make up the smell of the air.

Old pictures of the fathers of our country hung in each classroom with the American flag proudly hanging next to it. The walls were covered with the old-fashioned black boards, and the old glass bubble lights hung from the ceiling. The desks were the old ink well ones. Once you were out of the first grade, you had tables. Then as you passed on to the higher grades you graduated to your own unique desk.

The school had a big staircase that engulfed the end of the hall, an old drinking fountain hugged the corner of the narrow hall that was left, and the water gurgled out of the chrome spout. How you wanted to be able to venture up those stairs, but it was almost forbidden for those under the 5th grade. You just wanted to pass so you could climb those ominous steps to the upstairs, once there, you would find 4 more rooms and at the end of the hall was the principal office, usually a swirl of smoke arose from the office from a pipe. You knew you didn't want to see what that room looked like but if would almost be worth it just to see the upstairs.

Nathan saw his share of the big office upstairs from fighting or just some stupid accident as he was coming through the big double doors. Someone had straight-armed them and he went sailing only to land on his face and break out his front teeth.

But the highlight of school was when they had fire alarms; the upper grades upstairs would exit out a window, in the 6th grade room and slide down a long tube to the ground. A huge bell tower sat on top of the school, and beaconed all to come. Drummond had huge metal slides that would almost give you a nosebleed as you climbed to the top and slid down. 3 or 4 could pile on the teeter-totters. There were also the typical playground swings and a big metal merry-go-round, that sometime during the day someone lost his lunch on.

The school enrollment was around 90 to 100 students. Drummond was good for the kids, cause it didn't matter if you were rich or poor, it was hard to tell one kid from the other. A lot of the ranchers in the area didn't dress their kid any different than mine, so it was easy for the kids to fit in and not really realize what they were missing.

Life is like that; if you don't know you're in a bad way you think life is great and no one ever told them any different. Oh they knew others had more, and they did remember Utah. Probably the hardest for the boys was basketball; we couldn't afford extra shoes for them to play sports, so year after year they wore the same shoes tight and worn out. They would try to stop to shoot a basket and would slide past the basket and hit the wall, but they knew that we would change things if we could, but it just wasn't happening.

Life is grand

But life was grand. The kids roamed all over the mountains hiking, fishing, finding old antiques and dragging them home, to make forts in and above the ground. They found old 1930  and 1940 cars to play in. They spent hours playing and driving the cars that lay up in a gully, until one day as they were playing they moved the gear shift lever and the cab filled with hornets. They had disturbed a nest and the bees followed them as they ran as fast as they could for home. The old cars sat empty from that day forward, the kids decided the bees could have that area as theirs.

The kids made their own fun, they had each other to play with, and then they had their cousins down the mountain and a mile away. But that doesn't stop the young. I would see the kids when they returned home from school, and then they were gone until it was almost dark. They knew they had chores to do and would have to answer to Dad if things were not done. In the winter they made snow forts, had wars with snow balls, went sleigh riding and skiing down this mountain that could kill the most experienced athlete. One of the usual sledding activities was to climb the steep mountain over us and ride the sled down, jumping out of it before it hit the door of the trailer at light speed.

Summer time brought further adventure – hiking for hours in the mountains behind us, fishing for trout and outsmarting the bass in the bass pond. Swimming in the river was a daily routine. Digging a hole and making a underground fort with a periscope to watch the comings and goings of the valley. It didn't matter if it was summer or winter.

I really didn't know where they were half the time, but I knew each one would watch after the other. Sometimes they were crawling under a cattle guard and peering out just in time to see a huge logging truck full of logs heading for you. Back under and hold their breath until the dust settled and then all you could see were their eyes and a Cheshire grin. God seemed to bless us, because He knew I had no idea what these kids were up to.

Nathan, Corey and Russell formed a club. They heard this cool name and decided that would be their name, the Nincompoos. Corey took his Levi jacket and wrote in red marker Nincompoos.

It was great until mean ole Terrie said, "Corey, do you guys know what that word means?"

They all shook their heads no. She proceeded to tell them that the word was not cool, but stupid, they were crushed. Corey buried his Levi jacket; no one has seen it since.

They would pester old man Wibberding. How they loved to see him squirm, he was always yelling at them, and blaming them for everything, knowing now that they were probably to blame for most things that happened. He moved in after the kids were here, and he was squatting on their fort property. So they would just make life miserable, even though he was a sort of relative. They took blasting caps out of his garage. They said if he wouldn't have told us they were there we would have never looked for or found them, but it was the excitement of the hunt and to bug Bill.

We found out years later why they were such good fishermen, once in a while they would blast the bass out, and gather up the fish as they floated to the top. They were your typical Dennis the Menace brats.

They would string a rope across the road, and clothesline the neighbor kid on his little motorcycle, as he flew off his cycle, yelling at the boys. As they picked him up and brushed him off, good thing his cycle didn't go very fast.

We just didn't know all the things they did, and at that time I didn't really need anymore on my plate.

The kids should have never lived, for all the things they did, from crawling under cattle guards, I always wondered why they were black as Indians, They made fort 2 stories high out of junk wood they stole from every house in the neighborhood; if it was loose it was gone.

In the wintertime they would sleigh ride on every mountain around and especially on our driveway, which was three tenths of a mile long. Sometimes they made it to the end but most times they crashed and burned. The hill was steep and fast ice that was shined from cars trying to make it up. They loved life and nothing seemed so bad if they could eat some warm poor mans gravy and homemade bread, or salt beans. One day all the cousins were out playing and were over by a pond where we had told them not to go, and one of the boys fell in. They made a chain by laying down on the ice to get to him and pulled him out. By the time they came home they were all frozen. They all got lickins for not obeying and almost dying. But they were good kids and we hardly had to worry about them getting in trouble, they just had fun.

The river was the kids' playground and they were constantly covering 2-5 miles. They swam, and floated, just constantly gone. I guess there is safety in numbers, because all 10 of them would head down and hook inner tubes together and float away. I think the worst thing was the sunburns, Mr. Sun was merciless and sometimes he got the better of the kids. They moaned and groaned for a couple days after. I would get comfy leaves and boil them and put them on as a poultice. Don't know if it really worked, but we didn't have money for a doctor, and it made them stop crying.

The kids today don't get out and exercise like the kids did then. TV what is that? Out till the sun went down and on the weekend, camping together in a makeshift fort, old army tent, or just under the stars. All the kids played together from 12yrs to 4 and got along great, they all watched out for one another. They were close friends, all 10 of them.

Springtime

It's the month of May and our house now 12 logs high. A special thanks to Darrell Bradshaw for all his help, hiking up the hill and working for hours, then getting back in his truck and finally going home. We are waiting once more for logs. They say they're mudded out. One day maybe I won't have to sit here in Delightful or Dumb Dora, whatever mood I'm in at the time to call her, but I'll be sitting in my log cabin.

Our money is running short, especially when you have to buy insulation, spikes, pegs, drill bits, chains for the saws, let alone food for the family. We we're out of unemployment with no jobs until June. We're trying to sell the Bronco, and Bill's super bike, but no luck on either, we just keep hoping.

In June of '79 Bill found a part time job working for a rancher in Hall. He's been working so hard, 15 hrs a day, but he seems to love it. We found a truck we could use to get our logs. We had to replace the universal joint before we could take it so I ran to Missoula to get the part. The next day Bill and the kids take off, Saturday morning, to get the logs. Half a day goes by and I get a phone call. I just happen to be at Jean's. (Convenience of an 8 party line)

"Come and get me," Bill says. "The truck broke down. But don't leave till you change the tire one the VW because it's bald."

Oh hell, what next? The spare I had was the wrong size. Being a girl and dumb as long as I had a tire that wasn't flat and was basically round I could use it. So I put it on anyway and drove 80 miles with the car rocking back and forth. Bill had cooled off by the time I get there. He smiles when he sees me. We eat at Swedes place and leave about 9pm. I think they felt guilty for all they have put us through and knocked another $500.00 off our logs.

Bill starts driving back but can't stand the car, gets out and switches the tires around. He couldn't believe I drove it that way. But I did, so believe it... The next morning we have 2 flat tires. I'm going to quit asking what next.

Monday morning Bill pumps up the best tire and gets the VW to the Cennex, gets two retreads and went off to fix the truck and finally maybe get our logs.

Bill asked me to go to Hamilton to change a part, which of course was the wrong part. Women always do that. Men send them to the parts store knowing what they want, but the translation seems to get screwed up on the way. You take in the part, lay it on the counter and say one of these. But the parts place wants to know the life history of the truck, and my vocabulary for vehicles is, "I don't know!"

I get two miles down the road and a clunk, clank, squeak, bang. I pull over and can't figure out what is wrong and start walking back to the logging mill. It's a busy 2-lane highway. I'm in high heels and a long dress. Semis' go by and blow my dress up. I almost fall over from the wind. Two guys pull over and ask me if I want a ride. Mom always told me not to hitch hike, especially with 3 guys and a Saint Bernard. So I said, "Thanks I'm almost there" and they left.

What a crazy person I was, 4 blisters and a mile and half later I finally get to Swede's mill. Bill couldn't believe it.

"What were you thinking," he said, "Those guys were just trying to save you, remember you're in Montana now."

He drives me back to the car gets in and figures out what's wrong right away. The wheel was trying to leave the car and go off on its own. Bill apologizes for getting mad.

Today, Wednesday, we're looking at a trucker's strike. Not knowing how much food we're going to have for a while, Bill quit work for a while so he could build the house and the weather has been rotten as usual. The rain just keeps coming down.

The driveway is a muddy mess. The rain comes down it like a riverbed, washing what soil we have, leaving huge rocks to drive over in between the slimy mud, a type of clay that collects on your feet, so with each step your feet get heavier. Bill won't give up. He's outside putting up logs in 50 mph gusts.

Our dog Bilbo, a silver gray poodle, came home stinking to high heaven. The kids tell us that he killed a baby skunk and the mom got him. I guess! Oh Laws!

Tomato juice doesn't even touch the smell as I gag while washing him, so I try peanut butter.

I'd advise anyone not to do as I did. I used chunky. It looks like we rolled him for a cheese ball. It does cut the smell, but the problem is getting the peanut butter and then the nuts and grease and whatever smell is left out of a kinky curly poodle. Poor Bilbo Baggins didn't know what he did to get so many baths to still feel and look terrible. If you haven't seen a grease ball poodle take my word for it, it's not nice. The dog had a terrible complex, and the smell; we all were living by breathing through our mouths.

Today is our last three-meal day. We're cutting down to breakfast and dinner until things with the money get better. We're looking at bread, pancakes beans and rice. A good saying we read the other day will fit for the next little while and me a lot lately.

"Enjoy when you can. And Endure when you must." Cutting the meals down only lasted 2 days, I like food too well and we can cut other ways.

Well the house is up to the 2nd floor joists. Now to figure out how to get the nineteen, 600 lb beams up 12 ft up in the air. 600 lbs phooey, those beams weight 1,000 lbs easy. They pick up the front of a 3/4-ton wrecker when we're trying to lift them. I am stressed, and I need to visit my grandma in Utah, so I leave poor Bill to fend for himself. He said that I really couldn't do anything until he got these logs in position anyway.

When I returned from Utah, Bill had all

the beams for the second floor. He hired a self-loader logger to lift the logs up to the second floor. Now we need 60 more logs, and then up with the second floor ceiling.

Wash Day

I wash outside in a 1925 washer; it has three big plungers that go up and down. The wringer swivels between wash area and the tubs of rinse water. The sun beating down on me feels good; because the water is frigid. I use a stick to help load the Levis and shirts into the washer. The big plungers make a big sucking noise as they go up and down. Twisting and turning to almost a rhythm, the motor clicking, wringer grinding and plungers sucking. Out of the washer, into the wringer, into the rinse water tub, then stir with a stick. Out of rinse water, into wringer, then another tub of clean water. Then wringer again, and into basket to carry over to the clothes line. Why did I ever complain about washing, when all I had to do is turn a dial and wait 20 minutes? We never appreciate what we have, until we don't have it.

The hornets are everywhere and they swarm me. Hornets and I don't get along. I'm wearing a long sun dress and now and then one gets under there, and then watch me rip at things, jump and cuss. I come out on the better end. I am at least still alive, cause I killed that sucker after he stung me on the rear and leg. Then I itch...not a pretty site. Oh well back to the task at hand, washing and wringing and hanging out.

I have to stay on my toes, Tiffany loves to help me. I've warned her and warned her not to get her hands close to the wringer. I was getting the last load done and she decides, while I'm over by the clothesline, to run the last things through the wringer. She stands on her tiptoes reaches in the cold water and pulls out a shirt. She decides that she can feed it by herself into the wringer. As it starts she changes her mind thinking I will yell at her, so she reaches to pull it back. The washer grabs her fingers, a scream like I've never heard from her then, "Mommy!" in the midst of her cries.

A mother just can't seem to move fast enough. I ran as fast as I could. The wringer was up to her elbow by the time I reached her and hit the release bar. I started to cry to see her arm all skinned and red. Then I began to shake all over. Her arm swelled up, it was bruised and scraped. We waited hoping that we didn't have to take her in to Missoula, for we just didn't have the money, but we couldn't take it any longer, her arm looked terrible. So we made the 50-mile trek to the hospital.

But one more time our prayers were answered; it wasn't broken. Just hurt a lot for a week, a Popsicle made it feel a little better. Now I'm very careful when I wash, and Tiffany, well I've lost my helper. She won't even go near me, if I'm near that speckled green monster, with the arm eating thing going.

Hot summer

Bill gets our last logs today, July 10th. I can't believe it. He borrows an old dump truck from ole man McMahan. Everything went ok (what a shock) his stuff never runs. But don't hold your breath.

We have the house up to the second floor and are ready to put the flooring on, so we can walk around up there and finish with the second half of the house, then the major carrying beams for the house and then tongue and groove again.

Bill is working on the house a couple days after and a splinter gets in his eye. I work and work to get it out. He calls me blind and we drive over to the neighbors, but they must be blind too, cause they can't see it either. This gave me a little satisfaction that I can do some things even if he doesn't think I can. He is plain miserable, which makes the whole family miserable. He is up all night. At 7 a.m. we drop the kids off at Terrie's and head for the hospital. By 8:30 it's out, thank heaven. Hell, he was surly, and a wife is the last person he should be around when a little boy grown tall is hurt or sick.

Back to a normal day. We start putting the flooring on today, July 15th, but first we have to carry 600 17ft 2x6's 50 yards up the hill then put them through the window at the bottom floor. The kids help me but in 90 degree heat. It seems like it takes forever. We looked like Egyptian slaves hauling that lumber. The kids are wearing towels on their heads to keep the sun off, as it beats down on us unmercifully. 3 little kids working so hard, the hours seemed to tick slowly by, and the sun seemed to intensify as the afternoon clicked on. After 4 hrs of steady work we had it moved. Now to get it up on the beams, it seems somehow I always get the low end of the deal when it comes to work I guess, cause I hate heights and balancing on beams 10ft in the air.

Bill gets on the beams while I get the 2x6 from the pile, measure and cut them to 15'5". I lift them to the top floor, and then run over, put the ladder up to help Bill. I crawl up push against the flooring to hammer it in place. Then down the ladder, move it, back up, push again, then down, move the ladder, cut some more lumber and start the whole process again. I can't do it fast enough. Then I mention that I think I have the hardest job. Bill says, "do you want to trade jobs." I say, " no cause all you would do is yell if I didn't do it right." You'd think I'd lose weight instead of growing as wide, as I am tall. One of these days!

Bill is working really hard, and I'm just not used to the whole rotten ordeal. Why can't I just pick out colors, carpet and lights? NO, here I am working off my tail, that isn't coming off.

Mosquitoes

I really haven't figured out why the Lord put those things on the earth? Mosquitoes will suck you dry, especially here it Montana. I grew up here as a little girl, the bugs would bite me and my face would swell up like a balloon, but life was just that way and you lived with it.

The bugs didn't seem to irritate me like they do now. We're trying to build the house; early in the morning things are pretty good. Then the sun begins to warm the chill off the air and that annoying buzz starts to hmmm in your ear, and then it gets louder as a dark cloud heads in your direction. They swarm your head and body. They go up your nose and in your ears, I try to flay my arms like a crazy person to discourage the vampires but it just excites them more. I put out more scent, and they love it.

I run for the Deep Woods Off, spraying every inch of our bodies. Now you're covered and they are hungry but can't stand to land on you, so they swarm over your head. Nathan, the other day, asked me if anyone ever died from mosquitoes eating them. Dustin had 150 bites just on his face and arms and neck, He can't sleep with his head under the covers, and that is the only way you can survive in the trailer. I never knew mosquitoes would be blood brothers to my kids. You pray for the sun to beat down and get hot. Out in the sun they thin down to a small army. But if you are any place that has shade, Katie bar the door, they will carry you off. If working on the house isn't hard enough on my patience, these varmints are driving me dingy.

Chapter 5
Blessings and Animals

Bill and I headed for town to get supplies. As we round the corner after a long day in town, Jean meets me in her driveway, and flagged us down.

"I've got something to tell you lady," I couldn't figure what she could be so serious about. "It's your son."

"Oh hell, now what," I thought.

"Your son, Nate and my son, Russell were playing with matches today and started your mountain on fire. It got away from them and spread like wild fire. Mom saw the smoke and wondered who was on the mountain by your log house. She got the field glasses and there were those two 7-year-old boys jumping and running around trying to get the fire under control. Nathan had the sense to run in the trailer and get the fire extinguisher and put out the fire. We went screaming up the hill, beat both kids, and took them home."

Needless to say Bill was hot, and Nathan got beat. I've never seen Bill so mad. Everything we own in our life now is on that mountain and could have been destroyed by kids playing with matches, let alone they could have died themselves.

Later Bill marched Nathan up the mountain, and asked him to look at what he did. There before him was a huge burnt area, every plant, blade of grass and weed was charred to the ground. Then Bill took his head and smacked it to the ground, trying to get him to realize what he had done, not noticing that a rock was there. Nathan raised his head and blood was running down his nose, and over one eye. Bill felt terrible about the cut on Nathan's head; it was an accident just like the fire. How easily things happen. We never had to worry about Nathan again with matches. He hated them, and wouldn't touch them for years, not even to start the fire in the stove. He got wood and got it ready but someone else could handle the matches.

EX Wife Yuk!

If life isn't difficult enough, and the Lord hasn't tested me beyond hope, here comes a biggie. Bill's ex-wife calls us and says that she's having trouble with her 10 yr old son (which he has never seen) and she is bringing him out for the summer. Oh laws. A day I'll never forget Sherry, Bills Ex calls the night before and says she'll be there in the morning. Bill has to go to work. Guess who gets to entertain her until he gets home? How am I ever going to introduce myself?

She calls about 11am, "I'm here. I'll just wander around town until you can come get us."

I guess I'd better hurry. I wonder what she will look like. How do I meet her? What do I say? I asked Jean and Terrie to go with me. She gave me so much grief when Bill and I got married, and wouldn't give her consent until an hour before the ceremony. She has tried to put him in jail, because she didn't think that we were paying enough child support. And now out of nowhere here is the wicked witch from the South. Butterflies were swirling in my stomach giving me an uneasy feeling. She was in the Sky Motel room 1.

I just bravely walked up and knocked on the door. Chris, Bill's son answered.

I said, "Is your mom here? Can you wake her?"

My first look at her, lying there she was so pretty, so tan, blond, make up just so. Little body. Everything I wasn't. I wanted to leave. My heart kept pounding harder and harder. Why me? Why now when were in such a mess. All these things went through my mind in a few seconds.

He walked over to wake her. We all met and it really wasn't too hard, I really wanted to scratch her eyes out, just pure instinct, ya know ex-wife rage. We were all so sweet to each other I think it was quite phony; she probably wanted to rip my lips off, just like I wanted to rip hers off. What a picture her no lips, and me a scratched up mess, cause she had some fake fingernails that could cause serious damage. Well we held our cool, and She followed us home, and I asked Terrie if we could wait at their place until Bill got home.

We had a party for Chris to welcome him, and Sherry decided to make a play for my husband, if you can believe that one. She about fell all over Bill, saying, "what a mistake when I let you go." Boy, I was steaming. Every chance she got she would take advantage to fall on him, to touch him, and be alone with him. At 11:00 p.m. that night she left. I don't know when I'll ever see her again and none to soon...

Chris has been hard. Bill went out of his way to be extra nice. Chris stayed with us 3 weeks. It was such a challenge for the whole family. I was proud of Dusty and Nate. Everything they had they shared with Chris without a second thought. It wasn't so easy for Chris, he had to eat our food, learn to share, and what it was like not to get everything he wanted and to mind. He helped on the house a lot. He followed Bill around like a puppy; he really loves having a father. He is got awful homesick. I know it was as hard for him to be thrown in a home that he was not used to and live by their rules, as it was for us. But we all worked together and made it work. Chris is a good kid and learned to help and have fun with the family.

Rafting on the Road

Once work got too long and hard we would head for the river. We had a big raft, and inner tubes, life jackets, and just plain fun. My cousins came over from Idaho and asked if they could borrow the raft and take the kids down the river, I agreed. The kids and I have been down the river time and time again. It's a great way to beat the heat and just forget about our troubles, as we dangle our feet in the water and paddle down the river. Cars go by and wave and honk, envying our easy life. Ha!

My kids ran all over these mountains fighting off snakes, bats, and any other thing they could find to make life interesting. Rafting with relatives sounded rather uneventful. When my cousin Buddy does anything, he does it in a big way. He asked every kid in the neighborhood, which were all cousins numbering12, ranging from 12 to 3 yrs old. They went into the river and everything went great. The water is always cold and sometimes a fish will nibble on your toe, or a snake will slither past. Our kids knew the river like the back of their hands so I had no fear that everything would go great. They all get out of the river about 10 miles down the road. Buddy loaded the raft on top of his van.

"Alright you kids get inside,"

"Please Buddy, can we ride on top of the van in the raft? We will be careful."

"I guess it won't hurt, I will go slow and it's only a short jaunt back to the mountain."

Shaun, Scott, Chris, and Russell all climb to the top of the van and hold on. They are all laughing but Dustin and Nathan said "no we will ride inside." The other boys seem to be having a riot on top.

The raft starts to lift some from the wind whipping underneath, Shaun notices first as he feels the raft lift even more and the craft wants to leave the top of the van, then Scott's eyes widen, the boys look at each other, nod and decide they are going to move down by the ladder at the end of the van. The boys start to get more silent, as the van picks up speed around corners, and up hills. The kids start to tighten their grip and fear begins to engulf them. But boys are not going to say they are scared and say uncle, so the ride on top of the van goes on, the wind whipping through their hair, as the van went faster, and faster.

Buddy yells up to them, "Is everything Okay?"

They all yell, "Yes, it's a blast. Go faster."

As he rounds a curve and heads up another hill, the raft starts to leave the van. Shaun and Scott get scared and finish their plan to go to the back of the van and slide down the ladder that is part of the van. When they did this the extra weight that was holding the raft on was now gone. Tragedy hit, the raft suddenly tore loose. Chris and Russell are inside. Russell took a hold of the two oar hangers and held on for his life, he turned completely upside down and rode the raft to the road, as it skidded along the pavement, and exploding with the impact of the road.

Chris tried to ride it out but had nothing to hold on to. The raft ripped him off the top of the van, his body hurled past Shaun's head. Flying through the air, the raft caught the wind and had slowed down. Chris was traveling through the air without anything to block his fall, except an inner tube around his neck and his life jacket, onto the black roadway. His body smashed into the road head first. He skidded along on his face and chest leaving sections of his scalp behind on the road. The inner tube stem had ripped into his lip and took the whole bottom of his lip off.

He lay in a heap on the road. Buddy tries to stop the van, but things happen so fast, that seconds seem like hours, as all this flashes before you. Buddy stays by Chris, as Carren his wife drives up the mountain to get me and tell me that Chris has been hurt. I load into the van, kids screaming, and crying they know that he is dead.

Blood is everywhere when we pull up. His head is starting to swell, I don't want him to panic, he is at least conscious. I try to not look alarmed, Chris looks terrible, but if I let him know I know I will throw him into shock, so I tell him it's not bad, only a few scratches and bruises. We drive to Drummond. He is throwing up now, and still with pressure on his cuts, is bleeding pretty bad. We get him to the ambulance shed. This is a volunteer ambulance so you have to wait for a crew to arrive from working on cars, or hanging out clothes, or plowing fields.

I call Bill at the ranch and tell him that Chris has been hurt bad. We are taking him by ambulance to the hospital in Deer Lodge. I follow with the car so I have a way back to the house. The kids are crying, and know that Chris is going to die. I don't know how we are going to tell his mother.

I pray on the way to the hospital "Please Lord, help us in our stupidity to make it through this mess so Chris will survive without any life affecting injuries." Tears trickle down my cheek. I think as I drive, we are so poor can hardly make ends meet. And now this.

Chris is tied down as they stitch his head, nose, eyes, and lip. The rest are cuts and abrasions that just hurt a lot.

Bill gives him a blessing, and we have to call Sherry. "Oh he looks pretty good, you won't even be able to tell," as we roll our eyes.

I didn't know if his face would ever recover without plastic surgery. It looked as if he had been in an Indian raid, Custer's last stand, and was scalped by the enemy. It was horrible. Please God help us!

Chris remained in the hospital for 5 days. Each day Chris seemed to change, his face transformed before our eyes. I know it was Our Heavenly Father that made his healing possible. Chris got on the plane and flew home on the 13th of Aug.

. **Gored by an Elk.... NOT**

The Mighty Hunters

One day Shaun and Dustin went hunting with their dads, first of the season. I drove all of them up to the top of Wet Mulkey and let them out. They were going to hike down and hunt. They would for sure get the big one before dinner they said. In their travels Shaun sees an elk antler, and picks it up and shows it to Dustin. Dustin looked, to no avail, for the other antler from the huge animal but it was not to be found. Dustin's nose was out of joint cause  he didn't have one, the ole lip came out; he was good at the pout.

Luckie felt sorry for him and said; "give it to me and I'll break it on this rock and you will each have a part of this huge antler."

Well, the boys smiled and gave him the antler. He swung with all his might against a huge rock. Whack! The sound echoed and then they heard a thud and Luckie fall. The antler had come back and hit him in the nose, splitting it open and breaking his nose. The antler was not phased by the pounding.

Luckie was staggering around like a drunk and holding his nose. Bill ran down the hill, as the crow flies to get help, and the boys administered first aid, or let's say moral support, as Luckie was in misery. Bill got to the car after running down hill for 7 miles. He drove up and got Luckie and took him to the hospital.

They asked him what happened, and of course Bill pipes up and says; "He was gored by a elk, it was spectacular you should have been there, he barely survived with his life."

Well it spread through the hospital like wildfire, that a guy in emergency was gored in the face by an elk. People came out of the woodwork to see the guy who survived an elk attack. Luckie had to set them straight, but most people wouldn't believe him, they just knew Bill had told the real truth. (You have to watch Bill like a hawk.)

Animals

Wild animals everywhere, from mountain lions, bears, coyotes, deer, mountain sheep, snakes, rats, bats, skunks, magpies, and the stupid sage hen. I really don't know how those birds live or exist. But they manage somehow. It's fun to try and dodge them as they wander out on the road as you drive by. It's a real trial and you have to be on your toes, because if one makes it on the road 5 will follow and won't stop for anything. But they are so cute. Then the magpies, what a challenge they are, as they steal food from our dogs. One will circle around him and get him barking and then pull his tail, while the other steals his food. It's great to watch.

The eagles are everywhere here, as they scoop down for snakes, fish, and rabbits. I sit on the deck and watch them soar through the air, with them squealing and calling out to one another, either mating or fighting, I really can't tell but it is fascinating to watch them fly and cross and then dive and fall together and then soar again.

The coyotes are thick around here and at night come up to our house after cats, and mice I'm sure, cause why not? Easy picking. I can watch them out the window as they yelp their blood curdling call to their mates and family to come and get it. But we manage cause after dark we usually stay in, except to get wood, since we have to burn the stove 9 months of the year.

Deer use our mountain for a refuge. They come close to eat the grass over the septic tank, cause, as we all know the grass is always greener over the septic tank. After eating their fill they bed down just below our porch and dot the mountainside. Sometimes they will walk right up to the porch. If you sit perfectly still they don't know you're there. What beautiful animals they are.

The problem with the deer hanging out here is that the mountain lions live in caves behind the house and when they need food they are out and about. We don't see them a lot, but a few times is too many when you have small children, or a fat, slow moving body. Anyway, one day we woke up to see a dead dear lying in the driveway. We walked over to see it and the whole inside was gone and mountain lion tracks in the snow. We are glad those sightings are few and far between.

The big horn sheep live down the road apiece and are just fun to see as they come down to eat the gravel and salt they put on the road.

The skunks are a real trial, I think they are everywhere, but ours are pretty cute the way the mom will go up to our dog water and get a hold of the side of the pan and rock it till it turns over and then she and her family will drink away.

The last things are the bats. I think they live in an old gold mine up the draw from us. They come out thick in the summertime, swooping and diving for their dinner, as they eat hoards of mosquitoes. They fly so fast and sometimes come too close for comfort, they fly under the porch awning and out before you know it, but let me tell you they can turn sharp. Bill just laughs as I scream as they dodge me and go for another mosquito that is trying to eat me.

Love you no matter what

Another chapter of our life; so many new and different things have happened to us since we have moved. We have learned so much, how to endure in some of the hardest times, to enjoy a small pleasure to the utmost. One thing I have learned since I have been here is how much I'm loved.

My kids love me so much they tell me every day, hug and kiss me. What a feeling to be loved by so many loving people. Today I turn 31 years old.

I hit my 30's and my whole life changed. I know women hit the change about 50 but my whole life is hitting it 20 years early. If I can make it through these trying times I'll be a better person. I'll know how to live in the hardest of times to go without a paycheck for months on end. Without any running water for 8 months, 10 below zero inside. Trying to shower using buckets and dumping on you after you have lathered up, and it's so cold your feet stick to the metal shower floor. My little kids have experienced it all too. If only grown-ups could take life like a child does, just take it in stride. All they need is that loving kiss good night and a loving I love you in the morning to carry them through.

The Weekend

Working away from home, has also slowed the house to a crawl, but somehow we have to eat. Bill is working on a survey crew, so travels all week and then comes home on the weekend to work on the house. I do what I can but I need my Bill, cause I usually do it wrong.

Bill got home early from St. Regis as I greeted him with 6 kids, we were tending Bryant's also and he took it in stride. We spent the night over at Terrie's house. It was a lot warmer and more comfortable than 8 people in a 8 ft wide trailer.

Saturday Morning we come over to work on the house early. Darrell Bradshaw helped us all day we were really blessed; we almost had a terrible catastrophe. We dropped a heavy chain, which swept the circular saw down the stairs. Christina was just about to come up, the saw just missed her and the chain skinned her head. I don't know when I was so scared, but the rest of the day on the house went real good. We finished all the tongue and groove on the top of the roof. The guys really worked hard.

About 5pm I asked Bill to take the kids and I to get a treat, so he says, "Let's take the old wrecker."

Bill, 6 kids, 2 dogs and I all pile in the old beaten up, rotten running truck. Kids are hanging from every corner as we putt to town. We get gas and then drive it to get a treat. Bill pulls it in, stops it while I run in and get 12 root beer bars. Then he tries to start the bomb. R-r-r-r no luck, over and over r-r-r-r it just won't turn over.

Bill says, "Okay it's in 2nd you steer while the kid's push. When we get to the middle of the road, turn it toward the tracks. It's downhill, it should start."

I hit the middle and head down hill, the thing has no gear, oh oh! Not in gear, oh no shift it before Bill finds out too late. Bill's yelling!! I'm tired, I yell right back.

Drummond knows our vocabulary now and Bill is fuming. If you saw this truck you would realize what he is pushing. It's a 1 ton pickup with an army pickup bed on it and a boom and extra weight so it would lift heavy vehicles. It has bullet holes through the roof, and holes in the floorboards.

"Now don't try to start it until we get past the train tracks."

We clear the tracks. It just won't start, Bill yells again. I reply in the same manner. Then I look down, I can't believe my eyes. I didn't have the key on. Like a stupid person I told him and he found a new word in his vocabulary to call me.

The ole wrecker starts right up. He gets in; I smile and say, "Want a root beer float bar?

He smiles, and says, "why not."

The kids have been super. They all minded so well it really wasn't as bad as we thought the weekend would be. Monday was a holiday so we worked on the house all day. We really need God's help to get things done on this house before it gets much colder. I really don't want to spend another winter in Dumb Dora.

Finally Friday, the end of the week, I almost dread Saturday to come cause we work so hard on the house all weekend. Today we got a loan for the house $1,500.00 and we ordered lumber and every cent is gone now. Prices are just skyrocketing. I hope we can finish this house with not much more money; we have been pretty good with our money. That's the first money we have had to borrow in a year and half. We still need lights and plumbing. We can live with kerosene lamps, but I'm tired of living without water, and a tub, especially.

Bill says we'll have one soon, I can hardly wait.

I went over to my brother's to visit, not a good time, Terrie and Luckie were not in good moods, and they decided to go out. Well my dog Barney the Basset hound was under their trailer barking at the cats. Luckie was afraid he would break something under there so he gets a broom and chases him. Barney gets scared and runs for his life. Rounding the corner, he loses his footing and trips over a pipe. Luckies fears came true water went everywhere. The guy was furious. Barney had broken the pipe right off where it entered the house.

Off to Missoula, before the stores close, cussing part of the way I just take it in stride. If it would have been one of my kids, I would have felt bad, but it was my dumb ole dog Barney. You just expect crap from him, and Luckie caused it, by chasing him. The night got better; we stopped for pizza after the plumbing store.

All Bassets act the same, they are just bread to love and get into things

Chapter 6
Brrr it's Cold.

Oct 16th. I was washing my clothes today, outside. The wind was blowing and the cold water that I wash in almost seems warm to my half-frozen hands. I can't seem to do the clothes fast enough. People never appreciate what they have until they don't have it. I listen to my friends complain about washday. All they have to do is walk over throw a few clothes in and push a button and it does the work. These hard times have helped me grow so much and to appreciate what and when you have it, cause you never know.

I had to smile when I was hanging out my clothes. Bill tries hard for me. He built me the neatest clothesline out of old insulator poles. We put clothes line rope for the lines and as you hang clothes the thing starts to sag. For 3 months now I keep pulling up the slack and cutting off the excess. But by the time I get done with my clothes I get a backache from reaching high when I start and almost crawling to hang up the clothes after the sag sets in. I just smile each time. Because Bill tried to tell me to put wire on it and I said no. It would rust the clothes. So I don't dare say anything, because I'll have to eat crow. And that's pretty fowl.

Oct 24th it's been awhile since I wrote my thoughts down. I love this journal; I enjoy the people in the church also. They are so kind and show me a lot of love that I've never known before. I want to so much get back to the church, but I don't want to go without Bill.

The house right now is tearing him apart, because I'm a nervous wreck, I want out of this mouse nest, spider web, and cat box, of a trailer. And he knows it. So we try, that's all we can do.

The logs are up and finished, and the tongue and groove is now on the roof, now to get the roofing and insulation done. And then maybe it will start looking like a house.

All Hands on the Roof

Saturday was such a great day cause we had a lot of friends come up on a miserable wet day. And work all day. On our roof it has taken Bill and I so long no matter what we do, but with help it sure makes things easier. Charlie, William, Elaine Parke, and Luckie all came up bright and early to help us Rick Lacey showed up in mid morning.

We really appreciated all the hands. We have never known such friendships; it's great to know such fine and loving people. We got half of the roof boxed in, insulation, plywood and tarpaper, before the rain. It was so slippery up there, they had to use corks to stay on the roof. (Those are logging boots with spikes in the bottom). I hope one day I can show them how much I appreciate what there doing for us. When I see all those hands working in my house, it gives me hope that maybe by Christmas my house will be done. Thank God for leading us up here where people are so giving.

Wood

Oct. 28th Daylight savings time ended last night back to standard time. We worked so hard today went up and got two loads of wood, stayed up there 6 hours, boy am I pooped. Uncle George, Bill and I loaded wood, cut, fell, rolled, carried, split, you name it trying to get a winter of wood in one day. I don't think is going to happen but we're giving it a good try.

You have to know Uncle George. He does everything in a big way, and the trees he goes after are huge, as he cuts them in huge chunks, then rolls them down to us on the road. You have to be careful or they will kill you as they roll over the top of you, as they did with Dustin. They just laid him flat, but being young he got up, a little dazed but lived. Now if it had been me I would have still been laying there. It took only 3 to 4 chunks to fill a pick up of the huge slabs of wood and then the long process of chopping them when we got home. When Bill was gone it was almost impossible for me to chop, and the kids would get the wedge in the middle and then bury the wedge, until Bill got home to hit it hard enough to split the massive wood.

I'm so tired I can hardly sit here. The kids are in bed now. We just finished two chapters of <u>Charlotte's Web</u>. The whole family enjoys the little book. We read together so much, a special time for our little family. Bill is really tired also. I have to admit he and Uncle George did work harder than I today. But also I'm a girl and the woods aren't exactly what I'm used to. The woodpile sure looks better.   We have one more tree that we already fell that we have to go get tomorrow. Woe is me. Tired city!

Well off to the shower, have to be fast though as a 5 gallon hot water heater just gives you enough time to wash the necessities and skim over the rest. All right bed here I come, let the others fight me for the room; hope I beat them for position.

Today sure feel tough. I guess moving wood all day yesterday did me in. The cold weather helped complicate my many aches and pains throwing in their ole frog voice. But it got me out of going back up and getting wood again.

Went to town with Terrie today, they were supposed to get their money for their ole '37 ford pick up, they sold to Bob Crocker. They have had more problems. They have been trying to get their $2,500.00 for 5 months now. I guess they're going to court over it, cause Bob didn't come through with the money. Terrie and Luckie are in such a financial bind; I worry about them, creditors knocking down the door. Terrie has held together pretty good. With all that has given them problems, they marvel that I can live the way I do with all the mice, and cold and you name it. But I can handle it. I don't know if I could handle being in debt up past my ears. I guess each person is given his own trials to bear. I sure hope everything works out for them. Cause they need it! Got home late. Bill had dinner ready, skillet pizza. He wasn't too happy about my rummage sale buys. In fact he threw a fit. Ranted and raved, over a 15 cent doily. I guess he is just tired. Give me a break!

Oct. 30th, Day before Halloween, the kids are all excited to wear their ugly masks to school. Then to primary, then out to trick or treat. Woe is me.

Went and got wood again, just Bill and I. We took our saw, boy what a difference, without Uncle George's big saw. We ran out of gas half done but Bill had enough gas to cut them into big honkers. We could hardly lift them on the ole truck. It looked like we were hand loading a logging truck pieces 20" in diameter and 4 to 5 ft long (Hernia city). I'm not feeling the best today anyway, some logs rolled down the hill over the road and down the other side.. So down the hill I go to push them back up. They rolled down there with such little effort why are they so hard to push back up the hill?

I'm pushing up the ones that over shot the road. In the mean time trying to dodge any others that fly by me (talk about suicide!) Getting wood can be hazardous to my health.

I hear a howl, as I'm down in a gulch. Chills roll up my spine another howl and more shrill this time. Others answer. Bill and I stop work. It just gives you an eerie feeling. I think the coyotes or wolves had a deer down and were telling the pack to set the table, chow was on. The forest is still a very hidden place with a lot of corners not discovered.

Bill is already in bed. The kids sacked out, me alone, to think out my thoughts. I guess I'm not alone; the mice sneak up on me and keep me company. I wonder if our life in the trailer will ever be in the past instead of such a rotten reality. I never really thought it was as bad as it is until I hear people shudder when I tell them things that happen, or they come in and look where we're living.. They tell me how they would go nuts. How do I do it? I really don't know. I just know that we are supposed to be here, on this mountain and in Montana.

Nightmare on Front Street

Woe is me! I never thought that it would take me so long to get back to writing in my book. When I drew the bag of candy and jack-o-lantern the day before in my journal, the day started out pretty normal, still not it the house, so the drudgery of washing outside in the brisk fall air is still a reality. I looked at the few clothes I had, and almost everything was dirty, so I decided to even take my underwear off and wash it in the green monster. Wearing my old worn out Levis, pretty tight, and a sweatshirt, I began the chore. It was a brisk cold day, but the sun was shining, a good washday. Terrie, pulls up in her green station wagon, and asks me to go with her to Primary. She needs my help to paint faces on the kids, because they can't wear masks in the church.

"I can't go Terrie; I just hung up all my clothes on the line, including my underwear. I'm like, you know naked."

"Oh, who would know, you'll be fine. Those Levis, you can't even tell. Now get in. It's to primary; we will be back before you know it."

Terrie, can always make things sound better than they are, so I agree and jump in after draining the water out of the washer and turning the rinse tubs upside down.

Primary is an organization in the church for the 3 to 11 yr old kids, and they love it. Primary seemed to go great. I asked Terrie to stop at the local market, to get some paper cups for MIA that night, and some apple cider, 2 gallons. MIA is a church activity for the youth of the community from 12 to 18. Since we were the party planners, we ran in, grabbed what we needed and ran back out, the kids were all in the car 7 of them, my three kids, Terrie's two boys, and Scott and Russ the other cousins. Tiffany had gotten in the front seat. So I never said anything, put her on my lap and closed the door. It was 5:30 and I wanted to get the kids home so Bill could take them for the most fun night of the year.

As you can tell, this is before the ole seatbelt craze, and safety factors came in to play. Cars were made to get down the road, the more we could shove in them the better. So we piled kids to the roof if we could.

The kids just love Halloween and can hardly wait to fill their paper bags with goodies.

As we pulled out of the parking stall of Mordon's Market, dusk was starting to fall, the time when you should turn on your lights, but it really isn't necessary to see with them. We started down Front Street in Drummond; remember this town is a busy metropolis, maybe 200 people in 20-mile radius, no stoplights, one street through town, which is 1 mile long. It has 3 bars, 2 stores, 3 gas stations and 3 motels; mostly on one side of the street because it is an old railroad town and the railroad parallels the road. On the railroad side is the train station, a stockyard, a repair shop, and a sort of ambulance/fire shed, all the comforts of an old cow town. And an old water tower that was used to fuel the steam engines, but now is water for the city.

We had gone about 3 blocks, when I saw this brown station wagon turn across our lane of traffic. "I yelled Tiffany!" and wrapped my arms around her, so she wouldn't go through the windshield.

I remember everything going in slow motion, as the two cars came crashing together. I remember my head and neck being in a position that I don't remember ever being in before. As it bent over and touched my shoulders, the windshield made a sucking sound on my eardrum when the side of my head impacted with the glass. My head had a feeling I can't describe, but it was warm and yet cool. I could hear things but yet I couldn't hear anything. I remember looking up at the windshield and seeing some stuff all over the window, but I couldn't figure out what it was. People were calling my name but I couldn't answer. I wanted to talk to them but I couldn't. I didn't know where I was, or why I was there. I didn't know what had happened. I was all wet, Terrie thought that I had lost all control, and wet my pants. Little did she know that the apple cider behind me had come forward and broken all over me.

The kids in the car bounced around the car like rubber balls, bouncing off of the back seat and each other's heads. Nathan crushed his entire sinuses, his eyes blackened and nose was bleeding. Tiffany had coat hanger wire in her hair, because she was dressed up like Pippy Long Stockings. It could have been so bad. Both cars were totaled. Everyone seemed to make it though the ordeal except me, and my kids.

Someone called for the ambulance, but the battery was dead. One of the drawbacks of being from a small town is a volunteer ambulance and fire department. In the mean time the house burns to the ground as they have to come from all directions when the siren sounds, and they dawn their gear. Living 8 miles from the fire station doesn't help either. Oh, back to the ambulance, it was an old station wagon looking thing but the best we had at the time. It's not always a plus being in a little back in time town. Because when you need an ambulance you don't always get one.

They moved me from Terrie's car to Linda McFarland's car to try to keep me warm, I was freezing to death. Luckie got there to take me to the hospital my legs buckled as I stumbled over to the old 1960 Cadillac, what a bomb. At least the back seat is huge for me to lay down, as they drive up the winding road. Tiffany was put in the make shift ambulance with me, cause her cheek and eyes were swelling excessively.

Once we arrived at the hospital, the little nurse that was on duty was so excited; I really don't think that they get much action. She ran around like her head was cut off.

"Oh my, Dearie, I do hope you're going to be okay. I'll take your blood pressure."

She tried two or three times to get my blood pressure, but I didn't have any. This panicked the nurse.

"Oh dear, oh dear," she said as she patted my arm till it was beat red, and swinging it below the table. "There has to be a pressure here, I know you're not dead. I can see your eyes blinking," as she still pounded on my arm.

She finally located the doctor, and he told her to get an x-ray of my head, she cuts off my shirt, and then goes to remove my pants.

I grab them and say, "I don't think so."

She pulls on them again, I said, "You don't understand, but I don't have underwear on."

"OH! No problem dearie, you don't have anything that I haven't seen before," as she takes the scissors this time and cuts my pants off of me, leaving me naked to the world. She covers me with a white sheet. And then says, "See it's no different. I've seen it before". Now that was reassuring to me for sure, as she precedes to tell me how some bottoms are bigger than others, only different …

The doctor arrived, and said I had a ruptured eardrum, I had a skull fracture and contusions, and my jaw was swelled out like I had those great big candy balls stuffed in the corner. They asked to keep me overnight, but overnight turned into 5 long days.

Everyone was so kind to me. I hated to complain, about my throbbing headache. I hated using the bedpan, and eating nothing but broth, tea, and juice for 3 days. I knew what each meal would be as they carried it into me covered with the stainless steel cover over the plate and duplicate small ones hiding the other food. Or let's say lack of. I finally said please don't bring me that tray. I'd rather not eat.

"Why?" the nurse asked.

I told her I knew what was in there.

She looked at it and said, "oh no, they forgot to put you on regular food. We got that notice yesterday."

This hospital left something to be desired, the staff was great, but the facilities could use some fixing up, a two-room hospital with 2 beds in each room. I lay awake and listened to a heart machine next-door beep away, with each beat of this guy's heart. I asked the nurse, what was wrong with the guy. She said he had a heart attack and was on a machine to warn them if his heart failed. Hours the machine beeped away in a systematic rhythm. Then I heard the machine go to a long beep, the nurse came flying down the hall, she's in there for a moment, and then the sound became regular again. Once more I listened to the machine tick away. I thought about this poor guy across the hall. And once more the machine went to a long sound. The nurse went running again. Oh I thought, "He's dead." The nurse comes out laughing.

Again and again it went on through the night. I called to the nurse. "Is that guy okay?"

"Oh sure, it's that stupid machine. I just have to run and kick it to keep it working."

I thought, "Boy I'm glad I'm not on that machine. You'd listen to your heart beating away. And then think, Oh no, I'm gone."

I'm a member of The Church of Jesus Christ of Latter-day Saints, and some of the priesthood came up and administered to me. That is when those in authority lay their hands on your head, and give you a blessing. Dale Duffin and Allen Bradshaw administered to me, in this blessing they told me things that neither of them could know. My Blessing: "The Lord is very pleased with you Pennie to ask for this blessing. He knows you have many problems besides this accident at this time. He knows you are a strong spirit and is proud of you. He wants you to know that you will recover from this accident. But will have discomfort for sometime. But you will recover, and have no permanent damage. He also wants you to know that you have been worried about raising your family. The Lord wants you to know that you will live to be a companion to your husband for sometime and will live to raise your children. Your husband needs your example; once more the Lord wants you to know how pleased he is with you for asking for this blessing."

I was so overcome with the blessing, tears rolled down my face I was so touched for the Lord had told me of fears that I have had for years and only my closest family has known them. I have been told many times that I would die when I was in my 30's like my mother. My Grandmothers both told fortunes and had predicted my mother's death and others. Too many things that they could see had come true.

The night of the accident while I lay in bed my head hurting so bad I couldn't describe, I wanted to just have the pain cease. I would drift off into another world almost, and something would wake me. There beside me sat my mother. All in white as beautiful and caring as I could remember. I couldn't speak. She would arouse me and say you can't leave your children as I did mine. Many times during the night my mother brought me back into reality. Or an image my mind had simulated so real like, morning came and it seemed so faint but yet so real. I know angels watch over you. Mine just happened to be my Mom.

Here Kitty Kitty.

Another day, then into 5 days. The last day I was there I was lying in my bed and an alarm goes off. Nurse's are running down the hall, but not bothering to get us patients out. As the fire truck pulls up to the front door, and the volunteers file out, with their big rubber boots and fire hats. Not the same crew as miles away, but trudging through the halls.

"Excuse me!" I yell. "Do I need to be rescued here or something?"

"Aha. No, the cat got into the alarm system and we need to find it."

Oh Calgon, take me away. I know I can recover at home better. Even with the mice I sleep with. I convince the doctor and homeward bound I go.

Finally Home

November 6th. I stayed over at Terrie's for two days to keep warm. The insurance company totaled both cars – $1,000 for one car and $1,500 for the other, what a mess. The phone is ringing off the wall so I go back to ole Dumb Dora where we can't hear the phone. Bill is being darling, keeping me down and leg up because I developed a blood clot along with everything else.

Saturday a work crew is coming up to help get us in the house soon. Bill told me about the kids wanting to go trick or treat the night of the accident, so he gave them grocery bags, and let them go door to door in the small town of Drummond. They ran from house to house swollen eyes and bumped heads. One man said, "Let's see inside your sack. Do you have a lot of candy?

To his and Dustin's surprise they both looked in to saw a high heel. Bill had given him the sack from the shoe repair, if that man only knew what they had been through that night.

The man just laughed and said, "It's a weird night" and dumped candy into their sack, because it was late and then clicked off his light.

Recovering

William, Charlie, Elaine Parke, and Ernie Wight all showed up at the house bright and early. At 12 noon up came Phyllis Wight with lunch: two loaves of hot homemade bread, it seemed like 10 gallons of soup, homemade noodles, big chunks of beef, homegrown carrots (sounds like a T.V. commercial). It was so good. Janet Parke brought a cake Margaret a salad. We had a regular feast. We could hardly waddle out of the trailer. I only hope I can repay these people for all they have done.

I have to stay down, my leg really hurts and my head is trying to compete with it and my earache is running a close second. 4:30 everyone is still working, the wind trying to blow them off the roof. Charlie has his rubber boots on and William is starting to swing like a monkey from the eaves. They're doing so great, from the first time they came to work on the house and both had nightmares the night before about getting on the roof. It's funny how friendship can conquer fear and they sure have been friends. My brother showed up to work on the house, after he got home from meetings in the big city of Missoula. He was trying to learn how to teach all of us who don't follow the right path all the time. He's pretty special for a brother. We've always been close all through our life no matter what life has brought.

My Brother....

In all the time I have written in my journal I have never really told anyone or written my feelings of my brother. Luckie and I have been through so much together, we had to be close. Mom and Dad divorcing; going back and forth between parents; neighbors interfering, and turning us in to child services for neglect; our mother dying at the hands of a drunk driver; a stepmother that beat me, locked me in the closet, poured liquid detergent down my throat, and other things I will not discuss or just don't want to. This caused Luckie to have terrible feelings for her, and he had a hard time conquering them in the long future that lay ahead.

Being poor, peer pressures, our marriages, and our problems. Luckie and I are closer than any sister and brother that I know. We always made each other come to reality or feel better. I wish every family could have the love and caring relationship carry though out the years as this one has, you may get mad at the person, but you never stay that way. Love overrides everything.

I've seen Luckie change so very much from being a wild teenager, a philosophy fool to now a Branch President in the L.D.S. church I have to say the latter is the best. We both have had so many problems lately, that we don't have much time for each other anymore. But when things get tough who do we turn to, but each other and our mates. But that tie is still strong. A love I can't explain. I hope when times settle down some, we can take the time to have our long talks that straightened out each of our lives so many times. I love you Big Bro. Remember I'm always here, the little sis you always worried about...

2 weeks now my head has been pounding constantly. I forgot what it would be like not to have a headache. The Doctor gave me some Valium and codeine to help with the pain. Valium, boy do they ever knock me out. I really hate taking drugs, because of my stepmother and her bad drug addiction. So my body rarely even sees an aspirin enter into the stomach zone, let alone heavy drugs like these.

Well my body did a rebellion and shut down. My brain didn't know what to do, the main sending center, wasn't getting the signal from the gray matter to the limbs. I would try to lift my arm but would have to look at my arm, and say, "lift arm". And then my body would respond like in slow motion. Needless to say, I only took one. I decided Tylenol will work just fine.

November 24th Snow

Saturday, came our first big snow storm, over 8 inches and colder than blazes. Snowed all day, but lightly. It's just so cold it's not melting off, and now the cold north winds are starting to blow. They blow so hard that it chills your bones as you walk from trailer to car or house to house. It sure is looking like last winter as the temperature dips down below zero and forgets to come back up. The wind is whistling through the windows tonight and the trailer this morning was almost unbearable under two wool blankets a sleeping bag and 3 people in the bed, you could hardly move as not to get cold and freeze. I forgot how cold winter could be... it's funny I never thought I'd forget after last year and all our problems.

Bill has been working every free moment on the house. Put all the food in the pantry cleaned the west side of the house put the stove in and been working on the flooring. He worries so much; he has to be away from home and just doesn't know how his little family will survive. But the house is coming along so good it won't be long and we'll be in our new home.

The winter stayed and never left, the snow just got deeper, and the cold wind stronger and more often, as the temperature drops out of sight.

We try to keep our family warm at night, as they huddle around the little wood stove in the trailer. Bill brings home wood when he can. We are constantly feeding it into the little firebox. The stove is glowing red. The kids are asleep in their beds. Tiffany is in our bed for 3, and the boys on the makeshift bed in the kitchen not 3 feet from the stove. I sit writing in my journal and watch as the little stove is transparent in color, no black is showing just a glowing red. But the little home is toasty.

I've been so down and Bill hasn't been too up either. We yell at each other a lot, just over anything. We're trying so hard to get in the house. But the harder we try the be hinder we get.

Bill still hasn't kicked the bar scene, I don't know if it makes him cope better, or what, I guess I can't understand because I told myself I would never really drink, when my mom was killed that way. So I had something to believe in, but Bill grew up with friends and a love of alcohol and he can drink about anyone under the table. He is a funny drunk, and his eyes twinkle as he smiles at you and stumbles to the floor. I couldn't threaten him like I used to do in Utah, for we had nothing. Everything was tied up on this mountain. And jobs, well lets say it is manual labor. How could we come from so much to nothing? I marvel that we are even here, and sticking it out. It is hard to see your kids not have the things other kids have, especially food.

Here Piggy Piggy

I made it a practice to buy bread at the day old bakery, but even treats there were too expensive to buy. The kids were without until one day I saw a guy loading into his pick up boxes and boxes of everything.

"Ah, excuse me but what are you doing?"

"Oh, I use this for pig food, they love it, they don't care and it makes them fat."

"Could you tell me what you paid for that?"

"Oh, a couple dollars."

So we found inventive ways to get food, so they could have treats, pig feed. I went into the store and told the lady that I had pigs at home, and needed some of that pig feed. She said sure, and carried out baskets and baskets of goodies, and for $2.00 you could fill up the back of a station wagon. Twinkies, donuts, ding dongs, cupcakes, and bread. When we pulled up the kids came running. Some of the food was hard and had to be tossed, but most were just smashed or getting old and stale. But to our little pigs it didn't matter they loved it. It kept them happy, and felt like a real treat. Those kids could hardly believe their eyes, as they rummaged through piles of Twinkies, donuts, pies and bread.

"Oh mom, you're the greatest," Nathan said with a mouthful.

We had to wrap everything the best we could and box it, so the mice wouldn't crawl all over it and eat their share. I wonder how my kids can survive with these varmints, they are everywhere. You can't go anywhere in our trailer without finding mice tracks and droppings on everything you own, clothes, towels, plates, silverware. Any foods that are in sacks have the corners eaten out. The varmints crawl down in the cereal boxes after they have gnawed through the box. Sacks were just a bother to them, didn't even slow them down. Its funny how you change the way you live when money isn't in the picture. You just need to exist, and to feed your family is one of the top priorities   (I hate those beady-eyed creatures.)

The weather and everything just seems to be unbearable. No matter how we try, something just keeps knocking us down. I don't quite understand. I guess this is a learning process. We put ourselves in this predicament so I guess we just have to live with it. It is just hard to realize how much my life has changed. Sometime I just want to twitch my nose and have things back again, nice house, sports cars, money, now that would be really nice. But if I give up, Bill will turn and run. This is also way harder then he ever imagined.

How can life be so different? Oh well buck up and stoke the stove, before we freeze to death. Not a pretty picture finding a fat lady frozen next to a 10 by 20 stove and -mice are having a hay day. Oh this is depressing, quit while I'm ahead.

Chapter 7
Don't Open the Door! Crawl... FIRE

The wind was howling from the northeast. The little trailer shook as you catch the door when someone comes through it. Or the hinges almost fly off. The temperatures are dropping below 40 below zero. In this little trailer of ours the windows become non existent as so much frost collects on the inside that you could almost make snow balls from the stuff you can scrape off. The stove is red hot from packing wood in it all night

The night seemed like any other night, just colder than usual. My feet seemed to stick to the floor from the cold, as I got closer to the rear of the trailer. I couldn't put another log in the fire, cause the stove was too hot to touch. So I prayed that it would keep the boys warm for a while. I knew the fire wouldn't last the night, as it never does. By morning the dog water by the stove will be frozen solid. We can blow smoke rings with our breath. The kids huddle down in their sleeping bags and try to keep warm.

"Night mom they echo."

I give them a kiss and hope this terrible night brings a warmer and better day.

I shook the snow that had blown through the door and window in the back off the covers. A good ½ inch had blanketed the bed. You couldn't feel the stove in the back of the trailer, so I crawled into the cold bed and covered my head with the covers. If you leave out any part of your face, you get frostbite on it. By the time that I go to bed, I'm exhausted so I drifted off quickly to dream land.

A few hours later, the stove had taken more than the little stove could take and the wall beside it. The heat transferred and the trailer was on fire. The first to notice was Dustin; he lies in the bunk next to the ceiling, and can't stand to have his face covered. He wakes up with his eyes and nose burning. It is hard to breathe, he starts coughing and chocking.

I hear a voice from the other room coughing, "Mom! Mom!"

I say, "What?"

"I can't breathe," Dustin says.

"Why?" I say, as I try to get courage to stick my head out of the covers.

"Because of all the smoke," says Dustin.

"Smoke!!"

I jump up. The smoke had engulfed the little trailer; you couldn't see your hand in front of your face. The smoke burned my throat, as I gasped to figure out where is this smoke coming from I say to myself, as I'm leaping for the front room. Smoke in a trailer fire, smells different. It isn't your typical back yard burn your eyes, it has a smell that I won't forget, old varnish, layers of old insulation smoldering, so thick that I wasn't sure we were going to make it out of this one.

Bill wakes up with a jolt, and Bill being a born boy scout, knows about the rules of a fire, and is crawling along the floor trying to see where the kids are, and shoving them back to the back of the trailer as I leap over everyone. I'm going to be super woman and find where this fire is. I don't see a flame, I open the door.

"Shut the door, do you want this place to explode with all that air rushing in?"

"NO fire on the roof," I say and then Bill opens the closet next to the stove. Billowing out of this 5-x3 closet a black smoke oozed from every crack. The fire was contained in this closet next to the stove. Even though we had Z brick and asbestos, the heat seemed to transfer into the wall since there was no air space in-between.

We have no water it has long since frozen solid. Bill grabs his gloves and starts tearing out burning pieces of wood and throwing them out the door, and into the snow. Canned goods bulging and steaming from the heat were tossed out also. Bill worked, his mouth covered with a neckerchief. His eyes watered, as he worked to get the fire out with buckets of snow. I was out in the yard handing him another bucket of snow. Your adrenalin is running high, so you don't notice that you have no shoes on, and standing barefoot in the snow at 20 to 30 below zero, the wind howling around you, but you stay focused on what's going on with your family, a survival instinct kicks in.

Steam would hurl up in his face, and ash went on his clothes and face. The weather is indescribable as soon as any moisture touches his coat it freezes on because of the extreme cold. The trailer is now an icebox.

The kids are in the car in case the whole thing goes up in flames. This is no party either. The doors froze shut from the bitter cold and the inside like an ice box, just no snow and wind. They huddle together, not knowing what is going to happen next, watching their parents frantically fight the fire. We had to because there was no way a fire truck could get up the mountain, we are on are own. Except with the help of our Heavenly Father and He did bless us that night with our lives.

Finally Bill gets the wood stripped out, and the fire is under control enough to get snow in there to cool it off. Tears stream down the face of the kids and me. We are so lucky to be alive. But maybe it was the Lord trying to answer our prayers to rid us of the mice, and we saved the thing! Oh what have we done?

We take the kids over to Terrie and Luckie's and stay for the rest of the night. I think that I was hoping that Dumb Dora would go up in smoke and end this whole ordeal; maybe we are not supposed to be here. Tinfoil now covers the wall behind the stove. And we are all back in Dumb Dora, at least for the time being. Our clothes smell of old burned wood covered in stinky lacquer, and of course in those days lead…

I really couldn't air out the trailer much, because of the stubborn weather, it just stays cold, day after day. We get used to the smell, but kids at school tell the kids that they stink like smoke, but they just shrugged their shoulders and say, "Because we had a fire! Duh!"   We thank God for having Dustin wake up and for hating to sleep with his head under the covers; for saving our lives, because we would have died from smoke inhalation.

That's it we're moving into the house, no doors, and 4 windows in the house, plywood flooring, electricity here and there but we have to do something. We have everything we own in the house, thinking it would be a good storage shed. But long extension cords will toast your fridge, and other appliances, then add cold, moisture and stress; a broken fridge, broken TV, mildewed clothes and sheets, you name it.   It seems every time we turn around ole Montana weather knocks us down. But we're making it, I hope soon. I don't know if our marriage will take much more. The knit picking on each other is getting unbearable.... 3 days before Christmas we move into our log house.... No doors just blankets cover the openings. We have windows from a neighbor's old chicken coop and a huge window out of a house that Lacey's were tearing down.

We are set. It did seem like heaven in the huge house with a huge ole mohair burgundy sofa and chair. An artificial oriental rug covered the cold wood plywood floors, the wood burning stove kept the house bearable if the wind didn't blow our make shift doors open. No walls were up yet so we had to staple a blanket to the door to keep the varmints and the cold out.

The weather just seems to get cold. Temperatures dip below zero so our blanket door is now solid. As we bring in wood we just kick the frozen cloth to close it, then at the end of the night, stack a few logs at the bottom and nothing can push it open. There is every animal you can imagine, from skunks, bears, to mountain lions, and yes the dreaded mice have moved into the house now. There's no food in the trailer so in they come. I set a trap and the food will be gone next time I looked, so I started getting smart and putting 2 to 3 traps in a row, if one trap didn't get them the other would. I would set a trap, walk into the other room and the trap would snap. I would have to empty it, out to the umpteen cats, and set it again. One night I emptied the trap 18 times before I gave up and went to bed. Every morning we would find mice in the traps. It was unreal. You wouldn't think a door would keep so much out, from cold to varmints.

What a difference, this place seemed huge to the cramped quarters of Dumb Dora. Plop, plop, fizz, fizz oh what a relief it is.

This is our house in the spring with 2 rainbows, there has to be a pot of gold here somewhere.

Chapter 8
My Dream House?

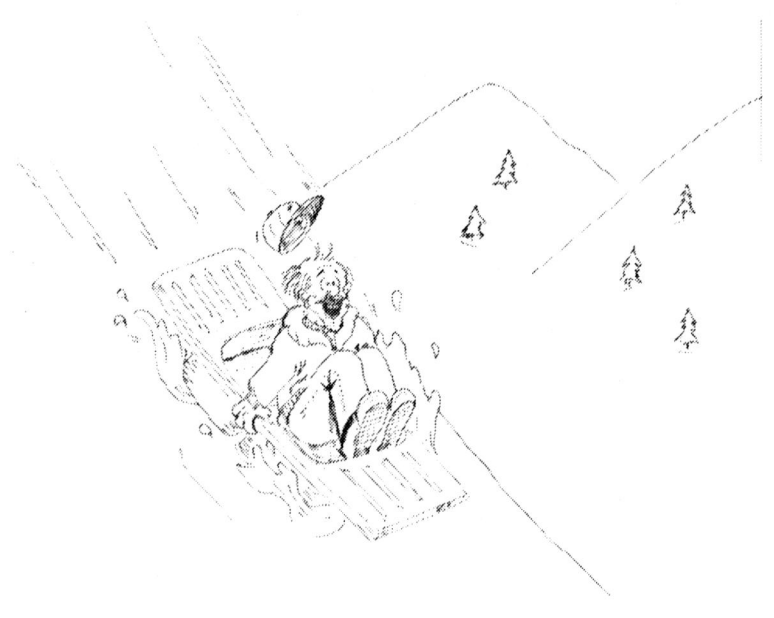

Christmas Eve

Different than from a year ago, we have a whole lot more elbowroom. The kids are so excited and can hardly wait to go to bed. The clock hits 9:00 the kids head up the old ladder to the upstairs an open room 30x28 with 3 lonely beds next to each other, in an otherwise big empty house, after either giving away most stuff, or having the elements ruin most of what we had.

The excitement is over whelming to the kids who are at the perfect age for the bearded guest to come visit. Our Mountain is impassable except for our 4x4 and sometimes ole Tilly tomato. Time to get the toys out and play Santa. Our first Christmas in our new home.

The top floor of our house, without windows, makes you lose all track of time. I can't sleep, never have been able to since I took over the job of Santa. I get so excited to see the joy on my little kids faces. The kids start to stir, Dusty gets out of bed, stomps over to the clock then yells to his brother Nate to get up lets see what Santa got us.

Dad yells, "No! Go back to bed until ten."

The boys almost fall over with disappointment "10 o'clock its 7:30, Dad, isn't that late enough?"

"Okay just wait for us to get downstairs."

I go down after Bill. Someone has to hold the ladder for me, cause I'm petrified it will fall on me. (This is just a old tin ladder that is propped up to the upper floor, it shakes and rattles and sometimes moves, not cool, for a mom who hates heights, and then have kids and husband that tease me as I gingerly come down the ladder. They shake it to and fro and say it's falling as I scream bloody murder, then get down and try to swing at who ever is near as they run past laughing. I guess it's fun to see mom go crazy, which is quite frequent.)

It is so steep. The kids come down it like it's a slide. Run to their socks and gifts like they set them out, knowing just what was theirs. The wrappings are all over, kids with dirty faces and toys and clothes scattered, in our cozy log cabin. What a warm family happening.

Trip

Bill's sister Kathy showed up for Christmas on her way over to his sister Barb's in Seattle. She talks us into going over also. Bill really needs a break. Terrie offered to tend the kids, so off we go in Tilly tomato, that's our little red Volkswagen. We have $100 for a 1,300-mile trip. We drove all night got to Port Orchard a 4 a.m. There was so much fog we couldn't see anything. We drove around and around trying to find Barb's house, we finally had to give in and call her. She gave us instructions and within 15 minutes we were visiting with her. We hadn't seen her for 2 years. Seattle is nice, but get me back to backward Montana and lonely Drummond (Buzz out City).

I can't believe Barb likes it here, people everywhere. Bill and I leave after 2 days take ole Tilly tomato on the Ferry across the Bay to Seattle to head home. Gas is from $1.10 to $1.15 a gallon; money goes so fast our $100.00 is almost gone. Bill shows me where he worked on the road, he was helping put in the new freeway system, but it wasn't done yet.

"How awesome up here honey," he worked surveying. The mountains were straight up. He helped with leveling and seeding. He tells me of a sink he saw in an abandoned house on top of one of those mountains.

Scotch me. I say, "lets go get it, this would pay for our trip."

Our Sink or Porcelain Sled

So we reach ole Ritz Montana top of the pass about 8:30 at night, snow everywhere. The moon is full or almost, really helps us see

"Well, it's up there!" Bill points up this steep mountain. Now remember this chubby body does not like to hike, and a steep mountain is even worse. We park Tilly tomato, off the road and start climbing. Bill takes a hold of my hand to help me up. I feel like I'm going to die. I can hardly breathe. I have to stop.

Bill asks, "Are you okay?"

"Ya, just let me rest" Look how far we've come already." We look down the snow covered mountain at our car, a small spot. Just about there, we crest the hill, I'm breathing hard.

Bill says, "Shut up!"

He starts whistling, making noise. He doesn't want any wild animals jumping out on us. All the way up we are following deer tracks, now were amid hundreds of tracks. I see the outline of the cabin ahead. We stumble up the stairs, dig our feet into about 10 inches of snow. Bill crawls through a broken out window. He flashes the flash light over the room.

"Well here it is. How do you like it?"

What does he expect me to say, oh, it's not the right color, after hiking over a mile straight up, "It's great!"

It was a huge sink with 2 porcelain drain boards. Bill pulls it from the wall and we lift it out the window.

"Are you sure this cabin isn't someone's summer get away or something, and when they return they see that someone has stolen everything, even the kitchen sink."

"Look Pennie, are there any roads in here?"

"Well no!"

"Do you see that anything has lived here but raccoons and bears?"

I looked around the house, windows broken out and weeds, branches and debris lay on the floor. That's all it took as a coyote howled, and the hair stood up on my head.

Going down the hill was a real joke. Bill left me in a cloud of snow. The sink literally took him down the hill. He looked like he was riding a toboggan with a faucet and drainpipe. A few times he did a few good somersaults. I'm just trying to manage to get down without ending up like a snowball in an avalanche. I criss-cross the hill and finally get down to the road.

Bill starts the car and pulls it over to the unused lane not plowed. Now to get a 6 ft sink into a 5 ft Volkswagen twist and turn struggle and move. We finally got the sink in but no room for Bill to drive, and no room for me to ride. Bill scoots the seat all the way forward and can hardly get his nose off the windshield, and me, I sit behind him cramped with a drain pipe in my ear and a faucet in my back and Bilbo my poodle in my lap. What we don't do to save money. We both start to laugh; now we're stuck! Out we pile. Bill pushes and I try to drive. We get back onto the road, pile back in and we're off.

Only 120 miles of cramp to City Drummond. We're finally home but can't get up our driveway. It is 5 below zero in the middle of night and I am exhausted. I get to hike up the hill and my lungs burn as I huff and struggle to get my well proportioned round body up the steep hillside. The house squeaks from the cold as we go through our blanket door. The door is still frozen solid, but it's still good to be home.

We have no cupboards, so we set the new sink on our old washer that doesn't work and our old dryer that doesn't work. The two drain boards rest comfortably on the top of each and the sink hangs in-between, now just stick a bucket underneath and we are in business. Just take water and fill it up, we can wash dishes, then pull the plug, drain into a 5 gallon bucket and make the trip to the backyard to dump it out.

This made for yet another chore that the kids had to do, so of course it would cause fights. They are at the age that no matter what I tell them, they just did it, or it's not their turn. From getting wood in, to emptying garbage, dishes, work on the house, but kids will be kids, and I have to admit they are the best,

January. Below zero to 20 below with snow and wind. The conditions are a little better with more room but we still go outside to dumb Dora to the toilet but we have an electric heater in the bathroom and when you sit down you almost sizzle. What a difference from squatting in the snow bank last year. We don't have any water out here when it's so cold, so carry a water jug with you to flush the toilet. Just a fancy tin outhouse let's say.

It sure will be nice not to have to go outside to the bathroom one-day just walk in another room. What will it be like?

Money is tight, weather so cold Bill hasn't been able to saw trees for 2 days. Snow is still coming down. I'm staying up to tend the fire when everybody is asleep but I need the time alone; I need something to cheer me up

Building a house, and living with no money is so stressful. Putting down flooring, Bill helped and worked on frozen water lines. He is working on getting us a real door that shuts instead of the frozen army blanket on the opening...

It's another day of below zero weather; the wind is drifting the snow, so our driveway is no more. I've been keeping the stove cooking all day; we would freeze if I let it die. Our new home is so nice, maybe not to others but after ole Dora, this place is a palace. It has plywood floors and no door, no bathroom, or water, no cupboards, no closets, no stairs, but Heaven. We sure appreciate everything we

have.
Full of Surprises

January, what a strange month. What a change in the weather, all the snow we had is turning to slush; 26 inches one day, 6 inches 2 days later. The whole nation's weather is unpredictable. I'm sure the cold will hit us again. They always have a January thaw then watch out and buckle up, it's going to get cold.

Watching TV ... Well sort of

When we watch TV someone has to go outside, move the antenna to get the least snowy figures. Sometimes it is a real trial, then all of a sudden it will come in clear as glass, and then we see the Lone Ranger in some foreign language talking, just get interested and it goes back to snow. Anyway back to what I was saying, maybe Bill and I should buy gold. Since September it jumped from $200.00 to $765.00 an ounce, unreal!! Like we would have any money to invest in gold. Let's get real here. We can't even get water and a door on our house. The nation's in such a terrible turmoil, Russians trying to over run little countries. Iran has 53 Americans in captive for 2 ½ months and the U.S. tries to negotiate.

My family and I are doing great here on our little mountain. We only made $5,000 last year for a family of 5 and making it.

I can't believe we can do it. Bill's doing better at logging, if the saw keeps running. Yesterday was the best ever, 60 trees. I just hope he is careful; what a dangerous job.

Chapter 9
Insanity sets in.

Hand me a Cushion

10 days later the cold weather came back just as the ole veteran Montana people said it would. The temperature is 47 below zero. If you have never felt 47 below zero, it is not nice, every thing cracks. The air is so crisp you can hear any little sound and it magnifies it a hundred times. The animal's feet bleed, the dog and cat water outside freezes in just minutes. We have to go for wood and our cheeks burn and our hands go numb. The snow has no moisture to it at this point. Your feet squeak with every footstep. It's just eerie. You have to put a scarf over your mouths, as your lungs burn just breathing the air. Nothing starts! Schools close because of the long distances the kids come to school, and know that they can't get there, because the buses can't start.

Bill has to get to work so we have to get ole Tilly tomato going. We get propane tank, with a weed burner on it and lay it under the car to try to warm up the motor so it will turn over in the bitter cold. Dustin went outside to get more wood and noticed smoke coming from the back end of the car, the Volkswagen was on fire.

Dustin comes running in frantically, "the cars on fire!"

We all run for the door and our little VW. Sure enough smoke is billowing out the engine compartment.

Bill whips open the engine door, the belts and paraphernalia are smoking big time and the insulation is on fire. I know that baking soda puts out fire, so I tell my kids to go get some. They run and bring flour. Not a good thing.

Bill is a little stressed by this time, and does the usual, "PENNIE get something!!!"

I run back in and get baking soda and dump the box on the car. The belt's a little worse for wear, the paint a little scorched in places but it's running. As Bill heads off for work the little car coughed and sputtered as it inched down the mountain. Bill returns home. No one can work, the machinery won't start, and the saws freeze up, let alone your body.

Drummond is in the middle of nowhere, and when it gets this cold, nothing will run, not even those semis's that go down the road and run constantly, their fuel gels and they stop. Little Drummond had 47 semi's parked everywhere in town. That doesn't sound bad unless you know how small Drummond is, one main street that goes for a mile, and these semis are packed in here like sardines. If they weren't frozen up, the road was closed because of the weather and blowing and drifting snow. Truckers were 5 to 6 to a room and thankful for it. Loads of fruit were freezing in the trucks because there were not enough shops to keep the trucks warm.

Our family was having difficulty ourselves. The poor windows and lack of good doors, lead to us taking turns sitting inches from the stove. The little family huddled next to the stove, trying to make it through this cold spell, if you walked more than 5 ft away you could see your breath. I had a chair so close to the stove the side of it turned black from the heat, but lucky for us, it didn't ignite.

We took the cushions off the couch and chairs and shoved them in the windows to block the cold and draft.

I love heat, well let's say it has to be just right: not to hot and not to cold. But Hot would be good right now. I can't get warm and the kids are dressed like they are going to a blizzard when they are inside, sweaters, long underwear, and two pair of socks, slippers, coats, hats, and still fight over who has position on the stove.

Well in this house it is too cold, so I want to be warmer and the only way to achieve that is to sit on the stove. I inch closer and closer to the stove, touch my back side to the rim of the stove, oh the heat is unreal, it feels so good the best I felt all day, so I warm up to the stove a little closer and a little longer, all of a sudden I knew it had been too long, I jumped back, but too late. I had burned my bum. Now how do you explain to anyone that you burned your behind? You don't. I just sat down gingerly for a little while leaning more on one cheek than the other. I must admit it was warm while it lasted.

We put up wool blankets over the doors to try to slow down the cold gale coming through. The stove was wide-open 24 hrs a day and we couldn't leave the side of it. The kitchen was unbearable. And we had to let the animals in so they wouldn't freeze to death.

Finally Bill had enough. He gets the ole wrecker running and goes and borrows my brother's diesel blower heater that they use in Christmas tree lots and big shops. He sets it in the middle of the front room and turns it on. Move everything within 5 ft. because it will ignite it. The house smelled like diesel. But it was starting to thaw out. We could actually walk around, and try to function. The sound of the blower was deafening, it echoed through the house, no one could speak within 30 ft. of the massive machine, but what a blessing.

I have never experienced anything so miserable in my life. And to have your little family have to go through it is worse. Bedtime was a real ordeal but we had lots of quilts for the kids and once in bed you covered your head and laid still to warm just one spot, then you breathe under the blanket, the warm air from your breath starts to lull you to sleep, unless you're Clausterfobic and then you have to leave your nose out and chip off the ice in the morning.

Bill and I have a waterbed and we crank that heater, that is a problem sometimes because you can cook yourself like barbequed frog legs, but our bed was so warm to crawl into we loved it. When I crawled in I would almost throw Bill from the bed, as I struggled for a comfortable place, trying to get me enough room to just roll over.

One morning I was just waking up when I felt uncomfortable and felt my bottom touching the base of the bottom of the bed, and as I lay there I thought I could hear, drip, splash, I wake Bill.

"I think the water bed has a leak," I say, as I get out of the bed.

The floor is wet, but not too wet cause we are upstairs and have a tongue and groove ceiling that doesn't stop water, just channels it faster in some areas. I run down stairs and turn on the dining room light that was just below the bed, the leaded glass ball light was filled with water and when the electricity hit it, it exploded, let alone set me with a shock. The rug and floor were swimming in hundreds of gallons of water, what a way to wake up on a cold winter morning.

I mop and wring and squeegee what I can out of the room rug, and then we carry it outside and put it on the porch. Within a half hour the rug was frozen solid, who knows when that will thaw, and our bed oh Hanna. When or how do you find a pinhole in a king-size mattress? Well, it turned out to be more than a pinhole, but a seam ripped open. Off to town we go to get a new mattress. We pump water from the bed and then try to figure a way of filling up the bed with no water.

Why can't our life just be simple? Choices we make I guess…

We still don't have water, and at this rate we won't get any. Bill does bring in a bucket for us girls to use. Bearing your cheeks in this kind of weather is down right deadly.

We worked on the house today, really couldn't do much else. We finished the stairs. What a relief to be able to take down that creaky old ladder. Stairs that I can stand up on and walk, and not hold on for dear life as I struggle to the top, and then crawl on to the floor once I get to the top. The joys of simple things.

Thanks Heavenly Father. I was just sitting here thinking as everyone is in bed and my turn to tend the fire, Bill and I have so much now, not so much material goodies, but what's inside that counts. Boy I love him so much, you really can't put in words how much a growing relationship for 10 years can make you love each other. We just smile at each other and know what we're thinking.

Feb12th – Bill got hurt logging. He was up in the mountains falling trees (that is sawing down trees) and then once you have them on the ground, you buck them (that is when you walk down the stump and cut off the branches). As he was doing this, the log rolled over knocked him down and pinned his leg between another log. These logs are huge and weigh a lot. His leg swelled and is black and blue, but luckily nothing was broken, and he was not killed.

I don't know if you know that loggers wear corks in the winter because of the ice and snow. These are boots with long spikes that dig into the logs and help them stay up on the ice and snow-coated logs as they walk down the logs like a tight ropewalker using a chainsaw instead of a balance pole. I told you this because I would have to wear these monstrosities just to walk around here.

10 days now, he is still off work, his leg still hurts, we used some home remedies for the swelling and bruising, but I guess these things just take time. We're used to living without any money.

Work has been off and on, the weather unseasonably warm melts everything then it gets bitter cold 20 below zero and 20 mile an hour winds. Miserable.... I have to help the kids get wood now that Bill is down and out.

It isn't a pretty picture to see me put on corks so I can stand up outside. The snow started to melt in the warm spell and then whap the cold comes back to turn everything into a skating rink, and so I don the corks, wool socks, the army wool pants, heavy parka, stocking cap and gloves, to chop wood. The ax is heavier than I remember, as I swing and it gets stuck in the huge piece of wood. I try to remove it, no such luck. I get a wedge and a sledge hammer and start pounding. The huge piece starts cracking and splits into 2 just rather large pieces instead of one massive one. I really don't want to chop again as I try to balance the wood and get the axe to hit in the right position.

Bill is watching from the window and can't take it any longer so he comes outside swings and chops the pieces in one-swipe, picks up the wood and hobbles inside.

"Don't do that again," he says, "you could kill someone, especially you!"

Utah

We need money so I decide to drive to Utah to sell our Bronco for cash. Terrie followed me down. I took Tiffany with me. While I'm there she gets really sick. I gave her baby aspirin, and that night her nose started to bleed. It wouldn't let up for 3 hours so I finally broke down and took her to the Emergency room. It took them 20 minutes to stop the bleeding. They had her sit up, blow her nose, kept constant pressure on her nose for 20 minutes. Then they packed her nose with cotton soaked in cocaine and then they cauterized her nose. Tears rolled down my face as I felt so bad for my little girl, she is only 4. Sometimes we don't think about drugs and how they can affect a little kid, or even us.

Our trip did get better. I sold the Bronco to a lot but really took a beating on the thing. Anything was better than not having food and peace of mind. I sold the Bronco for $3,600.00 cash, paid off bills and bought some food. Thank you, Father, for the blessing.

March 5th. The weather turned cold again. Today we had 14 inches of snow and later became depressed as hell. The water froze, the water line in the trailer broke and the battery in the truck is broke. We got notice from the employment agency that we can't get unemployment. I am bummed out thoroughly. I really can't get into working on the house and just want to Waller in self-pity.

It seems like all Bill does is chop wood and stoke the stove. I am sure grateful he is so good about keeping the house warm. Next year we are going to get our wood early, none of this garbage. It's so cold the kids haul it into the house in their toboggan, their cheeks and nose cherry red from the burning cold. How many other houses have a sled full of wood slide in the door, and fly across the room to an old Coca Cola Cooler, not the little type but 3 ft wide by 5 ft long by 4 ft high? It holds about 15 pieces of wood, the round log type in the box and the underside holds the kindling to start the fire. The kids and Bill hauled it home from the dump, to surprise me.

The kids are all in bed. Bill and I are in a little better mood. The stove is cooking strong, but the kitchen side of the house is really cold. I'm trying to get courage to boil the water to do the dishes, Oh sigh, running water, when will it ever come to be?

To do the dishes is a real ordeal in itself. First you have to haul the water into the house in huge 5 gallon buckets, and then pour enough water to heat up. We set our newfound sink between our washer and dryer that we aren't able to use. Then you put a bucket underneath to catch the drain water. Take it out the door and throw it over the fence. Whatever happened to luxury?

We carried the toilet upstairs set it in position but I don't know when the weather will turn warm again so we can finish the sewer line from the house to the septic tank. I just go up and stare at the toilet sometimes, and wonder what life used to be in Utah, when we had money and a real job, you know the story. I can't believe it's going on two years that our family has gone without. We just smile, but at times we need clothespins to hold the smile up.

The nights seem to go better; our moods or our nerves aren't so on edge. The fire has warmed the house. And I kick back to write my feelings in this book.

At times I can't express my feelings. Sometimes depression just overcomes me. I feel as if my life will never be normal. Water, Toilets, Walls, Closets, Tubs, Showers. When we started building this house I never dreamed it would take us so long. Sometimes I feel like giving up but where would I go if I gave up?

March 9th the whole family went to <u>Church</u> together for all the meetings a first for a long time, like 6 years.

I was thinking how that all came about, and it was because of our son Dustin. He was crying one night lying in bed. I went over to him and asked him what was wrong, in between sobs, he said, "Mom, if you and Dad don't change, you will burn when Christ comes in the last days."

When you have a 7-year-old son who is worried about you, it makes you start thinking that maybe we do need to change the way we act, think, and conduct our lives. Tiffany was so excited in Sacrament meeting; her first tooth was coming loose. She can hardly wait.

I love my family so much, and feel so good when we can go to church as a family. I hope Bill gets to love and care for the church again as he used to. Our family would have everything if we had God in our lives too.

As I write this book, it has been 23 years now, and we haven't stopped going to the little Branch, which loved us into the gospel. They would leave food in our car, come help us when I didn't think anyone knew that I was crying out for help. We have had blessings showered upon us more than I could have ever imagined. The time our wood pile was almost empty and we had no way to get any fuel to keep the house warm, and a miracle happened. I would put a piece of wood in the stove, and it would burn the whole day, and keep us warm, day after day this happened until we could get more wood. Our health has been great even with all the mice, now if that isn't a blessing from above. . Thank you Father for the kindness you showed us and for the loving people here around Drummond.

Ice Cream Dog.

March 10th. Woe is me. We're at it again. I think our family goes in streaks of crazies. First the family decides that since it's been so long since we've been out we should take the kids for a banana split, at the Frosty Freeze. But on the way cheap Charlie Mom talks the family into buying the stuff for it at the store. And make it at home. They all agree and we head home with the goodies. But now we have to get our chores done first, warmth is a key factor especially when you're eating ice cream. But now we have no fridge, so I tell Dusty to go bury the ice cream in the snow till we get everything situated. And then it was split time, Num Num.

We send Dustin out to get the ice cream since he knew where he buried it. He comes back in and says, "Dad! Barney ate the ice cream!"

Bill jumps up, "you better be kidding."

"I'm not Dad."

Bill goes out and smacks the dog Barney, no ice cream. Now every time Bill gets a sweet craving he goes out to beat Barney that cull dog. The kids were so sad, cause we had no ice cream and no money to replace it. But we did have a miserable fat Bassett.

Lets Hide

Today the school bus doesn't show up. The kids wait for 45 minutes then, Jeanie is down at the other stop loading the kids in and my boys get the bright idea that it would be better not to go to school. They run and hide in the weeds and snow. She pulls up, stops and looks for the boys then drives on. Dustin, Nate, and

Chuck get up laughing. Little did they know big mean mom was watching the whole thing from the window on the hill.

Mad! I yell at them to get up the hill, that they better get a hat on cause they are walking 8 miles to school, so head out. They start the long trek, I really wasn't going to make them walk the whole way but I thought a mile or two would cure their hiding in the ditch. But before I could lose sight of them over the hill Chuck's dad gave them a ride in. Come to find out the school bus driver was killed that morning in a freak accident, he was changing a tire on his truck; it slipped off the jack and pinned him underneath.

Tonight when the kids got home they couldn't do enough for me, so I wouldn't be mad. They made their beds, vacuumed, etc. Then I said they could play so what do they do? They throw a ball through the front room window, a perfect circle where the ball sailed through the window with great speed.

Dusty started crying, "why me?" he says, "I'm always so dumb."

I couldn't help but love him and fix the window with a piece of cardboard and duct tape.

Bill gets home, tired and crashes on the couch by 7:00. Logging is the pits for nightlife! He didn't even notice the big piece of cardboard covering the window, along with good ole duct tape.

April 10th

Tiffany lost her tooth on April Fools; she could hardly sleep that night, waiting for the tooth fairy. She was up by 4:30 with the little bag of money in her hand and a smile that could light up the room. (Just what we needed at that time in the morning.)

Rodney's wedding so I had to go to Utah. I didn't take our car as it had over 200,000 miles, so I caught a ride with someone else. The boys have to stay home with dad to keep the fire going and help with the house. They kiss me goodbye with big tears in their eyes, which made me cry. We drove all night; eight hours and we were there.

Our Step mom was sick in the hospital so I had to take charge to make it go smooth. Edie and I thought we would go crazy on Friday, sewing dresses, curling hair, tending kids, making the wedding cake, mints, nuts, punch, tablecloths, the minutes and hours ticking away and finally we got everybody ready.

I went shopping at Goodwill while I was there and fell in love with a chair. The price was right, $2.95. Okay it wasn't much of a chair, not a lot of demand for such a find, but it was great for me. I asked some friends to bring it to Montana next time they came. I headed home tired and anxious to see my family.

Tiffany just came up to me and asked me as she pointed to a mole on her arm. "Is this an age spot Mom?"

I had to smile, what kids come up with.

April 14th 1980

We hooked up our toilet today. We have no water yet but it's nice not to trek outside. We just get the bucket, fill up the back and flush. Oh, Heavenly Sound, Flush. What little things give us Joy!

May 13th Ranching again

It's been almost a month since I wrote in my journal. I can't believe how time flies lately. It seems we never have enough time. We still don't have the roof on the house. Bill's ranching again for Fred Parker. At least we're working.

The nation is in really bad shape. Depression has set in, nobody is working and in Montana you really feel it. We are one of the first to feel the crunch in these communities. When people don't build houses, loggers don't work. Prices are so high; the prime interest rate has gone up to 21% and now is dropping a little with the hope of helping the nation get out of the slump.

Trip to Spokane (ole blue Monster)

Bill and I had to go pick up some culverts for the ranch. Fred sends us over and back in one day. Bill calls and says come with me. I'll be over to pick you up in a few minutes. He fills up the two gas tanks on the Ole farm truck alas (Ole Blue) this truck has had its day, and shouldn't have anymore. It looks like it went through the war, it doesn't have a straight panel on it, doors have to be lifted up and then slammed by someone outside the truck, springs are sticking through the seats, it has holes in the floor so you have a good view of the road.

Bill drives up the hill sputtering and picks me up. We drop Tiffany over at Terrie's because she begged not to go with us in that ugly truck. The weather is kind of blustery and mixed up. We are getting a late start. Bill's really pushing ole blue 60, 65, now almost 70 mph past Missoula, almost to Alberton when all of a sudden everything goes blue.

The hood of the truck flies up covers the whole windshield. Bill goes to the middle of the road in a hurry. We get the truck slowed down as he sticks his head out the door window to see where the side of the highway is. He jumps out, crawls up on the cab and has to walk over the top to get the hood down. I was scared stiff, but couldn't stop laughing. We look like people you don't want to know. Well I guess we are. He finds some wire and a couple pieces of rubber beside the road and rigs it up the best he can.

He jumps back in the truck, shakes his head, "what next?"

Oh my, he shouldn't have asked, by now you know our record of unreal situations. On down the road we go get to a small town, St. Regis, eat a hamburger and have to find a place to free my bladder. That truck shakes everything out of you.

The weather's getting colder and starting to rain here and there. The engine's so noisy that you have to yell what you're saying.

Over the pass down the other side, Bill says, "boy the brakes aren't very good."

Should that surprise me when we're on an 8,000 ft. pass? My eyes get big and a lump rises in my throat as I look over the side at the steep drop off as we roll fast and wild, passing everything on the road, bouncing up and down and swaying from one side to the other.

"Slow this puppy down! We are going awful fast!"

"I guess we are, but I don't want to use the brakes too much," as he gears down and the truck moans and groans under stress. The road starts to flatten out, and I feel as though we might make it once more.

The rain really starts pouring. Bill turns on the wipers as the rain is coming down in buckets. Swish, Swoosh, Swish, Flop, The wipers on driver's side stops.

"Good grief Bill can you see?"

"No you drive."

"I can't! I can't! Not from over here."

"When we get to Wallace, I'll try to fix it."

Finally in Wallace, Idaho we pull over in a dirt pull out and Bill gets under the dash, feet in the air.

"Its broken, one of the parts is gone."

Why does that not surprise me either?

"I'll just slide it back on the arm, maybe it will hold. We can only use it when visibility is Zero." Oh Hell, off once more.

The rain's coming harder and harder, one swipe then he turns off the wiper. Idaho isn't on our side. We get over the border and have to stop at a weigh station. We pull on the scales, they have us pull over and bring papers in. I guess we looked like shady characters or the truck did. He probably thought anyone who was legal and in his or her right mind wouldn't be driving a truck like this.

I guess our papers were all in order, he sent us on the way, good thing he didn't see our wipers.

Coeur d'Alene, oh we're almost there and the rain's still coming down. Bill tells me to watch for the Culvert Company so we don't miss the road. We don't want to take this heap into the city.

Loaded pipes that stand 13' 2" in the air were higher then most semi's. I hope we make it under the underpasses. Homeward-bound better fix the wiper once more and switch gas tanks.

Out on the road, it's the 4 o'clock rush hour traffic. The wiper works twice falls off again, trying our patience, into the traffic rolling along at 60 to 70. All of a sudden chug, chug, and choke. The gas tank is plugged. We switch over to the other empty tank and pump for all we're worth. And pray we find a gas station fast.

We find one but the truck is too high to get under where the pumps are. Lucky for us the hose would reach but Spokane rations every car or truck to 8 gallons, which is nothing. Where can we get more gas?

Rain is still coming down so Bill has me under the dash, running the wipers. What a joy! Water's running down my back and I'm getting car sick from the bumping and swerving.

Bill finds a station 30 miles down the road. Once more we try to fix the wipers by taking a part from the passenger side. I still had to crawl under the dash and hold the parts so they wouldn't bind up.

All right we are cooking now. We get in a line with a bunch of trucks and Bill gets in the rocking chair. Let me tell you they cook. I just held my breath as we turned corners. Drummond's coming closer. We are so tired and the rain's coming down in buckets. It's 11 p.m., 12 hours later and over 500 miles we are home. We go to pick up the kids, Terrie says leave them till morning.

Raining Cats and Dogs – Inside the house

It's raining like cats and dogs all night, the mud oozing to our ankles. The cab's leaking down our back and dripping on my toes. I feel miserable, sure glad to get into our cozy house. Walk in the house, how good to be home.

"Oh Bill we are finally here," as the rain drips off my nose.

We push open the wood door (did you catch that phrase wood, not cloth) the door creaked like some horror movie and I couldn't believe what we saw, it sounded like some exotic rainforest restaurant. It sounded like waterfalls, and rain falling everywhere. Are we not inside?

It was raining harder inside then out. I started to cry, Why me? The floor's swimming in water, the couch soaked, the bed dripping.

"Well we can't do any thing about this now." says Bill, "so let's just go up and crawl into bed and deal with it in the morning."

Bill and I crawl in the bottom of the waterbed and listen to the drops of waterfall rapidly on the head of our mattress. How can I stand anymore?

"One good thing," Bill says, "we have a water bed and we won't have to squish this mattress out."

"Oh give me a break," as I curl up in a ball as not to let my feet get splashed on from the never-ending dripping and pouring of water. I fall asleep from fatigue.

Morning brought so much grief, the rain had let up some, so that we could round up some buckets and try to squeegee the house out.

Our roof only has tarpaper on it, and it was fine when cold and frozen, but when the rain came, so did the fountains in my house. As it rains, it pours off the rafters. They seem to channel the rain so it flows in big streams. Bill puts big tarps on the rafters and angles them down so the water runs in big buckets. We are constantly emptying buckets, every 5 minutes. We have to change buckets and it has to be Bill or me because 5 gallons of water is heavy for small kids, so our night goes on and we get grouchy. The kids know to try to help and just stay away and be quiet. Of course it can't be the normal rain that Montana has, but has to be a deluge with inches and inches of rain at a time, day after day, so we can't get on the roof to fix it.

We put buckets strategically around the house. My floors are starting to warp and buckle from the moisture. The house is a mess as I push every thing around trying to miss the rain. It feels cold and damp and depressing. I don't know how much more I can take.

The only one holding me together is Bill; he has such courage. He makes remarks like "well now we have running water" and "most people pay extra for fountains in the house." I don't know how he can smile so much. I guess because we have nowhere to turn.

We have to get big beams and bottle jacks to try and force the warped hardwoods to go back into place. After you spend hours, laying piece by piece of hard wood flooring and then see it buckle before your eyes, it's sickening. Bill rigs up the beams and jacks and positions them under the large beams then starts to jack and push the floor down, leaving them in place for a day or two and then going to another spot. After awhile the floor had seemed to go back into place. The water ruined everything. We poured water out of the TV set, stereo, and the couches would squish each time you sat on them for weeks. But the rain finally quit and our little family made it over another millstone.

Sour Milk   May 1980

Six months now without our food being cold. We're using grandpa's ole 1914 ice box to store the perishables. It was okay for January through April, but May in the house is too warm to keep lettuce, cheese, milk and etc.

"Come and get it kids, your hot cereal is ready."

"What is it Mom?"

"Oatmeal and Raisins."

"Alright they all shout".

Each of the kids picked up their bowl of cereal after I poured milk over it and proceeded to eat.

Dusty looks at his bowl with great concern, after half the cereal was gone. "What is all this white stuff floating around in my cereal?"

I look at his bowl closely. Oh, I don't want to tell him.

"Well son, I think its, Sour Milk!"

"Ooh Yuk! I think I'm going to be sick," says Dustin. "I'll never be the same."

Nathan's still eating his. "Can't be," he says, with a mouthful. "It's too good, looks like coconut to me!" as he scrapes the last remains in his bowl.   My stomach's queasy. I want him to stop eating but can't convince him the chunks are sour milk. Dusty gets an egg and cooks it quickly to settle his stomach; they throw it down and run for the bus.

A week later they get up in a rush, late start. "Get your cold cereal and run I say."

Dusty pours the milk and takes a big spoonful. "Yuk!" Spit! Sputter! "I think I'm going to die. The milk is sour again, taste it."

"No, and I'll take your word for it," I say."

"Mom, why does it always happen to me?"

"I don't know honey, I guess if I tried I would throw up. Dads had a few turns too. He's not crazy about it either."

"Mom, we have to get a fridge. I can't take much more, okay?"

"All right son, we'll try."

Setting out to make Life better.

Chapter 10
Is this Everyday life?

Rattle Rattle thump thump

I tell the story to my aunt and she says I have that old fridge out on the porch you guys can take. Anything! "the kids say." We plug it in. The noise from the motor's like an engine room in a battle ship after months of silence. We're not sure if sour milk is worse than that terrible sound emanating out of the kitchen. But we don't want the kids to get botulism or something like that, so we need to put up with the sound.

We can't handle the sound at night, we have to go down and unplug the fridge; it's just heaven.

Tonight is rather peaceful cause the kids are tucked in bed. Bill's on the couch and I'm sitting in my ole chair. My big $2.95 find that Bill's friends came through and dropped off. The weather the last few days has miraculously been nice. We have just an afternoon thunder shower here and there. Mostly here but I'm getting used to it. I can even smile as the rain runs down my walls and floors.

Bill put on some tarpaper last Saturday. It hasn't rained real hard since he put it on, so we haven't tested the new look yet. But it has to be better than it was. At night our bed lays under a beam, and the rain is like a Chinese torture, no matter where you put your head, the raindrops seem to find your forehead. As you drift off to sleep, a drip pounds down on you. I think I'm going insane.

We have been having Temple Preparation classes for a couple weeks now, and really do look forward to our lessons to further our faith and know more of the gospel. Both Bill and I really need to understand the principals more. This time we want to do it right. Times are getting too hard not to have the gospel on our side.

The lesson last night was on Family and Happiness. As he was giving the lesson, my mind wandered to my son Nathan, and when I went to teacher's conference. When he was in the first grade his teacher was telling Bill and me that she had asked her class what makes them happy. Kids got up and said candy, money, etc. Nathan got up drew a smiling face and said, "I'm happy because my mother loves me." Tears filled my eyes and his teacher's. She said that kid has it all together; he really knows what is important.

I love each of my children so much I wish I could only express how much. Thank you God for giving me such choice spirits to raise. I'll try my very best... Happiness Is: Three loving Children, One great husband, Unfinished house, No walls, No toilet, No water, 2 dogs, 3 cats, Dead mice! Friends, the Gospel, I have so much I really can't complain. I get depressed but I look back and we have come so far, that I have to smile, and look at everything around me with appreciation. If you have to work for it you sure enjoy it more, you don't take every little thing for granted. Bill and me or is it Bill and I are just preparing for hard times a few years early. But we know we can do it!

May 17th

We worked on the house all day. Bill's on the roof with Dustin helping him. I'm outside doing the wash; carry 30 gallons of water to the ole green washer. 15 in the washer, 15 in the rinse tub. It took 3 hours. Bob McMahan came up to help Bill on the roof, boy do we ever appreciate the help.

Nathan's sick, Sunday, the whole family's rather unorganized, so we don't make it to church. We stay home and work on the house. Bill goes out and works on the roof. This is one job I can't help him on. I hate heights and that is a tall roof. Bob and his family come up and help get the whole backside done. I get to stay on the ground and hand up the shingles. To do that you carry a bundle over to the ropes and pulleys hook them up and pull as they guide the heavy bundle over your head, my arms ache from the weight, but I'm thankful for some help. By the end of the day I am exhausted.

This Picture is of Spiders that moved in one night, it seemed they came with the wind, just like the volcano... millions of Spiders everywhere, and nothing you could do till they decided to catch a breeze and move on.

Volcano

A huge rain cloud's moving in about 8 p.m. We hurry to finish as a news flash comes over the radio, that the volcano. St. Helens has erupted and volcanic ash is hitting Montana. It's just scary; the road looks like an old desert road within an hour of the dark cloud coming down the valley. We can hardly believe our eyes that over 600 miles away this volcano is covering everything with ash. We get off the roof and then retire to bed and at 11:00pm we received a phone call telling us that there was no school tomorrow because of the volcanic ash, everything had come to a stand still. Visibility is zero, Interstates are closed down, and you can't drive cause it clogs up your air filters and who would want to. If you go outside you have to wear a bandana over your mouth so you can breath. 600 miles away and covering our ground like this is unbelievable.

The morning brings news reports of Washington State and the mess they're in, 7 inches of dust on the ground. It's just a gray haze outside. Ash has dusted everything. The beautiful green valley is now a creamy gray brown and the sun can't even get through the haze. Just an orange hew at times.

Now I pray for rain again, the only thing that can help us. I never thought I would pray for rain again, not after all the garbage I've been through. It's unreal how Mother Nature can mess up the ole world. The volcano had such power that it instantly charred people in their cars 15 to 20 miles away. Mud covered land for 50 miles and devastated everything in its path, even affecting us. They say it can change the weather all summer if the dust particles settle up by the North Pole. It will lower the temperatures for 2 to 3 months. What next?

Writing this book almost 20 years later, I will tell you it did alter the weather, our winters haven't been the same since the volcano and the snow just isn't as deep as it used to be. Before, we would snow mobile over the fence posts and constantly shovel snow off our roofs so they wouldn't cave in from the weight. At times the weather gets crazy and we get dumped on, or the temperature will drop out of site each year, but that's something you live with in Montana, a place to love and hate.

I almost feel like a normal person to have a few walls in my house, especially one around our toilet, even if we still have to pour water in the back. For the longest time we had no wall around the toilet down stairs, just a toilet in the middle of the floor, the few visitors that we did have would wonder just what was going on, we would tell them it was Bill's throne and I really think they believed it, especially if you know Bill at all. We had no water, but a toilet was nice. But to have a wall and a cloth door was heaven. Privacy at last!

May 22, 1980

School's almost out and the kids are rather down cause the volcanic ash has messed up their track meet. Air, you name it. You walk outside and your clothes are covered with white ash like you've been a chimney sweep for Mary Poppins.

June 20th

Haven't had a chance to write lately for the past month, all it's done is rain, rain, and rain some more. The rain dropping on our heads at night is getting on my nerves. I wonder sometimes what I did to deserve living like this. 2 years and still no running water (except on the walls). As you can see we haven't had a chance to finish the roof.   For the past month I have really been sick. I feel like I have pneumonia. Who wouldn't after breathing ash, and being wet constantly inside and out?

Wash Your Hands

Corey, my brother's little boy, got sick. His glands swelled and Terrie called and asked me to come over and look at him. I said it looked like mumps, but she better check it out, because I heard mumps are really bad for boys to get. Before the next morning it had moved down under his chin, his tongue had swelled so much that he couldn't speak let alone close his mouth. Terrie took him to the doctor here in Drummond. They hospitalized him immediately, they hadn't seen anything like this in 10 to 12 years and it was over in Vietnam. It was really scary not knowing what they were treating. They had a diagram drawn on Corey's neck in case they had to do an emergency tracheotomy, or something with a tube, so he could breathe. But with blessings, and the help from God, Corey came home after 5 days. I gave him a stuffed animal and it was his companion the whole time.

. Nathan waiting for Corey to get better

When it rains it pours (Greetings from I.R.S.)

Rain, still cold, hail, you name it, and then to get the dreaded letter in the mail from I.R.S. You scan your mail and then see it, IRS in the return address no one wants to see that, as you fumble it around and then open it carefully. They tell you that they want to see you in their little office, on a certain day and time. I call Terrie, my sister-in-law, to tell her the bad news; she had also received the greeting. We would both be going to hell the same day and time, just different auditors. I was just sick, how am I going to prove anything? What could be worse? <u>Nothing</u>! I hate to try to explain to people who don't even care why we have nothing and haven't got a clue what your life is all about. I was just sick to my stomach. Mice had made beds of my returns and papers, and the fire hadn't helped the deal either.

Bright and early Friday morning we get to be in Butte by 8 a.m. (Not only do we get audited, but it has to be at an ungodly hour). We have to travel for over an hour and find the place. I was sick to my stomach, even though I had worked for the place for 11 years; I knew how rotten these auditors could be. What an adventure, only I could get an audit to turn out like this.

Well to go on with the story. I was so worried about my audit, cause I had no proof of anything. The mice had shredded our checks and the fire had destroyed my 78 returns. I piled up what stuff I could find, mouse eaten checks, shredded tax returns, receipts, and mouse droppings mixed together.

It seemed like an eternity before we turned the corner and spotted the den of iniquity, the Federal Building. A lump comes to my throat, and my hands become sweaty. "Terrie, I'm not going to make it through this one."

Terrie had records of every kind, receipts, checks, you name it. We sat in a big lobby, then a guy came into the room, and called Terrie's name, and then called mine. We walked down the hall like it was death row; we were directed to rooms right across from one another. My sweaty hand gripped the brass doorknob. Oh well, here goes nothing, as I hold tight to my manila envelope of shredded treasures. Please Father, help me.

The auditor was waiting for me behind a big desk. A calculator was to his right, sharpened pencils, papers. He peered over the top of his glasses, he was rather small, mousy, the type you see in movies. I tried to be pleasant, we introduced each other, and he shook my hand, and told me to have a seat across the desk. I told him he wouldn't believe what has happened the past two years. He didn't seem to even care, nodding now and then, looking through the tax returns he had on his desk.

"You did these returns yourself?"

"Yes, sir."

"Do you have some proof to back up these returns?"

"Well, you see sir, I don't know if you really want it?

"Did I ask for it?" He replies in a snappy voice.

I hand him the envelope. "We have had unreal problems the last few years"

As he puts his hands in the envelope and pulls out the shredded mess, the mouse droppings roll around his desk. "What in the …. Do you mind? Removing this mess from my desk?"

I sweep the mess back in the envelope. And proceed to tell him of our dilemma. We started going over my return. I told him I didn't have proof, but honest to God it was true. That's all I had to say.

He slid my return to the side of the table and said, "Do you believe in God"?

I said "yes."

He then told me of his religion, how long he'd been converted and could tell I needed him. I backed up, put my emergency brakes on and held onto my chair. I wonder what he's auditing, I thought. He told me how they baptized, how he received the gift of tongues and words blurted from his mouth like I had never heard before, I sat in amazement. I was just relieved he was forgetting my return sitting in the corner of his desk.

He then remembered why I was there and pulled it back in front of him. Panic once more, I didn't know which was worse the religion or the return.

He listened to our life and said, "Pennie, you need to be baptized. I have a hot tub and if you want I can make your life better."

I stuttered, and stammered. "I'm really quite happy with the life I have," I said. "I appreciate your concern."

After 2 hours, we finally made it through without being baptized and without going to jail.

He got up and left the office, and I sat there alone knowing I was headed for the Deer Lodge prison because I wouldn't be able to pay any money back. I then thought of Terrie in the room across the hall. "How is she doing," I thought?

Terrie was going through Hell while I was being translated and being readied for baptism to get a new life. Terrie had the auditor that majored in Calculator 101 and he had that thing smoking.

He took every line in her return and she had to have proof for it. Also he added every receipt and made sure every penny was there if not it was disallowed or put to a debit.

My Auditor returned and told me that I had to do a few things for him and then I would probably be okay. I had to get signatures for supplies we bought for our house, and return them to him. Send for papers on the sale of our house. And promise to read a few scriptures.

I shook his hand, and walked out the door, a sigh of relief, as I walked down the hall, I heard someone behind me. It was my auditor running down the hall saying, "read *1 Corinthians 13:7* and call me if you need anything. God Bless."

I just stood in the hall, in shock. Terrie, walked out of her audit, and shook her head, that was hell! I owe over $1,000. I felt so bad for you, I had all these records. I knew that you must be sick in there."

"Oh I made it out fine, lets get out of here, and I'll tell you about it, before I get myself in hot water."

Terrie was ready to kill me, when she heard the difference in our two audits. I know without a shadow of a doubt that the Lord had a hand in my interesting day at I.R.S.

Mosquito's Again

Montana Mosquitoes, one day there can be none. And then the weather starts to warm up around the middle to end of June, without fail every year those little blood suckers come out of the wood work. They are everywhere, you walk outside and they swarm you, so you don't walk you run to cover, somewhere you can shut yourself in and then start smacking whatever came in with you. This makes a terrible mess on the windows and walls, but the kids have great fun seeing the results of the battle they had just won over the vampires. The mosquitoes go up your nose. If you wear Deep Woods Off, which I found works the best; they just swarm the top of your head. Everyone has a black cloud over their head just lingering, waiting for the scent to go away long enough that they can have you for dinner. Night time isn't any better, you hear that high pitched noise over your head and then by your eye or ear, you slap only to hit yourself, and then to hear that sound again, and again until you drift off to sleep. Only to find bites covering your face, arms and legs that happened to get exposed in the night. Perfume is a real NO NO unless you want to be a mosquito magnet. Then as the summer wears on the mosquitoes seem to thin down or we have swatted enough, dumped out any standing water in ole tires and flowerpots where they breed. Then we can co-exit outside together with our best friend Deep Woods.

Bring on the Relatives

If we don't have enough problems, Bill's sister asked us if she could send Jeff and Tammy over for the summer. Her two kids, who just lost their father in a car accident, have no guidance or direction in their life. So we're elected to be surrogate parents. It's not that we can't handle the kids, it's just the timing; no water, roof still not finished. trying to build the house, hardly any money to feed our own family. Besides, Jeff, is a growing kid that eats as much as my 3 kids put together, and Tammy well she is just picky.

And then Bill's ex calls and sends Chris for the summer, so now I have 6 kids and the same money ZERO. Kids are adjusting great, they love us. TV is no problem because we don't have one. The kids all pitch in and help when and where they can, with only a few complaints. We do have time to go swim in the river; it is our relief after a hot day of working on the house. The ages of kids: 16, 14, 11, 9, 8, and 6, now doesn't that sound like a nightmare, with no doors, just a sheet over the bathroom door and the girls' room. Jeff has a room to himself cause he wants it that way. Dustin and Nate share now. Chris sleeps on the couch, not my choice but he wants it that way... so I improvise.. I'm teaching them to make bread, and making dinner is just plain work, 10 lbs of potatoes for a meal, I go through 25lbs of flour a week. But I think the biggest chore is the teen-age girl, and a spoiled only child that has had anything he wants. But we are managing and the Lord is blessing us for our efforts, but most of the time it's crazy and fun.

Aug 15th, 1980

Rain came down in buckets, roof's not on, you know the old adage, just a few left but we don't have time until we get a cloud burst (and this is one). The rain didn't even slow down as it made its way through the tarpaper, insulation, tongue and groove and now my hardwoods. We caught 50 gallons in 15 minutes upstairs. I could still walk in water to my ankles downstairs and the floors were curling from all the water dripping through. As I crawled around on my knees with towels wringing it out and dumping more buckets, all the kids joined in. They didn't appreciate wet furniture, beds and things, so we all were mopping, dumping and wiping.

Bill decided the roof has to be put on! Bill stayed home and finished the roof the next day... Kids are up there with him and then it's FINALLY DONE.

How big are your Kids?

My Back was bothering me, so Terrie talked me into going to the doctor once more but this time I decided to go to the local clinic here in our small town. My lower back had been killing me, and I really didn't do anything that would have set it off, so it was a mystery to me why I was having all this pain.

I have a high tolerance to any kind of pain, but when I sat down I could manage, but getting back up I would have to work up to it, take my hands and push down on my legs while I was trying to stand up, hold my breath and cringe that was about it. I never really stood in the upright prone position but rather bent and doubled over.

I looked like a little fat ole lady waddling to the doctor's office. I should know from my last doctor experience that maybe I should just ignore the pain and it would get better. But I thought something has to be wrong, I'm so healthy.

I entered the clinic, and the nurse asked me what was wrong, as I shuffled in bent over and holding my breath because of the pain.

"It's my back," I said. "I just can't figure it out."

She led me back to the exam room and told me to disrobe to my waist. As I did this, I noticed that there were no gowns to put on. I was going to get the nurse's attention when the doctor walked in. There I stood; the only thing on from the waist up was a stupid look on my face. I folded my arms over my chest and said, "Hello."

I had never seen this doctor before; he was burly and matter of fact. I really couldn't believe he was standing there talking to me, me with nothing on from the waist up except my elbows.

He said, "Well, what is wrong with you?"

I said, "well, it's my back, it really hurts."

He turned me around and ran his finger down my spine and says, "Well from looking at you, you're 50 lbs overweight."

Well I could have told him that. Then out of the blue he says, "How big are your kids?"

Well when you're standing in front of a doctor buck-naked from the waist up and he asked you how big are your kids I thought he said "How big are your tits? I know why a doctor would use such language, but then why would a doctor let me stand there flopping in the breeze.

I didn't want to tell him I was a 42 double D so I said, "I don't know."

He said, "You don't know how big your kids are?"

I still heard the words wrong. And looked at him like "No."

So he said, "Well how old are they?"

I couldn't believe what he was asking me. I said, "Well they're as old as I am!"

He said, "Your kids are as old as you?"

Then I heard what he said, my face went red and I said, "NO! My kids, my kids, oh they are 6, 8 and 9."

"Oh, I thought maybe you were carrying your kids around on your hips to put your back out. But it must be from the work your doing." He told me to get dressed and he would get me a prescription.

I left the office, him thinking I'm a nut case and me knowing maybe I need my ears checked. I told my family about the crazy visit. So when Bill ever asked me anything about my body, he will ask, "Hey Pennie, how big are your kids?"

After a few days my back did seem to get better, maybe from pure embarrassment, who knows? But I sure was glad when the nagging pain went away, and didn't return for another year. I then ignored the symptoms and took good ole Tylenol and thought how big are my kids?

Bike Wreck

The summer is almost over; Jeff and Tammy are still here. Life is crazy with so many people in the house and things are still not finished. Dusty and Nate asked to have a picnic and go swimming with Chuck at the rest area. They would ride their bikes over to the old condemned bridge and then cut over the river to the rest area. Well I fixed their sandwiches and sent them on their way. I told them Tammy and I were going to Missoula, and to be careful but something told me that it wasn't safe but I ignored the feeling and sent them anyway.

Tammy and I set out for Missoula got about 5 miles down the road and saw Dusty, Nate, and Chuck. The bikes were strung along the roadway. Chuck waved his arms and Dusty was holding his face. My heart dropped, he moved his hands from his face. It looked like hamburger.

"What happened, son?"

"Oh mom, I was looking at the train wreck across the river, when I didn't see this big rock in the road."

I didn't want to show the fear that I felt as I loaded my frail little boy into the car. Nathan was kicking every rock on the mountain, trying to get back at the rock that hurt his brother.

I told Nathan to go on and have fun I'd take Dusty and his bike back to the house. By the time I reached the house Dustin looked worse. His face was swelling. I decided I would take my trusty VW to Missoula use it as the Wiseacres Ambulance. I had ole Tilly floored 65mph downhill. We tried to find a policeman but no luck. We chugged to the hospital and took Dusty to Emergency.

The nurses took one look at him and said; "good grief, hope the bike looks better than you."   Dusty nods, "ya it does."

They put him on the table. I take his dirty pants off and his shorts are dingy gray. A nurse takes soap and water and a toothbrush and starts on his face. My stomach gets queasy, my poor little boy. They numb his face. Lucky for me he lays there so big. After all is completed she calls in the doctor to make sure that Dustin hasn't a concussion or any broken facial bones, or any place else on his body. The doctor then asks him if he wants a bandage over his wounds.

Dusty says, "No, I want to show it off."   The nurse and doctor laugh, then Dusty gets dressed and a quarter falls out of his pocket. He picks it up and says, "I think I'll give this to the Doctor."

He walks over to the doctor and hands him the quarter, "Here this is for you because you worked so hard on me you earned this."

The doctor said; "No you buy something I'm a rich ole codger .

Chapter 11
Logging

Logging to make a living.

Bill hates logging, but sometimes you have to feed your family and do what is available. Bill has a terrible time being a sawyer, when he gets on a roll, and is clipping along cutting trees then the saw breaks down and we're back to square one. The company puts Bill on the Skid Cat

This is an okay job. You are paid by the day, but the work is hard and dirty. A Skid Cat is a bulldozer with cable and chokers on it, the front with a big blade. Or a Rubber tire skidder. This is like a bulldozer but has huge rubber tires that tips and rocks over the fallen trees and boulders.. Never could figure out how those guys could stay on that dang machine. I would call it something like the mechanical bull.

You get there early in the morning and you can see where the mountain lions have been laying on your machinery because the engine was warm when you left, as the rest of the woods were cooling off. The seat is frozen from the brisk Montana night. Here in Montana almost every month the temperature will drop below or around freezing, as the summer clicks on the air seems to get more brisk as fall is felt in the air.

Bill comes home and you can only see the whites of his eyes, he is covered in dirt, his skin is black, his clothes can almost stand in the corner alone as he falls out of them and into bed.

He said; "I wish I could fall into a shower," but we still don't have water, cause the house has rather come to a stand still. When you log you leave at 3 am and get home around 7 or 8 at night, and then have to fill jugs with saw oil and gas mix, sharpen saws, and hope your wife can quiet the kids before you bite their heads off.. And then do the whole thing over again. We have to get water heat it and pour it in a huge dishpan or old washtub for a good cleaning.

Skidding,

I guess I should explain it to people who really don't know what it is. You have to get all the trees that the sawyers have cut down and bring them over into a pile and then pile all the brush that is left behind the limbs that they have cut off, and the end pieces that don't make up a log. A log is a tree cut into certain lengths.

Bill ran this Skidder, but it isn't that easy. Add the horse flies, yellow jackets, deer flies, mosquitoes and dust that is so thick that you can't breathe. Most of the time you have to wear a mask to keep the dirt out of your lungs, but it collects on your face and clothes in layers. Or your face feels like it is going to fall off from the frigid temperatures that seem to linger from October through March or April. Then add the steep mountain.

Mountain, that is the key word. Mountains are not flat. You are running this Cat on a steep incline running over tree stumps that almost topple you over because they have been buried by slash or other debris and rocks. Then you have to climb in and out of this machinery to hook up the logs, being careful not to fall on the ice, frozen trees or hip deep snow. Then you wrap the chokers around the logs and drag them to the deck. When you get to the deck, you get out of the cat again and unhook the chokers. And restart the whole process over again.

Then you have to pile brush to clean up the forest. You gather old dead trees and junk laying on the forest floor, put it in a slash pile and wait for snow to fall. This is called burning slash and you can see the mountains glow at night.

The old trees may turn on you; the old sticks will try to pierce the cab of the Cat and sail at you like a spear. The Mountain is probably Bill's worse fear. He is rather new at this, and has watched many veteran skidder operators roll down the mountain, only to be life-flighted out of the steep terrain, if anyone is around at the time.

Throw me out please!

One such instance has happened to our cousin, who has run Cats for years in the woods. Sometimes the terrain is too steep and gravity is too little and the machine goes toppling down the mountain. Bob was skidding on very steep ground, when he could feel the Cat sliding and then losing its grip. It started to rock and then the mountain gave way as the heavy machine started to roll with Bob inside. The Cat had a roll cage that helps to protect you from trees coming through the cab. But when you roll it will keep your head from being crushed, at least the first few rolls, as the huge machine crashes down the mountain.

Bob had a chain saw inside the cab with him and each revolution that he turned the chain saw flew past him, one time cutting off part of his ear, and then slicing his face. Then Bob prayed that he could get thrown free from this killing machine. At that moment Bob was lying on the ground and looked up to see the Cat coming over the top of him. The Cat landed just inches away and upside down. The engine was running at high speed.

Bob tried to yell for someone, but the others in the woods were working and never thought anything of the Cat's engine running constantly. He lay there thinking and praying that someone would miss him or happen upon him. The weather was below freezing, snow on the ground and the wind blowing which made things even more miserable and visibility almost non-excitant.

One of the other workers stopped his saw to sharpen it and listened to the machinery, something was wrong. The sound was different, a high roar echoed through the woods, not the constant revving and pushing that he usually hears. He summoned the boss and coworkers and started to look for who was maybe in trouble. Then they saw the Cat at the bottom of the ravine.

When they did locate him the weather was too bad to life-flight him out. So they had to transport him best way they could out of the mountain and down where an emergency vehicle could take over. Bob survived with broken ribs, collapsed lung, and cuts and lacerations on his body and face. Bob was in the hospital for 2 weeks. But once more he has cheated death at the doorway. Bill had this on his mind and didn't want to have this fate.

Bill hated everything about logging, especially the dust and pollen that emanated through the air. This really affected his hay fever, and his attitude. Each night he came home more angry and hard to live with, tired and no time to work on the house. In the winter you had to hike up the mountain with your saw which most times is a 36 inch bar, a gallon of saw gas that hangs on ropes around your waist, 2 liters of saw oil, files, and a saw that is massive to do the job.

This job is not for the faint at heart. Most time he has to climb and then toss the saw and try to wade in hip deep snow. Then get to the trees that are marked for cutting and dig down so that you can cut it at the stumpage line. Just the adventure to get into the woods is a real trial. You have to have 4 wheel drive, and chains as the snow gets deeper, and hope that around each corner you don't come head on with a logging truck flying down the mountain. Each night I thanked my Heavenly Father for Bill making it home safely, at times it was iffy.

Fall time isn't as bad as summer with the bugs and dust, but winter starts early and he's had enough he can't take anymore. Bill jumped off the Cat in the middle of the day, as the Cat teetered on a steep mountain side, about ready to roll down the steep grade.

He says, "If you don't have something better than this for me to do, I Quit."

Bill tells me that he's "not a logger, not a sawyer, not a skidder, what I am, I'm UNEMPLOYED…"

So now I'm married to Billy Rancher.

This is my Dad and Brother Luckie Logging has been in our family forever…but Not anymore.

Chapter 12
Living with Poverty

Sept 1980

I'm so depressed I can hardly stand it. I've cried now for two days. I'm just tired of a lot of things, not living like other people, not having anything. I have to shake this depression, still washing outside with cold water; I'm tired of being a pioneer. What can I change? Not much, no money no time.

I had a good talk with Bill and he told me to buck up, things are not that bad. We do have a roof over our heads. And it finally has stopped leaking on us.

Autumn Leaves

Rain, rain, rain for two days now. The mountains around us have snow in them, but here it rains. I feel as though winter is closing in on us. Our woodpile is short. I'm still moody; I yell at the kids, bark at Bill and snap at the dogs and cats. The rain is pounding on the windows but the warm fire is a comfort.

Bill and I get in a good fight. I guess it's because of my depression. I'm fed up! Unfinished house, no closets, no money, no husband, no TV, no radio, kids fighting, and still no running water. We get in some stupid fight just before bed. And this girl isn't going to give up a good night's sleep, that's all I have. So we race for the bed, first one there gets it. We both jump for it. By that time were laughing.

I talk with Aunt Elaine; she seems to be my sounding board, along with Terrie. I don't know of another girl who would wait 2 years for running water, toilets, walls, you name it. I think I've been so patient, all my friends say, "I'd split that place," " I don't know how you stay and put up with it." I sometimes wonder myself, as the water was running through our roof like a sieve, now everything we own is early mildew, a real fashion craze in the garbage dumps.

Cleaning Dumb Dora or Hanta virus

A lady in Drummond stops me on the sidewalk "do you still have that blue trailer of yours?"

"Yes, but it's a mess,"

"Oh couldn't be that bad! Could we come to look at it?"

"Well NO! Not until next week, please."

I rush home and walk into the trailer to see what my job ahead of me is, before taking a tour through ole Dora I crack open the door to look slowly in. I know it's bad but can't remember if it can cause me a heart attack or not, sure enough cardiac arrest! What a Mess! No one can imagine how bad this place is.

Bill had let the animals have free run of the trailer now for 10 months. Barney's dog hair was an inch thick on the floor. Cat and mice piles helped it stick to the floor. The flies blackened the trailer windows and the hornets buzzing sound deafened me as I waded through the maze of everything we left behind. Where ever can I begin? What a mess, 30 some feet of total disaster. The kitchen drawers had mouse droppings so thick you could scoop them in a shovel. The fridge had food in it; I forgot we had in there, 2 rotten green peppers a dried up onion, orange, apricot puree that had turned to apricot wine I'm sure. And a pound of hamburger, which had come alive. I thought Dumb Dora was bad before, but this is the worst.

The cupboard doors swing when you walk through and you duck as you pass or you know you'll be knocked cold before you reach the other side of the kitchen. The water heater door is falling off. The clothes piled to the top of the only closet we have in the place, clothes that my size 16 or 18 body won't fit into anymore. Keeping them in hopes I shrink or could piece them together and wear them for a Coleman tent dress. Dog food is hidden in all corners; the mice had made a high-rise apartment house. Layered the paper and clothes in different layers and you could see where different mouse colonies had existed. Thanks to the cats, my friendly mice had moved to other quarters.

Well I have to start somewhere 6-garbage bags 30-gallon size I'm almost half done with the kitchen, 2 bottles of ammonia one economy size mop and lots of elbow grease. I can almost see the floors walls and cupboards. Doesn't look too bad, nothing anyone would want to live in yet, but it's better than when Bill and I lived there or moved into.

Stopped to take a well-deserved rest and get a root beer, gone a half-hour and I see a car on my mountain, "What the, Oh No!" It's the people to look at the trailer.

"Forget it! It's nice, but too small for our liking," she said.

I couldn't believe my ears. I just risked my life to clean up this mess and it's too small! When you tell someone it's 8x35, you would think they would probably know the size. I'm not a happy camper.

Now that I had cleaned the trailer, our pack rat decided to move into our house. I could now smell the familiar stench that only a pack rat has, and then finding droppings here and there, and when it's a pack rat they are not small. He would show himself now and then when I was alone in the house. He would come out in the middle of the room and sit and stare at me, like tempting me to get him, as I moved he would run. He did this over and over, and would drive me crazy. Just to have a huge rat in the house, piddling in everything and eating more than the kids, cause if he crawls on stuff he destroys it, or just devours cereal boxes, and pasta, cake mix boxes, rice you name it. I get queasy just looking at him. He is huge, has a rat tail but has hair on it, not a lot, just like he's had a bad hair day, dark gray and ugly. The eyes are beady and follow where you move, and they are fast. He has big teeth and I just want him out of here.

One day while I was gone, and the kids were home from school, Mr. Pack decided to play the hide and seek game. But he got more then he bargained for. The boys didn't even hesitate. "Let's help mom," they say as they get the .22 and then think about shooting up the walls, windows and furniture. They ran and got their air rifles and fired away… now not many people have kids shoot rifles in the house, but the kids figured I would rather have a dead rat, and could put up with some holes in the walls. When I arrived home the mighty hunters showed me their prize. There laying on the door step was the dreaded rat.

I said, "You shot that in the house?"

Then they weren't sure if they were in trouble or not. "Mom we didn't shoot real bullets, but BB and pellets."

That was bad enough; little BB's and pellets glistened in the light. You could see each one that was imbedded in the logs, or ricocheting around the house. As you walk barefoot and step on a pellet or BB, choice words ring out like … You little shysters…. But one less pack rat made me smile…

Witches

Halloween is close and to entertain the kids at school, Terrie, Jean and I donned costumes and dressed up like the Mulkey Gulch witches and off we went in Luckie's ole '37 pick up. All 98 kids in the school from 1st through 8th loved us and loved the treats we brought them.

We entered the school, and I gave out a witch cackle and the kids started to scream and laugh, as we went to each class room with goodies. When we reached the 8th grade, Jeanie's daughter Pam, yelled, "Mom those are my socks, and you're stretching them out. I'll never wear them again."

Jean just took it in stride and stuck her tongue out at her and tried to take her treat away from her. Everyone had a good time, it was fun to just let go.

Many other times I have dressed up and my kids just take it in stride now... Mom's crazy.

Oct.25th

Sitting alone tonight, the only noise in the house is the fire crackling. The rain is beating against the windows trying to turn into snow before morning. Bill is at priesthood meeting. I just returned home from a shower over at Terrie's (how good water feels when you don't have it). Once we have water we'll hardly remember when we didn't have it and how did we exist?

Our house is so beautiful. Even unfinished, everyone loves the feeling they have when they enter. A light scattered here and there, shadows dance around the room giving a soft glow on everything, making it feel so cozy. The stove feels good tonight as I curl up next to it, the kids are in bed.

The lamp we have is an old antique floor lamp and has a burgundy shade that glows red in the window at night. My husband has a joke with those that pass by and tells people I'm working... I could kill him, but the red light goes on and gives a warm glow. And I'm far enough up a mountain I don't think I have to worry about visitors.

November 7th

We made it through Halloween I can't believe it. Halloween in Drummond is a real treat, because you don't have to worry about your kids, as they run from house to house. You know almost everyone. Even the stores and gas stations give out candy bars. The Frosty gives out drinks or ice cream coupons, and the bar has a spook alley. We drive around the town, and then after they have their pillow case bulging, or are frozen half to death we head for home.

Bill's working late as usual, on the ranch now, and what a pit job, with rotten pay. We do get a thousand dollars a month, before taxes, but we don't get any benefits, as other ranch hands, no house furnished, power, meat. Plus our gas bill is high for all the miles that we have to travel, oh well it is a job…

Bill fixes fences; rides on horseback to gather up loose steers, feeds, hays, brands, and any other thing the ranch can find him to do. Ranching has slowed down some, the quiet before the storm. Having to go in early to feed the cattle, this is a job that just takes time, in the morning you load up the hay bales on a flat bed, and then you have someone else drive, or you get real good at letting the truck drive it self across the field as you cut twine and toss bales off the truck. Sometimes this works good, other times you better have your eyes looking about so you don't run over a little calf, or run into a irrigation ditch which will toss you off the truck The cows aren't due to start calving until January, I always thought that it was strange to bring baby calves into this world in January, one of the coldest months of the year. But what do I know? But there are always a hundred things to do, and in Montana the list just gets longer.

The house oh we don't talk about it anymore. It's at a real stand still, the paycheck is gone before we have a chance to spend it on the house, and then no time to do that either. Ranching is keeping Bill till late and then he is so tired he falls on the couch and sleeps, gets up and goes to bed.

Nov 8th (Wood Getting) asking for help

What a day got up like a usual day, going to get a lot done. Bill didn't have to work so we we're going to get wood and finish our water. Rain and mud, we can still go in ole Tessie Wrecker, she'll get us up the mountain. We get in to start her and R-R-R-R no deal... The battery's dead it wouldn't hold the charge we just put in it. Well off to town to get another, have to wait for them to charge it. Sit around Drummond for over an hour maybe that will work. Back home after 12:00 and haven't accomplished anything but getting up and yelling at each other. Bill puts the new battery in. $47.50, an expensive day. Now off to the woods. It still wouldn't turn over, well everybody out and push!! Bill, Dusty, Nate, and I out behind the truck, Tiffany our co-pilot inside. Down the driveway we go, Bill gets in pops the clutch and Tessie chugs, everyone piles in. Bill, Dusty, Nate, Tiffany, on my lap 2 guns and bullets, in case we come upon some game for food since its hunting season in Montana for a month or more, and then add my chubby self to the little cab. Let's say its cramped to say the least.

We are packed in the front of ole Tessie like sardines and I feel like I'm at the bottom of the can. My temper starts to flare as the kids skin my shins with their heels and smash me, my patience is like a thread.

We go up Dry Mulkey. On the steep grade Bill can't find the lever for 4-wheel drive for all the legs. The truck dies and won't start, Tessie is sliding in the mud backwards. It's not a pretty picture in that ole pick up.

Bill yells at me to grab the emergency brake like I was sitting there knitting or something. After I mange to push the bodies aside and yell back I find the brake, pulling with all my might but the truck still is sliding backwards and not following the road very well, favoring the cliffs on one side. Bill tries popping it in gear once again but in reverse this time.

He's yelling, I'm yelling, the kids are crying and Tessie just sitting there decides to do us a favor and turn over. The noise in the cab settles down we all apologize and head up to higher ground. What amazes me when you go get wood you pass thousands of trees, but you have to find this certain tree.

I say, "There's one."

Bill says, "It's not dead enough."

Sure looks dead to me, the needles half gone and orange. Onward and upward the mud's so deep. As we go up hill we're pushing mud with our bumper. (Oh what have I gotten myself into?)

"There's a couple of good ole snags" Bill says, and backs into this skid trail and we all pile out. Bill starts cutting and falls one, two, three trees, bucks them up as we start carrying over to the truck a good 30 to 50 yards The mud, that clay like slop that sticks to your shoes and your feet, gets heavier with every step.

I didn't come wood hunting with the right attitude cause I was really bummed out as I had 4 inches of mud stuck on me trying to carry these huge pieces of wood over to the truck. Bill starts carrying now; we have it piled high in the truck.

We jump in, once more Tessie decides not to turn over R-R-R, no luck. Bill thought he parked it on a down grade, but the ground was so wet that the heavy load made the wheels half sink in mud just like a little pig we are sinking fast; our wheels are up to the axles. I look and almost give up. Oh heavens we're going to die up here. The blowing snow is making our hands freeze and our noses numb.

We start pushing NO Luck! We might as well been pushing on a 747, it wouldn't budge. Well needless to say my patience had been trampled in the mud. I was cursing to myself and pushing on the back of the pick up. When I looked up Bill was kneeling down with the kids they had their arms folded.

Bill says "Honey, don't you think we better ask for help cause we sure can't do it alone."

"Sure," I said, thinking "a lot that will help."

Dusty said the prayer and Bill said; "okay, let's push at the count of three."

We all pushed as hard as we could the first time, no go.

Bill says, "Again."

Then I couldn't believe it, it moved 5 feet. My mouth dropped open.

"Who did that?" I went around feeling the little boys' muscles.

Bill says, "lets try again we only have 10 or so more feet to the road."

Again Tessie moved like the motor had started. I thought, "Ye of little faith..."   Bill jumped in and popped the clutch and Tessie turned over. Down the hill we slid, it was like the pick up had marbles under the wheels it just slid where it wanted to but we finally reached the bottom of Mulkey and our house was in sight. Oh how thankful I was.

Bill says, "We better thank God for helping us."

"Really," I said, "but He doesn't help those who don't help themselves," as I felt my sore muscles from pushing...

Christmas Treeing and I'm freezing

Bill is leaving for Bozeman to go and gather Christmas trees for Fred. He will be gone 4 days. The weather is 5 below zero. No wood chopped, no money. Bill grumbled and went out and chopped wood for over an hour. He says the kids and I can come up with some kindling. I really have a hard time without Bill. I never realized how much he does. Getting the fire started in the morning, what a pain.

The house is so cold when you step out of bed. The logs creak from the cold. I try to get my legs to work and get me down the long stairs and over to the cold stove. I don't know how to bank it well enough to have the fire last the whole night. Not a cinder's left glowing. Put the little kindling I can find a lot of bark and paper and blow, blow, blow to get a flame to stay going. Finally!

I get the kids pancakes because we are out of milk. I ask Tiffany to call me the time because we don't have a clock downstairs. She calmly says the time is 8:10. I scream, throw on Bill's slippers yell at the kids to hit the door, the bus will be here. I run out make two swipes across my windshield and start Tilly. The frost almost gathers on the window again before we all pile in.

I start down the hill see the bus and say, "good grief the Bus!"

I floor ole Tilly round the corner and the sun hits the windshield. Nothing, I couldn't see a thing so I roll down my side window and stick my head out and drive down the road to their stop. If we didn't look a site my hair in every direction, ole blue chenille robe... I tell the kids to hurry and get out of the car before everyone sees me. Too late; I just act cool and wave. I teach art to the jr. high and then back home to try to keep the fire going. Have to cut up a deer tonight; it has been hanging for over 2 weeks.

The time is now Terrie said, so I go over to her house, and we cut and wrap meat for hours, taking off all the sinew and separating it into small steaks and cleaning it.

I went home tired, and kicking myself because I didn't bank the stove good enough when I left, and now the stove almost out. I cut kindling with a table saw waiting for my thumb or whatever to slice off; I'm not too talented with machinery. So here I sit now, kids tucked away, no husband, and no energy, looking at my unfinished house with a sigh. Still no water and the kids are getting bummed out about it now. No TV, they have read every book in the house and school library. I'm beginning to regret moving away from my cozy little house in Utah. To pioneer life yuck! I'm tired of it. (My pioneer spirit has got up and split!!!)

Even now, Drummond still has Cattle drives like the old days.

Chapter 13
Cool Clear Water…

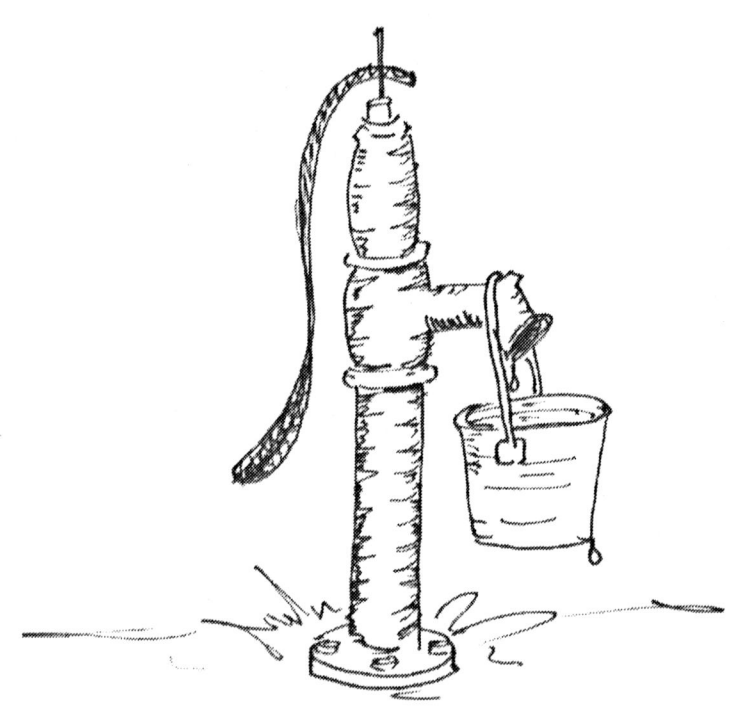

November 24th 1980 (A Day to Remember)

Bill's home from Christmas treeing. Saturday night Bill starts working on the water. After being in a motel with actual running water; we have to get this house finished or at least the water. He works on the water till 11 p.m. and then gets up at 5:00 in the morning. I was still snoozing.

He wakes me up at 7:00 and says, "I need a leak checker."

I said, "We don't have one of those."

He said, "No, I need you to check if there are any leaks."

"Leaks, are you kidding? You mean Water?"

He crawls down the basement and turns on the water.

Water! Oh I can't believe it. It came out of the kitchen sink, bathroom sink, bathtub It is unbelievable 11 months and 2 days since we moved in, since we've had water.. Now I can flush toilets, turn on a tap to get water and even bathe. What a rush... I can't believe this day has come I needed that!

The Tin Shower

We took the old tin shower out of Dumb Dora, because we were too poor to buy one, but it worked, and sometimes a bath just doesn't cut it. Now I don't know if everyone would agree with the shower we had, but it got you wet and that's all we needed.

A fond memory now, but a curse then, for 15 years we had the old metal shower, it measured 3 ft by 3 ft by maybe 6 ft. It was the typical old tin, that popped when any pressure was put upon it, so when you stepped in a sound would emanate, and then each time you tried to turn around in the thing you would hit each wall and a array of sounds would echo through the house, It had a hole in the top of the shower maybe 18 inches square, anyone 6 ft and over would have to stick their head through this hole, to be able to stand upright in the shower.

The shower had a old galvanized pipe that came through the tin wall and an old 50's shower head hooked to it, the handles were old and worn out from 40 years of wear. So being poor or lack of incentive, probably both, Bill fixed some vice grips to the handless bolt. The cold water would work just fine, but to adjust the hot you would have to find a good temperature and clamp it down and then shower away. This not being an easy task, as usually some one in the house would turn on the water or flush a toilet, and Katie bar the door, you would either turn to a Popsicle or be scalded to death.

It was almost a rule that no one would monkey with water of any kind while someone was showering. But when people came to stay, someone always broke that rule.

Jeff probably was the tallest of the people in our household that had to fit in the shower. He towered over the little shower. Jeff was a huge kid, not fat, just let's say large in stature. He was all of 6'4" if not taller, and had bright red hair, he never complained. He would be showering and I would hear the familiar popping sound, and then a yell as the water scalded him, then a thump as he exited the shower. Then back in when once more he had gotten the water back to tolerable temperature. It seems always when you had to exit the cubicle it would be when your hair or body was lathered with soap, and you couldn't see. But we managed and used the ole tin beast till all the kids had left home.

Once we had a couple missionaries stay with us for Christmas, and one of them was even taller than Jeff, which was a real trick in the tin beast. I tried to explain how everything worked, but as I was down stairs I would hear the familiar popping, a yell and then hear it again and again. When he returned downstairs he was a red flushed color, and had some cuts on his head. His companion was laughing at him, as he told him how his head stuck through the top of the shower. To wash his hair he had to squat down, which wasn't and easy trick if your more than 100 lbs, and then he would bump the vice grips and the water would turn scalding hot, he would jump out, and then adjust them, get back in try turning around and bump them again, as his head stuck through the top, bumping and cutting himself on the way out. He had to take a picture of the thing to send home, cause his family would never believe that someone really owned something like this and used it daily.

Then it was time for a new shower. We looked at plumbing stores for just the right shower that would fit in the small corner we had the other one in. We finally found one the right dimensions, not as small as tin lizzy but more on the smaller scale than the let's say rich man's shower. Did you ever wonder why the tub and shower are put in the new houses first? Well, I know now because they don't fit otherwise. We purchased a new whole shower and brought it home. The first problem was getting it through the door. We had to remove the door and squeeze and shove until we finally had it in then up the stairs. Another trial, up over the railing and then into the bathroom, which in our house is on the north side of the house. Our home is a hip style roof so it comes down on the side sooner than others. The bathroom door had to be cut off in height, then another door, so another obstacle. We got it in but then it got stuck laying partly on the tub and blocking the door. It would not budge. Okay I'm in the tub and the shower is blocking the door. Bill was yelling at me to push or pull, like I wanted to be stuck in the tub. Finally we got it moved and into place, a real shower with a door, in our bathroom Heaven.

Our bathroom also has a claw foot tub that was my grandma's and that was another chore to get up on the second floor. Those tubs, being cast iron, weigh heavier than I want to lift, but had to if I wanted to soak in a tub. So up it went also with help from our kids and Bill and me and a few friends. Now it's a tub for me to rest and take my troubles away, well almost. The biggest problem is that it is also under a large log beam and you have to be careful when you stand up so not to hit your head.

I just have a problem getting up out of the tub, as you know by now that I am let's say fluffy, and fluffy people fit rather snuggly and tight in a deep old tub. My well rounded cheeks hug the sides. To get out I have to flip over get on my knees and pull my self out of the chin deep tub. I always worry that I would fall and what a sight, if some one would have to find me in a naked state. Oh heaven forbid they would be scared for life, to see a saddle bagged hipped woman, with rolls from her chin to her toes. Not pretty, but they say it's what's inside that counts, and I have a lot of insides, so it takes a lot of fluff to cover that. After all that we finally have adjusted and are half normal, with doors, regular shower, and tub.

The road to our house

Our driveway was always insane to get up in the winter time. It took a real Mario Andretti. You had to get your car up to light speed, then maneuver it through the gate as you slide around the corner, white knuckles holding on to the slick black steering wheel, tugging and pulling as you bounce and roll, and then floor it to get up the rough steep incline. As you are almost to the top of the first incline you have to make a sharp turn and let your car bounce around the corner, quickly straighten it out and not let your wheels spin, and then accelerate again to get up the next steep grade. When almost to the top, you would then have to slide around the corner again and try to slide into place before hitting the house, trailer or other cars etc.

The truth be known, we didn't make it up that often. Most of the time we would make it through the gate and almost to the first corner and then we would lose all momentum and there we would sit, and try to back down. Bill was a master of backing down, but for me, what a disaster. I was all over the mountain, and never on the driveway. Usually getting it stuck so bad that he would have to get shovels to get me out, so he would ask me to park below and hike, which this body hated. If a car can't make it up, just think about a body carrying bags of groceries, and slipping and sliding uncontrollably. But I would stand on the porch and watch Bill as he got in the VW and would back up about a tenth of a mile and then come a running, slide through the gate barely missing the uprights and then bounce through and slide the rear end of the VW on the next corner and up he would come.

If you could make it through ¾ the driveway you usually could make it, if you had come up here 10 or more times. But if you were a novice, it was hopeless. We would have stuck cars all over our mountain, so needless to say no one drove up in the wintertime but our family. The springtime was a real challenge also, because of the mud, it was horrible. A spray would follow behind the car covering anything and everything within 50 ft. If you got off the packed road it was worse, which I usually did. Because you had to get a run then to, you would sink to your axels in mud. A few times I could barely open the door because the car was buried in mud. Let me tell you Bill was a tyrant when he saw that, and ranted and raved. But a few times even he got stuck, and I would have to smile. No I would chuckle, maybe even laugh out loud, because he deserved it.

Thanksgiving (Are We Crazy?)

No, just poor... Fred called to tell Bill that he is driving the ole Blue truck down to Provo Utah with a load of Christmas trees on it, and we would have a chance to see Bill's parents for the weekend. We had to be ready at about 2:00 p.m. so we gulped down turkey at Terrie's and then got over to Jens where the truck was.

We couldn't leave until Fred got there. He had the money and weight permits. The time clicked on 4, 5, 6, 7:00 p.m. No Fred.

8:00 p.m. Fred decides we should take the camper because of our kids, and he would take ole Blue, prayers are answered. We have to go in a caravan because you can't trust any of the trucks. They eat oil and miss as they go down the road. To Butte it is bitter cold, we have to gas, then head on to Dillon then start for Idaho Falls. It is after 1 am and Fred is really getting tired. We have to travel 35 to 40 mph. and Fred is starting to doze and the truck weaves. Victor flashes his light to wake him, mile after mile the truck sways over the line. Now Bill is starting to doze. I yell at him every other minute. Just let me drive. At the Idaho line they all stop, run around in the cold and try to wake up. Fred decides to stop in Idaho Falls for some rest. We baby him another 70 miles praying he'll stay awake.

Idaho Falls, what a blessing. We tell Fred we are going on to Ogden. We can't afford to stop. We stop and get donuts for everyone and then we push on. Just out of Idaho Falls Bill finally lets me drive and I plug on. Bill falls asleep and the roar of the motor and white lines going by the truck try to fix your eyes. I can feel the fatigue trying to take over my body. I am driving but I'm just barely keeping it on the road, but I have to go on have to turn my head from side to side, my hands feel numb at times. I'm hoping a deer doesn't run in front of us because I know my reactions would be slow or non-existent.

Bill wakes up 30 miles out of Ogden takes over at Tremonton. It is now 7:00 in the morning and we have driven all night. Ogden is up and stretching the ole government workers are on the road.

I'm trying to make a good impression in Utah to all the people when I'm in the mall. I feel like people are staring at me I start getting a complex, I even see a lady point at me. I get in the car all depressed and Tiffany says, "Mom how come you have your coat on inside out, with ole labels on the back." We both start to laugh.

We had a good visit with family for two days. Now we're back on the road this time in ole Blue, torture city... We load up Ole Blue and hit the road we have tires and wheels from my Dad and a wheel chair for Grandma, a fridge from Bill's parents, a couch and dressing chair from Ranae, my friend. We finally pull out at 2:00 pm after all our goodbyes. It takes $37.00 to fill the tank. We are getting between 4 to 5 miles to the gallon. We head on making pretty good time to Idaho Falls. Next gas stop, $28.00. Darkness is starting to blanket the valley; a storm is ahead of us.

We are out of Idaho Falls about 10 miles and the roads start to turn white and the tires slip every third turn. Bill holds tighter to the steering wheel. He told the kids not to bump him as the storm gets worse. The 5 of us are crammed in the cab of the ole blue truck. The frost starts to gather on the inside of the window, no scrapper. I pull out my drivers license, Bill says it works good enough to see awhile. The heater won't work the kids are freezing, even if we are packed in there like sardines. Heading up to the pass the snow is getting worse. Our muscles are hurting because we can't change positions. Tears roll down Dustin's cheek, because his leg is hurting so bad. My legs are numb from the knee down cramped next to the drafty door, as a layer of snow has coated on my pant legs. I'm cold, snappy and just plain mean, nothing is said; the only sound is the motor and the card scrapping on the window. Tiffany, on my lap, is falling here and there in her sleep, trying to stretch out and get comfortable. The bitter cold is unreal.

We get out at Dillon to warm ourselves and eat something. Down the road again, I pray that we make it home. We have such good kids. They never say anything for they know we can't do anything about it, and their Dad would have their hide.

Bill's trying once again to stay awake. He yells at me to talk to him.

I say, "Bill, I can't! You just stay awake damn it! I'm tired, miserable, squashed and frozen and I have nothing to say."

Drummond, what a welcome sight. Thank you for the help Lord, We only made it home because of you.

Christmas 1980

Christmas is close, I'm buzzing in and out of Missoula, trying to find presents for the kids with no money, The Prime interest rate up to 21% so I guess we won't be borrowing any money, like a bank would let us. They only loan to people who really don't need it, just for extras, that nicer car, boat, oh well, we can make it without them and we have so far. Prices are terrible. The Church is warning us to get food storage and get out of debt. Well we look pretty good about debt. We have none, but then we have nothing.

I was sick for Christmas and so was Grandma. I'm glad the whole foo fa lah is over. It always costs money that you don't have for things you really don't need.

The Special Things

How special the little things my kids do for me. The little notes, taking my hand and squeezing it 3 times (meaning I Love You), looking down and seeing a big smile and a wink. All my homemade Christmas gifts are scattered around the house. How special they are, for in a few years those kinds of things just won't do.

A toothpick planter, a clay molding of our cabin and mountains, a macaroni decoration on a block of wood with the Home sweet Home spelled out in beans and macaroni tied with a red bow. Only a mother could get these special gifts with all the love packed inside.

Everyday I receive something different, a note saying they'll help us or I love you, trying to straighten the house making dinner for me. I love you kids!

Being a Mother... I feel so good about my life, my husband, and my kids. A mother, what a very special person. One can compare, not just me. But what my kids call me, that special someone they always depend on and lean on when things go wrong. They know they can tell mom anything, you just have to ask, and then it all comes out with a stiff lip and tears rolling down their face. "I don't know why I did it mom!" "Do you have to tell dad?" I give them a hug, discuss the problem and dry their eyes. The day's a whole lot better and mom feels needed, a feeling I need so much at times. 3 little spirits holding on to this chubby body loving you cause you're you....

February 10, 1981 46 below zero

The weather today is unbearable, even though we're in the log house. The long night with the fire burning low, the house is bitterly cold. The wind is whipping through the old windows and make-shift doors. We huddle around the stove, the kids have to bundle in layers to go out and get wood in for the day. It's days like this that I wish I were a normal person in a normal house, with a furnace and money and heat... what a concept. Is it ever going to get better? I sit huddled in a blanket by the fire, but it is hard to tell if it is even going, when it is so cold outside. The house logs are creaking with the cold, what an eerie sound. I'm flat miserable, I sit and can't get warm, as one side of my face is beet red from the fire, and the other is cold so I keep turning like some stuffed pig on a spit on a rotisserie, never getting done. I'm just a tough ole ham.

Sometimes I wish that I wasn't so pig headed about staying here. How would it be to walk around your house without muck lucks for shoes, blankets wrapped around you, sweaters, and holding a cup of hot chocolate to keep the hands warm, trying to watch our only channel of white fuzz on TV. Sometimes we get skip, that is where the TV picks up waves from somewhere outrageous, usually Mexico or beyond, which only happens if you have a cruddy set up, which brings in the Lone Ranger in Spanish. Now that is a culture shock to see Tonto say adios.

As the kids bundle up and head outside the snow cracks and squeaks under each footstep. Their fingers go numb as they pick up the frozen wood that has been buried under a snowdrift. They bang on the door with their feet, to come in. Ice forms around the moisture on their mouths. Your lungs hurt and nose burns as you take in the cold icy air. They track frozen snow through the house to dump the wood in the ole coke bin. The fire just isn't keeping up with all the cold rushing in.

The car won't start, so even if I wanted to go somewhere I can't. Last week Bill had an accident on the logging road. He hit head on going up to get wood in Fred's pickup, totaled both vehicles. No one is hurt, just Fred's pocketbook.

Snow Snow Snow

The weather warming up the ole thermostat is almost hitting zero. Today Bill worked all day trying to start the flat bed so he could get hay for the ranch then at 6:00 it started snowing, and at 10:00 we have almost 8 inches of snow and still coming down. The next few days the snow just keeps falling. We have over a foot on the ground and as usual the kids are elated.

This is on the Flint Creek just south of Drummond

Chapter 14
Life in the Country

Ranching/ Calving

Ranching in the winter is a real trip. Living in the city for so many years of my adult life, I forgot how I grew up, the cold miserable winters, and the long days and nights of ranch and logging life.

Ranch life seems never to slow down. In the fall you preg check your cattle, now if that isn't fun as you dawn a shoulder length glove, get by the poop end of the cow and put your arm in to your shoulder and feel for the calf. Some guys are so good they can tell how old it is, how far along, but sex is another thing. If they do not have a calf, a lot of times you sell the open ones so you don't have to feed them all winter.

Then its time to work the cattle, separate the calves from the moms that have had them all summer. Winter time comes calving, and then tagging each of those little buggers, as the mom is trying to charge you. After calving and counting up your losses from sick calves, dead ones that just couldn't survive the cold or oozing mud, you scrape the pooh around the fields, getting ready to plant and water, move pipe, and irrigate.

A lot of ranchers around here move their cattle up on the mountain for summer grazing after branding in the spring, which is a joy in its self. The calf bellers and the hair stinks as it is singed and burnt with your identifying mark. Before you put them up in the mountains, you get on horse back, and check fence line, miles of fence. Mend broken wire so the neighbor's bull doesn't do the dance with your cute heifer, or vise a versa. Modern times have brought less horse back riding and more 4 wheeling. A streak flying through the fields with a shovel standing upright and a water bottle for refreshment, what more could you want?

Then summer, hoping the rain stops long enough to cut the hay and bail it, stack it, and get ready for 2nd cutting and hope for a third, but it doesn't happen much here in Montana. There's no 8 to 5 job here just long hard endless work. You're paid once a year, when you sell your calves and cows. Why do we do it anyway?

Bill has to get up and check on the calves at 2 am. That means going through the fields with a flashlight, and checking the first year heifers, because they usually can't have the calf on their own without some assistance. We usually separate the first year ones from the rest, so they don't get lost in a herd of 200 or 300 head, not a fun experience in a snowstorm and 20 below zero. So they have their own corral or pasture, just to make our life easier. Calving time usually starts mid January and lasts until April. It seems this terrible cold weather triggers the little calves to come, so here we are out in the middle of a corral,

We are looking for a sack hanging out or two feet, now where is this sack you say? Well it's the opposite end as their head. Then you help them to the barn, and assist the little mother to-be. You usually take them to a stall and decide what action to take next. Sometimes you're lucky and the calf just needs a little help to come into the world but most times it isn't that simple. The old barn lights burn long and strong, the barn isn't heated, but compared to outside it seems like a mansion.

Here are Little Mama and you. She is hunched over trying with all her might and just two hooves are sticking out of the south end of a north-facing cow.

Bill gets the rope, and secures the little lady to a post, and then gets busy putting chains around the unborn calf's hooves and securing them. As the cow pushes, you help her with a mighty pull. Time and time again, if that doesn't work you get the calf puller that fits around its hind end, which helps push the baby calf up and out as you pull.

If the calf is still too big, you go out and shoot the bull, not really. You either end up breaking the pelvis, or having to do a C-section on the cow. Now this gets pretty hairy and not the best conditions to be working in. for one thing, when it's at this point, the mother and her baby are pretty stressed. The rancher is not in the best mood either, it's usually after a hard day, 2 in the morning, and this calf is not going to make you a dime. You just hope that you don't lose the mother along with the calf. A lot of times you know the calf is beyond hope but you need to help the mother.

Now I got to help on one of these C-sections; just happened to be my turn to help Bill. The mother was in a bad way, but we were in luck, the Doctor was on his way..

We finally get home in time to get the kids up for school, and stock the fire, and feed the multitudes. Now the house has this great smell about it. If you have been around a ranch, the smell is Manure!!! It's horrid. It reeks, and the smell emanates everywhere. Bill's clothes can stand in the corner and his boots, after a few months the urine and crap, putting it mildly, starts to rot the rubber.
What ever happened to government work, white shirts, and 9 to 5 office hours? Oh Calgon take me away. Especially now that I have RUNNING WATER.

Bilbo and Eagle bait...

Our poodle almost died today in a fight with a Doberman pincher. Our miniature French poodle – what a mutt! He thinks he is some kind of tough stuff but finds out he is just fluff. Well once more Bilbo is temping fate. This wilderness is not for poodles.

"Let's go over to the Bryant's," yelled Nate to Dustin.

They take their camouflage gear and sticks for watching for rattlers (a common thing you do as you hike here). Over the mountain they go, along with the Bassett hound and the Baggins our little silver poodle. As they neared Terrie's house they saw Terrie outside working on her lawn. She noticed an eagle soaring overhead. The size and beauty of the majestic bird made her take notice as the shrill call they make echoes through the air.

The kids were running and Bilbo was running ahead of them chasing Killdeers when all of a sudden a big shadow swooped down and grabbed Bilbo. He let out a Yelp! Terrie and Trix both threw their rakes. They went running after the Bald Eagle who had Bilbo in his claws. He was huge, 8 ft in the air, packing my little poodle away. Up he soared as Terrie chased him with a rake. Oh no, not Pennie's poodle. The bird gained altitude. Bilbo was in agony and squirming. Then Bilbo either bit his foot or something, we don't know, but the eagle dropped him then swished down to catch him again. Terrie reached the scene and scared it away.

Bilbo was terrified and wouldn't go to anyone. He made a beeline for the house and hid under furniture until I could come and get him. I guess you couldn't blame the eagle. Bilbos just looked like the food chain, strange rabbit, but the eagle didn't care. Bilbo was sore for days after, lucky for him he was small enough the talons wrapped around his body and not into, as they usually do.

March 15th

Cloudy and cold, 35 degrees. Bill starts up the ole wrecker after we get home from church, well lets say tries, it just won't turn over. He tells me to help push and Dusty to get in and push on the brake when the truck starts rolling down the hill. Bill and I push and rock and push and rock finally the truck starts to roll. Dusty stands on the brakes but NO BRAKES! My heart sinks and my knees go weak as I see Dusty roaring down the driveway in that huge truck, a little white head barely over the steering wheel.

Bill yells, "Pump 'em pump 'em!"

Dusty's bouncing up and down on the brakes, we are running after him as fast as we can run, then all of a sudden they take hold and the truck comes skidding to a stop. Bill ran up opened the door and took over. Dusty's whiter than his hair, his eyes are like silver dollars and shaking as I was. How easy something terrible could have happened but the Lord is always with us. WE NEED HIM…

March 17th

Winter's back, it's been snowing most of the day. Bill is working long hours.

Going Fishin – March 28th

It's warm and sunny, going to work on the house. Luckie and Terrie drag us out of the house to go fishing with the kids at Millers Lake. They said we would be back early. We all get in Luckie's flat bed truck to go up to the lake. We go through the cow pasture for Bill. He wants to show us his calves. On the road again but spring run off produces MUD. The thick ooey gooey kind, oh heck, into the mud, and on we go, should we turn back? No, everyone says it's not bad so we trudge on to the top, then bog in mud to the doors. The truck comes to sudden stop, kids pile off and we pile out.

"Now what?"

"Go fishing," they all say as the truck looks as if it's no going anywhere. The truck is stuck. No heavy coats, no food, miles from everything why isn't anyone else worried. They walk down to the caterpillar to get it started. NO Way…

I guess we use man power. We go back and put twigs under the tires. Bill props up the front end. Luckie drives. I drive. Rock and roll, more twigs. Now these twigs are slash poles, not marshmallow sticks. These things are hefty and more work than I like. It looks as if we are building a bridge, as I look at the string of logs on the ground with the mud oozing through. At last the truck moves, don't stop now. WE DID IT.

On down the hill, Bill and the kids hike down, find fishing spots in the creek. Everyone stops for a while. There are so many fish you can see them but they won't bite. Shaun even hits them on the nose with a worm, nothing. So Luckie, Shaun, Dusty, Nate all go fishing with their hands. Talk about crazy. Fish swimming by and through your legs, everyone's laughing trying to throw them out on shore. Got one! Nathan gets so excited that he jumps up and smashes it. So he buries it. Then back to wading on to another hole.

Bill says, "get down here I have a hot hole."

You put in a line, smack a bite, another and another. Dusty, Nate, Tiffany, Shaun, Corey, and Christina, all catch one. Luckie's still chasing fish by hand. The wind starts to blow and it's getting cold. Seventeen fish, time to get home and cook them, and a warm fire.

Helping Brand and Vaccinate

Ranching sure isn't the easy life, as I thought it would be. As I drove past fields when I lived in Utah, and asked myself, how hard could that be – feed a few cows and plow a few fields? Oh, why did I have to find out this way? The family has been elected to help with the chore of getting the cattle in the proper places, to brand, separate and vaccinate the herds before they sell them or put them out to pasture.

Bill had me down at one end of the yard, trying to keep a mother and baby from getting out. And I was supposed to guard the door, so she wouldn't go that way. Well she came at me about 25 mph. I saw this big ole cow running right for me, should I move? Bill told me not to. She will surely get out, and I will get yelled at. I stand my ground.

Then just before she hits me Bill yells, "MOVE!"

I jump back and to the side, and then it happens. The mother runs past, grazing me and I go flying into a pile of fresh plowed out of the barn manure. I sunk through the goo. My arms, legs, behind and parts of my face dripped from the green goo. The kids ran toward me to help me out. And then started to laugh after seeing I was okay.

Bill says, "What were you thinking? Why didn't you move, she would have killed you!"
"I know but I didn't know which was worse, you or her."

He gave me a look like PLEASE.

Needless to say the ride home from the ranch was not a pleasant one for any of us. The windows were down and I reeked of every barnyard smell you could think of, and I looked worse. I'm not helping anymore. I'm leaving cows to the guys. Now home for a bath.

Haying

I lied again. All though the summer and into the fall, the rancher works late hours, putting up the feed that the cows have to eat all winter, move water pipe, pipes so heavy you can hardly lift them. Every kid in the community knows how heavy 4 in water line is, as you pack it over the long grass, grain and alfalfa. In the morning the water in Montana, even in the summer, is so cold that the lines are frozen, or it's just so cold that you're freezing. The long grass is scratching your legs, and then in the evening the mosquitoes swarm the fields, along with the grass hoppers and snakes, skunks, rabbits, and anything else that you can imagine is out there. You move water even if it rains, and you only stop watering long enough to cut the field, and then put water on it again, for second cutting.

Bill is on the tractor till late in the night until the dew comes on the hay, then goes home, rests. When the hay is dry enough he gets up and hits the cutting until the dew returns. The family would have family home evening out in the field around the tractor, as Dad ate his dinner, because this is the only time we would see him.

Bill and the kids loading hay

Fix fence, this means horse riding upon the ridge and around the lake. To find what areas of the summer pasture that the bulls and cows are getting through to other rancher's cattle, this is not a good thing. Horse riding is not Bill's favorite, but the beauty makes up for all the misery that he has to go through. Yes it is beautiful here. The air is so clean, and crisp. The only sounds you hear are the cracking of the sticks under your horse's feet, the insects and the wind rustling through the trees. It is awesome.

We don't eat the best – a lot of cream gravies and rice, bread and beans, for that is what we can afford. Needless to say I'm chubby. Tiffany and I are alone and she pops up with "Mom, my class doesn't think you're fat. 'Cause I told them in show and tell that you thought you were fat and all the first graders don't think you're fat, they like you! That's neat huh mom?" I agreed and smiled.
Isn't it neat that your kids think you're beautiful? They never see your fat or wrinkles because they love you for you.

Bill's working 16 hour days. We never see him, but that's ranching, and haying, or all the above.

Flood – May 23rd

We woke up with the ring of the telephone.

Bill asks, "who could be calling?"

It was George at 6am on Saturday.

"Guess I'll check and see how much rain we have."

I thought that comment was rather strange as Bill hung up from Uncle George. I jump out of bed. I couldn't figure why Bill was so upset. Now I can!! The river was everywhere Clawson, George's neighbors were underwater, 7 cars in their yard were submerged, chicken coop and you name it. We got the kids up and decided to hike over to the top of the mountain, we couldn't go on the road it was gone. The river covered everywhere. It was the only way to get to the relatives and see if they were okay now that the phones were dead.

"I'm not looking forward to the climbing over that mountain," I said, "but I don't want to stay here, dead phone probably no lights. I'll suffer through it."

I did suffer or should I say Bill suffered. He had to hear me complain and moan all the way up and then down the steep mountain. "It's too steep, my shoes are muddy, and my ankles hurt." Huff, puff. He was about to back hand me I know but we were almost to aunties. Everyone was outside looking at the damages.
  The kids got the raft out to raft around the field, by the house and mountain but not near the river. Unreal… Mother Nature can sure take care of things.

Bill was fooling around and answered the phone before it went dead, "Lakeside Properties." Little did he know. Good thing we were high and dry.

Clawson hiked over the mountain to talk to us. They had barely gotten out in time with a few things – guns, goats, and kids. At this time it was waist high inside the house. They said they're not coming back, everything is ruined. They're a poor family anyway, now they even have less. They said they have what is important themselves and the kids, which is so true.

The flood was caused by flash rain storm about 50 miles away that dumped a tremendous amount of rain. It came down the Clark Fork, and flooded everything in its path. The river has stayed up for a few days covering the main road into town. A few state trucks are the only vehicles getting through. Up the road some, the river is at least on the side it's supposed to be, so we can get to town with the old truck.

You never realize how your life can change from some freak act of Mother Nature. Thanks to our Heavenly Father for protecting everyone.

April

Seems like I never write my thoughts anymore just what happened today, blah, blah... The house is silent, not even ole fridge's rumbling. We put Bill's mom's ole fridge in here and it runs quiet. Heaven. Bill is in bed, the kids are all sleeping and I'm looking at my half finished house. All I can hear tonight is the scratching of the pen and an occasional crackle of the fire.

I went to Relief Society tonight; so many choice ladies and friends here. The beautiful young girls, their youth glowing about them. The young mothers, some a little over weight from too many babies or lack of exercise and energy, probably the later. Middle age spread is wider than the young mothers but they have learned to control mouth and elbow disease when elbow bends mouth need not open. Grandmothers, the wrinkles tell of the years they've spent, a story on their faces. The laugh lines, the sorrow, are written clearly in time. The figures seem to broaden, the body grows shorter but how wise they have become.

April 5th

The weather's cold and blustery. Wind is terrible, trees blowing over, porches flying apart. It's causing white caps in the river. Now we have rain and snow. Bill at work loses his favorite calf and 2 more die from eagles.

Diet

Today I start the dreaded diet, I'm really down, and my weight is a real problem. I can tell the way Bill looks at me. He's disgusted by the way I look. The kids would never hurt my feelings but I'm not happy. I can't buy a dress that doesn't look like a tent, no stylish clothes, the bigger the better. I need help but get none from Bill. He either comes down too hard or teases me till I cry, either way it's misery. I feel trapped I want to lose weight but yet I can't make myself diet. I start then say to hell with it. You never think you're as big as someone else who is your size or even smaller. You look in the mirror and you always see a smaller person. I've gotten to the point my mirror doesn't lie to me anymore. I try to suck it in or turn sideways but I'm almost the same in all directions. I mention to Tiffany that I'm on a diet.

She says, "why mom?"

I say, "Because I'm fat."

She says, "You're not fat mom, you just have a lot of skin!"

Don't feed a little bunny Celery

Bill gets home late and the families in a bad mood. He tells me to feel inside his pocket. Now I know Bill, and you never know what he has up his sleeve or in his pocket. So this girl is not reaching inside. He pulls out this little tiny bunny. Its mother was killed in the haystack by the tractor. It came within inches of being crushed, so Bill picked up the little brown and white cottontail and thought the kids would like to raise him.

We found a box and some clothes we could wrap it in. We had a doll baby bottle to feed ole Hop a long. It seems like I'm meant to be a nurse maid for poor lost strays. I guess this rabbit isn't noisy like those rotten kittens I bottle fed. What a pain they were. On to the 6th day, with the rabbit not doing to bad, pretty cute little guy.

It's a cold blizzardy day. Now you say there is no such word as blizzardy, well there is. It is a day that is flat miserable. Our little Hop a long isn't doing very well either. I put some celery in his box, and he loved it. I was leaving to help Bill with calving and feeding. I put a pretty good sized stalk as I figured he could munch when he wanted. Well this rabbit munched a little too much, and when we arrived home his belly was swelled up and his feet stuck straight out. We tried to rub his belly and move his legs so he would pass gas. NOT! He would only pant harder. He died a few minutes later. Bill was elected to bury him, another animal up on dog gone hill.

Life is just plain miserable; Bill never has time to work on the house cause he's working long hours on the ranch. He comes home, and is too tired to do anything but fall asleep on the couch. Sounds like the same ole story so we just maintain. When things are bearable or you can make do, the drive just isn't there. We can eat and sleep without thoroughly freezing, we have the mice semi controlled. We set mouse traps every night and they snap before you shut off the kitchen light, empty it and put it down again. I do this 8 times before it slows to a slow crawl and I can get some sleep. I found out if you put a line of traps they can't jump over them and when they line the wall one usually catches one or more.

Temple Trip

We have been back in the church now for over a year and it has changed our lives. Bill has quit drinking and life is so much better. Money is still tight, but the family is happier and the Lord seems to bless us. Luckie, Terrie, Bill and I have all tried to be active at one time or another but now 10 years later it is here. We are heading up to Cardston Temple to do my mom's temple work..

We get a late start, so the trip is going to be longer than we figured because the border closes early. We have to go over to Browning and over the border that way, 200 miles further than we thought. At 1:30 am we pull into Canada and try to find a motel, no vacancy. We do finally find a room one between us, fall into bed. The night seemed to crawl I couldn't sleep. Could be the hard bed, firm I guess. It feels like they put the piece of plywood on top instead of under the mattress.

I finally fell asleep then Bill says, "Everyone up we have to get to the Temple."

My eyes feel terrible. Everyone's in the car by 6:15 am. The day is beautiful. Walking into the Temple I was excited my mom's Temple work I can't believe we made it. I go into the office they tell us that mom's records can't be located so we have to do the baptism also. The man suggests since Terrie's hair is short that she be baptized. Luckie baptizes her; Bill confirms her and I do the endowments.

So we proceed to the font, wait for Terrie to change then into the water. Luckie says the prayer and Charlotte's name and now mom is baptized once more. My eyes fill with tears, the Spirit is so strong. Bill confirms Terrie for mom and gives her the gift of the Holy Ghost.

Now it's time for the Endowment. I put on the beautiful white dress, receive mom's name and enter the initiatory room. I feel so pretty, maybe because I was being proxy for my beautiful mother. We finished the Temple session, the covenants and met the rest of my family in the celestial room. What a joy. I know how mom must feel, as she has been waiting a long time.

The trip was fun. We took the going to the sun highway and saw mountain goats. It was just in time for Easter. We got big smiles from our kids as we pulled into the driveway

Grandma Breitenfeldt

My little Grandma lives by us. She is 83 yrs old and the joy of our life has become a real trial. I never thought that I would feel this way. My grandma was my whole life, she is my ideal. Grandma never put me down my whole life. Even during my teenage years when I wore short skirts, stripes going the wrong way and ratted my hair. On a plump girl that is not good. But grandma would just hug me and brush my hair out of my eyes and try to suggest pulling it back. I would say no and she would say fine, and love me unconditionally for who I was. Now I need to return the favor.

I always went over and shared tea with Grandma. Being from England, she always had her tea, so I would have Mormon tea, that was hot water milk and sugar, and of course cookies. How I loved the times with my sweet grandma.

Grandma is sickly and demanding. All of a sudden her granddaughter has to make all the decisions about her life and mine and I hate to see her sad. She has been really depressed. She doesn't want to live alone anymore and I really don't blame her but knowing my house by now, it would be impossible for grandma to live here. I went to check on her Friday and Grandma was packed to move things out of her drawers. She has caught stuff on fire, set the fire alarm off in the building and gotten stuck in the tub. She's over dosed on her pills, stumbles and just stares at the wall when we try to talk to her. She forgets to feed her bird and herself. If we don't come in grandma goes all day with tea and toast. She weighs 105 lbs and is losing.

The decision has been made for us. I received a call from grandma's land lady. They don't want her there any more. They don't feel that she is capable of caring for herself. What are we going to do? We call our Dad and he says find a rest home. How do you tell a little lady, your best friend, that she has to be put into a home? I took her by the hand, looked into her eyes, and said grandma you know I love you, and would never do anything to hurt you. And she looked at me and agreed. I told her what was happening. She just said I trust you. It was the best grandma has been for months.

We took her to a rest home in Deer Lodge, Montana. We fixed her room with her chair, TV, and pictures on the wall. I promised her that we would see her a couple times a week and take her places, even though it is 35 miles away. We kept our promise faithfully. Grandma stayed there for 6 months.

I received a call late one night from grandma. "Pennie," she said, "can you come and see me? I itch all over and it just getting worse."

I drive over after midnight and find her in terrible pain. She has had an allergic reaction to the pills she has been taking causing her to have huge hives covering her whole body. So they gave her something for the hives and we got her settled down, the more I see her, and take care of her, the more I love her. Time and time again grandma gets sick, she has reactions to the different medications, bugs are crawling all over her, how terrible that would be to not know that these things are not real, and see them everywhere. I reassure her and brush her forehead. I need help with this sweet little lady.

Dad said he had a retirement home in Utah, where he wanted to move her, so we packed her up one more time, thinking this would be the best for her. But little did we know, moving old people from what they know is not the best thing. They get comfortable in their surroundings and fall in love with their young doctors, cause at that age everyone is younger than you. But I guess you can only do what you think is best. This upset grandma and she wandered off in the middle of the night looking for me, who was 500 miles away. I came down and visited, and got her situated and relaxed in her new surroundings.

Grandma finally adjusted to her new home, and her son took over my job. I visited her when I could, and always got a hug and big smile, she never forgot her Pennie. Grandma lived to be 91, and then fell asleep and didn't wake up. How I miss my little friend, her loving smile and our warm cup of tea and sharing time together

Grandma at 90 and at 1 year in England

Chapter 15
Cats and Bad Luck

June 13th

Bill stays home we have to get something done on the house. Bill's parents are coming and we know they will be looking at what we have done in a year, not much. Well maybe water, some walls a sink, toilet, tub, and studs.

Anyway, Bill and I work all day on the kitchen, we're going to lay the linoleum. First we have to lay sub floor tar paper, move the wood stove, ice box, electric stove and fridge (Hernia city). Bill and I are tired; the day's been long and tiring. The kitchen looks like a disaster, let's just get it done. We roll out the piece of linoleum cut it to fit and roll it back. Bill and I start putting on the glue. We make1 gallon stretch and have to wait till it's not sticky and almost clear.

While we are waiting our little kitten sneaks in the house and walks in on the floor. I grab her and try to wash her feet. I put her down, not thinking anything of it, and 15 minutes later she is lifeless. She has no muscle control and can't even hold up her head. We can't believe that glue is so powerful. It says vapors are harmful; ventilate area, no dah. The little cat died within the hour. Bill got to do the funeral stuff with the kids. I cleaned up the kitchen. We are dead tired, but not as dead as that cat.

Bill's parents arrive. They bring another set of grandparents and sisters. Also Bill's nephew and niece show up to stay the summer. Calgon take me away…

Christina and the Dead Cat

June 20th rain and cold. Christina and Tiffany were playing and found a stray cat. It was really cute with long black and white hair and of course the girls fell in love with it. But they didn't want it to run away so they thought and thought how can we keep this kitty safe and be our little kitty? They found an old bird cage, and Christina decides to put this 8 inch cat through a 5 in hole. What comes of that is a really upset angry cat, cute or not. So the cat went crazy and bit Christina on the hand. She screamed and dropped the cat, the cat ran and hid and the girls went to find their moms and get things to feel better. Terrie cleaned it out, and washed the bite, plus put Neosporin on the cut. Band-aid and kiss, things were great. In the meantime this little cat grew real weak and died, so they buried it, major funeral and the kids got over it. They just know about life up here and how hard it is to live. Only the strong survive.

Terrie called this morning Christina was taken into the hospital last night, the cat bite had become infected. Christina woke up with a fever but it seemed to break so Terrie sent her to swimming lessons. Christina was moody but most of the time that's normal for Christina. Well last night Christina was complaining of her arm, her hand was swollen from the bite. Terrie looked and her lymph glands were huge. So off to the hospital they go. The hospital is very concerned. Terrie and Luckie had to come home dig up the cat put it in a bag and put it in the fridge, for the health department. This cat has been dead for a few days now, what a joy. And stink, you can't believe the smell of rotting cat guts in your fridge, num num. They need to check it for rabies. They are going to pick it up and fly the dead cat to Bozeman for an autopsy. If they can't tell whether the cat contracted rabies they will have to start rabies shots. Just another trial we don't need right now.

Dead Cat

The hospital called and told Luckie that they couldn't pick up the cat but he needed to get the cat to Missoula in record time. So Luckie grabs the stinky cat out of the fridge, sticks it in a cooler and heads for Missoula, cooking along at a cool 85 or 90. He hears ringing in his ears. It's the thing we all hate to see in our rear view mirrors unless we are broken down, but speeding, it is not a pretty site. Luckie pulls over and the policeman saunters up to the car, not wearing a smile.

"Do you realize how fast you were going?"

"Yes sir," Luckie says in an excited voice. "Ya see I'm rushing this dead cat to the hospital."

"Dead Cat! Hospital! Oh by all means leave and hurry, without any more explanation," says the officer. As he goes back to his car he gets this puzzled look on his face, raises his arms for Luckie to stop but the little car was a streak by now. I'm sure he thought Dead Cat. I can't believe it. I've heard them all now. Luckie headed down the road with his dead cat in 3 zip lock baggies and a hefty to the E.R.

Christina's fever broke today. It was 105 last night so they washed her down with cool cloths. Today she is up and running, you can't keep kids down. The time is drawing near to determine whether or not she has to take the shots. They get a call 2 of the test for rabies has turned out negative but the last test takes 21 days the doctor feels pretty confident that it isn't rabies. What a blessing.

June is always the worst for mosquitoes and they are horrible. If you're outside you are slapping at your body, or stink like repellant. The mosquitoes are crazy, they smell blood and swarm. It's like the movie *The Birds*, or the bees or something. A black cloud of mosquitoes cover me from head to toe. They go up your nose when you swat at them you can feel hundreds hit your hand. The repellent keeps them 2 inches away. The only good thing is that eventually these suckers die! It gets rather warm and they can't take it. And I SMILE!

Bad days seem to always come

What a day, everything seemed to go wrong, if it wasn't the mosquitoes eating us alive. Bill and Jeff get home to tell us that you would think it was Friday the 13th or going on Monday. Full moon, you name it. They got 2 trucks stuck, poured oil in the wrong hole in the swather. Jeff knew that Bill was going to kill him, and Fred was going to fire him. I assured him that Bill has had his bad days too, like when he wrecked Fred's truck, a few cows died on us. He was sawing some wood and cut the ends off the boss's ping-pong table. I don't know if that made him feel better but you know misery loves company.

Summer is flying by. Not much is getting done on the house. Just life, and its ups and downs, having 3 more kids in the house is insane when you don't make anything and then feed 3 more teenagers. Jeff and Tammy don't have a dad; he was killed in a car wreck and we keep them every summer. What a challenge at times – moody girls, and rotten boys. Everyone has to share bedrooms and do their share of chores, what a headache. So with no money and 6 kids under 14, I come in to find one or two boys hand cuffed to the log posts in the kitchen. I calmly YELL, "Jeff, come and get these boys."

Then I start dinner, this is no easy adventure because with teenage boys they seem to have a hollow leg and for one dinner we peel 10 lbs of potatoes. I make poor man's gravy (that is flour, bacon grease and canned milk), and biscuits. One thing I can do is make a little food stretch and feed a lot of people. Even though the kids ate a lot of starch they all looked like starvation orphans over in some third world country. I was the only one here gaining weight. How can this be? I work my butt off but it just keeps hanging around, and around.

To Dog Heaven

I guess we all have to face our pet dying and leaving us. I returned home from girls' camp to find my little poodle sick and hurt. He had a run in with that Doberman pincher again and came out on the raw end of the deal. His nose and face were torn up, his neck swollen to twice its size, and puncture holes in its back. I called the vet, he says to bring him in. I bring him into the office the vet looks at him and says that's one tough little poodle, other dogs would be dead by now. He says this has been done almost a day or two ago. The swelling in the neck is all infection. He gave him a liquid medicine and weighed him, 7 lbs. "Get chicken broth down him if you can, he has to eat."

I take him home but he can't keep it down. I just love him what else can I do? My little poodle, that I talk to when things are so rough, now what? Who do I tell my inner thoughts to, that won't say I'm wrong, who listens and loves me. I can't lose my little friend. Always staying at my heels when we walk unless I say, "go ahead" as he moans when he sees a killdeer or magpie to chase. Then through the grass and swamp ears a flapping, only seeing his head long enough to jump up and see where he's going.

I don't know how to express the love a person can have for an animal, a bond that no one can break. No matter how rotten you are or the dog, you stay friends. This morning Baggins my dog lay limp, and lifeless. I know the time is near. He can hardly breathe as the infection squeezes off his airway.

The family is in tears. Our little gray friend is dead. No more will I see his loving brown eyes begging for a treat or a love now and then. I won't feel him jump upon the waterbed, after all the lights are out, and snuggle by my feet. Or wake us up with his singing; we always thought he should be on Johnny Carson. But now we have to bury him, this is hard for little kids to understand; death, even if it is a pet. It hurts and it's not fun. But we manage a funeral and bury him on the hill above the house. We call it dog gone hill, because 3 dogs have died now from the hardships here in Montana.

Adventures in Travel, or who let these crazy women go to Utah?

Off to Utah at 11 pm at night we loaded Terrie, Tammy, Dusty, Nate, Corey, Christina Tiffany and I in a little car. Now you can tell this is before seat belts were even stressed. It's throw the kids in the car and let them bounce all over tarnation. The more you can stuff in, the more cushion you have, or maybe the more insane you are. All the above worked for us. We just needed to get away and when that time comes there is no stopping a determined crazy mother. We have 3 in the front, 4 in the back and one in the back window. Ye haw, we must look like hicks from? I know Montana...

We are not on the road a half hour and a drunk driver tries to hit us head on. We pull off the road and he barely misses us. Let's hope things improve from here, but it's not to happen. Kids are fighting, moms are yelling. We get gas in Butte in case Dillon is closed. I hear a rat a tat

"Terrie I think you have a hole in your muffler," I say.

She replies, "no sweat, if that all it is."

So on we putt. Pop a no Doze. Have you ever taken one of those pills? Holy Cow I started to buzz. And then jitters set in. I'm sure the 32 oz coke didn't help either. Caffeine city when I'm not used to it. The kids fought till they fell asleep. That's why we decided to travel with 6 kids in the middle of the night.

It's 3:30 am and we pull into the gas station called Boozers in Idaho Falls. We are a little more than half way there. It seems when a car slows down an alarm seems to wake all the kids. They all need to go pee. So they all pile out of the car then pile back in with food and pop or should I say junk food.

I drive now; start up the ole blue comet bump bump something is picking up the car. I stop the car the muffler is busted off the car and hanging down so every time we moved it dug into the pavement. I tell Terrie go see if there is anyone in there that knows anything about mufflers and see if we can get if off. Terrie comes out of the station with a real loadie, not that you have a real choice at 3:30 in the morning.

He looks under the car, "yup," that's a muffler."

"I know that, can you take it off?"

"Well," he says, "do you have a coat hanger?"

"No!"

"Well than I guess I'll just remove it."

He goes in the station for a wrench, crawls under our car and dirt drops all over him.

We said "sorry about the dirt but we're from Montana."

"I know about Montana," he replies. "I used to live there, Cut Bank."

"Oh that a terrible place," I said,

"I know," he says. "I don't live there anymore. I moved to Casper."

"That's not much better," I replied.

He says, "I don't live there anymore either, and I'm not going to be here in Idaho Falls long either."

"Sorry about your clothes," we say.

"Aw don't worry I need to do my laundry anyway."

"Watch out! Your hair is going to be burned by your cigarette,"

"Oh I need a hair cut anyway." He then gets a knife to cut the bands off the muffler. He says to us, "you know I'm a proney."

"What?"

"Accident-prone."

"Oh hell, then be careful," we say.

His friend roars around in this unbelievable car, both doors open, the seats look like a cotton batting factory, he pulls up to the side of our car.

The one under the car yells, "Did you feed the squirrel?"

Both Terrie and I are amazed what a flaky pair we have here. But nice, fortunately for us they ran out of gas. He throws our muffler in our trunk, waves goodbye and is off. He didn't even give us a chance to pay him. How did we make it this far? We pull onto the freeway. Our lights don't work. I finally hit the dimmer switch. Only the bright's work both dims burned out, now on to Ogden.

Get the Whale out of the Water

I don't know if I have ever mentioned my life long friends Launa and Ranae. They have been my salvation. They always buoy me up and want to hear the stories of my crazy life in Montana. They never say anything about my size, or how I dress, but seem to just shower me with love. Thank you girls...

Utah, vacation land, my friend Launa and Randy, take our family water skiing. What a day we all travel up to the dam 17.00 of food pop cookies, gas up the blazer and boat. Randy brings the boat from the other shore. We have 7 kids and carry 2 sacks of food, a cooler, 3 blankets and 9 towels. Hell knows how far. The sand burns our feet as we try to find a place that doesn't have people. Being from Montana you forget that people do exist, and large quantities of them and they all have the same idea as you. That is to leave home, bring their SUV, (non existent at that time, then it was your average 4 wheel drive Blazer) the great ego booster to have a boat and paraphernalia, and go to the dreaded beach.

Now we are on the beach. Everyone starts peeling off their clothes, to show their perfectly tanned bodies. Oh heaven forbid, I forgot to tan this oversized body, let alone tuck all the excess skin in the too small bathing suit that is stretching about my rather large fanny. I must learn that large fannies do not bend at waist and look down, because all the other people see is this huge black blob with two Ripley legs hanging from it. Unsightly. So bend and squat to place your towel on the sand and try to tan this body.

Now the boat, the kids go out and try water skiing. They are all like fish, and everyone is having a great time. Now they all yell for me to come and join the fun. Well my body is like a lobster now. So I slowly head toward the water. I used to water ski, in my teen age years. Oh what a picture that was, skinny body, big chest, two-piece, pretty cute, now what? The big chest has just gotten bigger; the rest of the body has exploded to rounding proportions. Okay here I go, how hard could this be. It has to be just like riding a bike, once you learn you never forget.

I put on the skis and sit my little butt in the water, tips up, and signal for Randy to hit it. The boat roared and the throttle was thrown forward, and the back of the boat lowered in the water, all you could see was a boat and a large wake with a black butt hanging out. I looked like a backwards waterfall or something of that source.

"The boat's running crappy," Randy says.

"Sure." I say.

Each time I try I almost get up but my legs won't get my lead butt out of the water. I felt like I was straining pine view through my teeth, arms, legs.

"I give up," I say.

I'm out in the middle, so they try to pull me in. It takes the whole boat load and 10 minutes of pulling, I'm finally in. They were thinking of using me for a buoy and just drag me back to shore. Ya know water sports aren't fun for fat, out of shape moms. That was the last time I put on a pair of water skies. I tried a water banana, and a kneeboard and thought I was going to lose my new false teeth, so I left them in the cooler. That was the hit, everyone laughed. And I tried not to!

Wedding Cake

Terrie and I swore that we never would make another wedding cake but funds were short and since we knew how, well at least we had made one, we were pros by now. We could make Kevin's wedding cake and save them some money. Now to start our masterpiece, 8 lbs of powdered sugar, 6 cake mixes, 1 can of shortening, a dozen eggs. My sister Edie has worked for 2 days making 60 orange and yellow roses out of frosting.

I sit down in front of the largest layers and started slapping frosting, now smooth with water and a wet knife over and over again. Terrie is frosting the middle layers. Edie keeps mixing up more frosting. I keep smoothing, my cake is sweating. We froze the cake thinking it would be easier not so! It gets wet and beady. The frosting is trying to slide off the cake and the second layer is trying to slide off the first layer. 4 hrs later, 545 roses, swirls, bows and what ever, we place the top on and all of a sudden the frosting on the top layer starts peeling off. I mean flat falling off in sheets. What do we do? Make a new top layer.

We mix up cake and throw it in oven. We ran and to Kentucky Fried for dinner, came home and the cake is done but stuck in the pan. But with a little prayer we got it out in one piece. Now put less frosting on, this is when less is better. It worked, now add roses, bows and wishes. It's finally done.

How can people make these things for a living? After all that hard work, they let someone cut it into pieces. Pull it apart layer by layer, not even thinking that it took someone hours, I could be a mad housewife, a craved mad women if I did this for a living. Good thing this is my LAST cake.

Summer (Hay Fever)

Yuk, this is the worst, hay fever time with someone who has allergies. Bill is one mean dude, which in turn makes me a cranky woman not a good combo. Plus 3 extra kids help throw a monkey wrench in our moods. Being broke should come in stride but no. You seem never to take that well. My stove blew up on me (sparkler city), my nerves are fried.

A bad day has turned into a bad month and now two.

Bill comes home and said, "Well, I Quit."

I couldn't believe it he really did it, he quit Fred. We travel to Missoula to put in applications, fix the stove; he actually has time for something besides farming. He is going to work for Gene McFarland, sawing at 95 cents a log. New chain gas, oil, tape, wedge $70.00 later maybe we are ready to make money. Good thing we have the saw. Go grocery shopping and spend $75.00 and the food is gone in 3 days. We have 4 more months to feed 3 teenagers and my 3 kids.

Jeff decides to move over to Parkers. He doesn't have a ride and bicycling 10 miles to work is not fun. It has taken some of the stress out of our life, less food, wash, and fights. The Kid eats like a horse, because he's huge. We love him but he can put it away. Packages of cookies, 8 to 10 lbs of potatoes, milk, bread, cereal, you name it, Jeff ate it. Don't get me wrong Jeff is like one of our own, but he understands how hard it is on us also, and decides to make life easier... Thanks Jeff.

Camping

I don't care if you are rich or poor; I think camping is the pits. Well at least for the poor wife or mother having to pack up the food and gear to get there. Tammy and I pack the car and I mean PACK and tie the raft on. I find a clothesline rope for one end and use the rope on the raft for the other. I feel pretty good so we start down the hill.

"Can you hold on to it Tam? I think it is trying to lift off the car."

We pick up speed on the Frontage Road almost to 35 mph. A gust of wind picks up the raft and whips it off the side. Tammy and I get out and slide it back on, get back in. I don't even get the key turned on and the wind takes it off the other side. Well maybe we need to turn it over. So we untie everything from the bumper, turn over the raft so the raft bottom fits over the top of Tilly our VW, tie it down. Boy that doesn't move, jump in and all we see out of the windshield is the bottom of the raft. Well I can't drive like this. So once more we get out, untie the raft and decide to blow up the raft at the ranch when we get there so we proceed to let the air out of the 6 man raft.

Ssh ssh out goes the air by the side of the road, Tam and I sitting on the raft, now jumping up and down laying any position we can to try to get the air out. It looked flat laying out on the road. But as we folded it to go into the car the air seemed to grow I shoved it in the car. Now have you ever tried to shove a 6 man raft, half full of air, inside a VW along with a 10 by 13 tent, coolers, sleeping bags? Well needless to say the backseat was over full so we needed to get the raft in the front seat. You ought to try this. You push and tuck with no progress, finally it was in but where does the driver sit, let alone a passenger? This driver is not small.

Now I finally get the raft over enough to squeeze in but now I can't find the gear shift and key. The whole car looks like an air bag has exploded inside. The only way we could fit in is to have Tammy sit on the door jam, one leg through the window, Tammy hanging out the door, me trying to find gears through an air bag. All you can see is a head a body hanging out the window and a huge orange and yellow blob covering the inside of the car.

The air is seeping out slowly so that Tammy, after 10 miles, can get in the car. We don't fill up the raft because of the wind we know we could never hold on to it. So we get to blow up the raft by mouth.

Bill and I start a fire, listening to music reminiscing of old times after midnight. The kids had a ball. I have to admit sitting by the fire and watching the fire's glowing embers that it looks like a million city lights far off as you go into a daze. Pretty relaxing until you have to head for the sleeping bag and the hard ground.

Bed isn't too comfy the back of the ole bomb (back ache city). Morning feed everyone, clean up and head home.

Haying

2 acres of alfalfa (oh heck why get fancy) good ole hay. We have our heifer, Lucy, to feed this winter since Fred said we needed to move her now that we don't work there. Now to cut and put up the hay 2 acres doesn't seem like much unless you use Bob McMahan Sr. equipment. His old tractor limps around the field. If it dies you use your truck to jump the battery. Around the field a couple times, a section breaks out of the blades. Bill hammers and cusses, another night gone. The mosquitoes are intense in the long hay. 3 nights of cutting, now 5 and finally the last blade is cut down. Bob's farm hand doesn't work, so we pick up the hay by hand. We have 4 pitch forks that are used by Dusty, Nate, Bill, & Chris then by me, Bill, Tammy and the boys. Tiffany is giving moral support. I never ached so badly. We're trying to rake and drag the hay into stacks so that we can pick it up. I never dreamed I would leave IRS and my cushy life for this.

We had 46 stacks in all. We have to haul it over to one large stack in the corner of the field. Bill and the boys work for 2 days and finish half the field but 25 stacks are left. Bill has to leave.

"Can you finish the hay, we have to get it into the large stack?" Bill says.

I'm left to get the hay in and Bill is going to Alaska to help Barbara. She is trying to run a fishing boat by herself, so she needs someone to help for a month to six weeks. Bill offers to help and thought it would be an opportunity that he wouldn't ever have again. It's like briar rabbit; oh please don't throw me in the briar patch... So our adventures change to another key, and off and running again.

This is Barbara on her boat fishing; she has caught a shark not salmon here.

Chapter 16
Trials and Survival

Going Fishing in Alaska

We are packing our wash, telling each other that everything will be okay for a month while Bill is gone. I really don't know why single Rocky didn't go to help Barbara. But I guess that is another story.

I pack Tammy, my niece, up to go back to Seattle cause she can fly out of Spokane for $48.00. Good-bye, I don't need any more headaches. We wait at the airport for over an hour because we forgot about the time change. But at least the little VW got us there. Bill is on his way to Alaska, fishing with Aunt Barbara for a month, learning the trade, making some money (I hope).

Since Bill has been gone I've been busy school shopping, church meetings and doing that stupid Hay!!

Bill is working hard and missing his family, here are a few pictures of him with a shark, and salmon, that he said was great eating. It seems that Bill has been gone forever, rain and high gale winds have kept him in Alaska longer than he planned so we just keep plugging along. He said that the other fishing boats that are around you just get hidden by the 20 and 30 ft swells, he is pretty lucky not to be puking his guts out. He has lost weight and works from sun up to sun down, and doesn't think that he's ever dry.

It doesn't sound as if Bill is having anymore fun then I am, but truthfully he loves it. He said the scenery is gorgeous and on a little 40 ft trawler you see it up front and personal, shark, whales, salmon, dolphins. He found a glass ball on the ocean that had floated from Japan, what a

find. Pictures and more pictures we can hardly wait to see the beauty and hear about everything.

Barbara is a hard worker and is amazing in all she does. It's an experience that he won't forget, and thankful that he can help her out. A big plus is to see God's great creations, even more beautiful than Montana, which is hard to beat.

It's been raining hard the last few days and coming down in buckets. It even rained inside my house again through a few cracks we don't have sealed and don't think of till it starts leaking. Half inch of rain in half an hour on the 20th of August. FLAT RAINING! Our driveway looks like it too. It looks like the Cascade Falls with deep gullies for 3 tenths of a mile.

I'm sitting here alone. All the kids are in bed and the time alone is nice at night, to slow me down before bed. I wonder what Bill is doing, probably ice fishing or just crawling into bed, dead tired.

I have so much to do around the house. I just need to find the time to do it; clean Dumb Dora again, sand floors, varnish, sigh!

Aug. 22nd.

We killed a rattler 4 ft long down by our pump. Corey was running down to the garden to get the chickens out of my tomatoes when Poosie the dog started going crazy. There was a rattler coiled and striking at the little dog. Corey stopped, started yelling "Rattler, Rattler." Chucky, the kid who lived down the hill ran got his rifle, and put the barrel down by the head, the snake started following the barrel of the gun, and Chucky just let him have it.

Then they put it on a stick proud as peacocks and carried it up the hill. Well I'm the last person you want to bring a snake to. I freak, of coarse that's who a nine year old and a twelve year old decide to bring a flippin snake to. They tap me on the arm and watch me go bananas as I jump around the room. Those kids had a riot chasing me around, as this ugly snake hung from the stick and then slithered on the porch a few times. They picked it up once again to torment me. I yelled and got mean and the fun was over so they left their prize to show the rest of the family.

I can't believe that I had been down there, and not seen that snake before. Where are you Steam Boat Willie? I miss you. Life is going on, school starting. My helpers all headed back to learn their ABC's. A storm is brewing; the wind's blowing, the weeds bending to touch the ground. The wind whistling through the old windows makes it sound worse than it is. It's kind of scary when you're all alone.

Today our little family got up and had family prayer, to keep Dad safe and that he would come home soon. We miss him so very much. He's never missed in their prayers or thoughts and now in mine. When two people are apart how the heart grows fonder. You realize all the little things they do to make you happy and how much of your life revolves around them and how much you're intermingled together, depending on one another.

Birthday and Movie

The kids wanted to go to town to see a movie, so we ventured in ole Tilly tomato and headed for the Zoo. We decided to go see the *Aristocrats,* a Disney movie, and *Condor Man.* They are a dollar movie, at least we could afford that, we thought. But things didn't go as we planned.

We're tooling at a cool 60 mph. when I see a red light flash on my dash. Oh, I can't believe my eyes. We have just lost all our oil. We are about 9 miles out of Missoula. I get out of the car get the extra oil that we pack in the car, because it's old and we know it can't run without the black gold. So I loosen the lid and open the engine compartment, and dump the oil, all of a sudden I see a puddle of oil coming out of the bottom of the car. The dip stick looked like it had been licked dry by the oil monster. I stand up and glance back at the road. I could see where the oil started pouring out of the car and followed ole Tilly to her resting spot.

What do I do now? I can't believe this happened to me. I wonder if the engine is blown. We hardly have any money but let's pile out kids and go over the fence. Leave Tilly with her emergency flashers on. The kids are crying and I tell them don't worry we'll work it out.

But the biggest problem is getting mom over this fence. The barbed wire tugged at my pants and I knew threads were going to give away any moment. Then people would notice us. Lucky for us a garage was across the fence.

"Do you have a wrecker?"

"No," he replies, "why?"

I explain to him what happened. "Do you think I blew the engine? I shut it right off, could it be a seal or something that made all the oil spill?"

He shakes his head. "Ok where is your car?"

He ventures over there works on it for a while and then says, "It looks like you lost a bolt and dumped your oil. But I don't know if we have anything that will fix it."

Back over the fence, he returns with a bolt and some sealant. The whole time I'm saying a silent prayer. It works. Tilly turns over and is running. I pay him $10.00 then venture into Missoula and check to see if the bolt will stay, before returning to the long dark trek back to Drummond.

The kids get back in the car and say: "Heavenly Father sure helped us, didn't he?"

I said, "He sure did, and we need to thank him." It is funny how the Lord takes care of you if you put your life in his hands.

Life in Montana is never dull,

I am talking on the 8 party line, to Elaine and arranging a ride to the funeral when Nathan interrupts me on the phone (which is easy to do on an 8 party line).

"Mom, help us, we need help! Mikey is hurt, the go kart tipped over, just help us!"

Mikey is a crippled kid that the kids played with, he couldn't do a lot of the things the others did, but his best friend Chuck would pull a wagon behind his motorcycle and off they would go for a great day.

I slam down the phone run to the truck. No shoes, curlers half up in my hair and jump in the ole orange truck that we have borrowed from a friend, because we have no vehicle, battery cables still on the hood. I pull out of the driveway down the hill; the cables fall off half way down the mountain. I jump out of the truck. There lay Mike in a heap on the highway, fluid running out of his nose, his face scratched blood dripping from his ear, arms like hamburger. He is in shock, I try to get him to lie down but he won't, he's just screaming. I talk softly to reassure him he's fine, put him in the truck not knowing if the ambulance will get the call. We could have him in there in 10 to 15 minutes. Pam puts in a pillow.

He keeps calling my name, "Pennie can I sit up?"

"No Mike!"

"I'm scared," he says.

"I know dear."

"I'm sick, Pennie."

"Just throw up on the floor." so he does.

I'm too hyper to get sick. Back into Drummond Clinic, it's closed, then to the ambulance shed hammering on the door.

"I have a boy in here that has had an accident, I need help," I say to the assistant.

She runs out, looks at Mike and calls for help. Within seconds people from all over converge upon the parking lot. The ambulance pulls out, she's taking his blood pressure and Mike wants a drink.

They take him out of the truck and load him in the ambulance and off to Missoula. I'm left with a car that is filled with throw up. Oh now I'm sick, where can I get a rag to clean up this? I also get dry heaves, as I clean up the mess. I go to Missoula with Luckie and Terrie. We stop by to see Mike in the hospital and brought him a stuffed animal and coloring book. He had a skull fracture, spinal fluid drainage out of his ears, but doing okay now. Another blessing from our Heavenly Father, that he wasn't hurt from crazy country life.

Wood Again

Bill still not home from Alaska. It's a day for hard work. I clean house, then Luckie and Terrie ask to use ole Tessie our wrecker, to go get wood. So get the kids, saws, and jump ole Tessie; (Terrie, Luckie, Me, Dusty, Nate, Tiffany, Shaun, Corey, Christina and I). Uncle George and Aunt Elaine are in their ole pickup with Trixie, Scott and Russell. We head up Dry Mulkey and find a lot of dead trees. They start sawing once we're on top and the rest of us fix lunch. 3 houses threw food together and made a real smorgasbord. We go 2 truckloads of wood, throw the kids on top with the saws, pull start George's ole truck and go down the hill. Why do you take all those kids with you? Well back then our kids didn't have TV and the mountains and getting wood was an adventure.

The following Saturday we get up by 7:00 am clean the house make rice for breakfast, do dishes, vacuum and then get into ole dirty clothes as we're going up to get another load of wood. We gas up ole Tessie; get the kids, saws up the mountain we go again 10:30 am. We didn't want to take the dogs so they ran up the whole way behind us, 5 miles or more up hill. Worked hard and filled the truck, then Terrie and I took that load down while Luckie and the boys stayed up on the mountain. Terrie and I Trixie, Tiffany, Christina, Russell, Nate, Scott, and 2 dogs, we must have looked a site coming down that mountain. Unload the wood at my house, make sandwiches, lemonade and go back up the mountain, we eat. Then Dusty gets stung by yellow jackets 4 times; once on the head and on the cheek and arms, poor kid. Let's just get off this mountain, load the wood, everyone tired and tempers are on edge. I feel like my body was tipped upside down and someone left the top off me and drained all the energy out. Stop and unload wood at Luckie's, then head home to bathe a tired family.

Bill still not home, getting more and more depressed. City people don't realize when they see the smoke billowing out our chimney in the fall, and it looks so cozy, they should know the planning, blood sweat and tears that goes with that warm fire, long hard back breaking work. But to keep us warm in the winter is worth it.

Listen to Dusty practice on his trombone. Now that may not sound like much to you, but if you hated horns like I do it's a real sacrifice to listen with great concern and smile. Brass instruments drive me up the wall and the way Dusty plays right now I was hanging from the ceiling. For 25 to 30 minutes listening to *Mary had a little Lamb*, and he had to be sacrificing the lamb... terrible but better than I could do by far.

Montana is shutting down all lumber mills and logging is at a stand still. The cattle business, well you can't give them away. The wood market is terrible.

Tilly is still hanging in there. It has a flat tire in the driveway and I can't pry the puppy off. I jump on it, try everything, there it sits, I get to walk. I finally get a pump and go out and use a bicycle pump and pump my heart out. Then the kids try, the tire is holding air, at least for the time being so I can get it to town and maybe have someone look at it.

Bill Home!!!!!

September, I have to get him from the bus in Missoula, what a relief to have a husband back. He was gone for almost 3 months. It is so nice to have him back and have the responsibility of saving our family from financial ruin, or at least starvation.

Bill's logging. He had to put a splint on a broken leg today up in the mountains. He was the only one who knew how to set a splint. Having a scout leader as a sawyer is a plus, I'm sure. Then they waited for the helicopter to lift the guy out of the woods. I thank Heavenly Father that Bill is careful or blessed by him as he works in that dangerous environment.

I have lived in Montana for years, and moved over and over. I've watched my Dad work hard then fall in bed at 9 pm only to rise early by 3:00 am to hit the woods again. To drive up a slick, steep logging road, and then slide down it, having masterful skills at driving, doing this day after day. That is one thing that Bill has decided not to do is drive truck. That we can't afford one might be a deciding factor, but I think it is because Bill just plain hates logging and will soon move on to something else.

Nathan knocking teeth out

Nathan's forever accident-prone. The first time that Nathan knocked his teeth out, was in the third grade. They shattered and lay on the ground. Nathan sat there waiting for me with his teeth in an envelope. They couldn't fix them with caps till he was 18, so they put some fake teeth in its place, and as the time passed, Nathan's front teeth became darker and blacker. He had to live with teasing and ridicule because we couldn't afford to have them fixed properly. But it wasn't too bad because there were kids with big ears, buckteeth, bathroom problems, and just normal dirt. So he took it in stride and just put up with it. Well once more the school called and his teeth lay shattered again. A door this time hits him in the mouth. He is really depressed as he knows money is tight, but we manage to get him some front teeth again, and give him a hug and assurance that everything will be all right.

Bill laid off.... what's new?

This is a regular occurrence in our life, logging is just like that. If the weather is bad, you have to stay home. If the road is mudded out, or the land is too dry you have to go on hoot owl. That means you work from 12:00 midnight till 8 in the morning. Or the mill has too much wood, who knows? But once more we have no money coming in, for weeks.

Tree Hunting

Winter is closing fast, already into December, snowing and getting ready for Christmas. One thing about Montana, we can afford a tree for Christmas because we just have to go in the backyard or the mountain behind us and get one, if picky mom can find one.

If you know me by now my trees are special to me. I have to find the right one, which is not an easy task and it happens every year. Bill's temper was starting to fly when I couldn't decide. Bill says we are getting this one by the road. Up a steep frozen mountain, throw it on the car and we're off.

At home the kids pull out the decorations and decorate the tree while I have the 12 days of Christmas to do. When I arrive home I get the car stuck on the mountain. I high center it on snow. We hike in 5 inches of snow with temperatures below zero. I'm crying. Bill's yelling that I have lived here long enough that when it snows this much you know you WILL get the car stuck. But I am stubborn and I always have to try, not a good thing when you have an irate mad husband...

School Play (Christmas)

Tiffany's excited. The school programs in Montana are a big thing and every kid in school has a part. You sing, play an instrument, or dress up like something: scenery, bells, animals and dance, shake or whatever. Moms are so proud, and cameras go crazy. Then Santa comes at the end of the program, the tattered red suit, the beard tangled the fur matted, but the kids are elated. Boxes of bagged candy sit around him, each kid comes up to him and he hands him a sack of hard candy, peanuts and an orange. The kids could hardly wait for the treat. How easy to please kids that don't have much. I look at kids now days, would a sack of peanuts and an orange light up their face with excitement?

Christmas snow again. No money so I made everyone prayer rocks. I painted pictures on a rock and put a poem with it. The kids got cheap roller skates; the house has become a skating rink. Snow, and more snow, cold, and wind that never stops, so I sit inside and try to enjoy it. We all decide to go sleigh riding. We head up Rattler Gulch; it's plowed for the logging trucks so the road is in prime shape for a runner sled. Bill and the kids get on the sled, lying down; we are 6 miles up by the mile markers for trucks.

Bill advises the kids to hold on tight, and if they feel like they are going to crash, don't, they will kill them selves. Also the cattle guards are going to grab your sled, so brace yourself. Off they went. Tiffany's too young for this insanity. I also thought the boys were crazy. Bill leaves everyone, his weight helps to make his sled go in fast gear, faster and faster he goes. A cattle guard, his body moves forward as it tries to throw him off then situated again as the runners hit the glistening snow. I follow with the truck, 40 miles an hour and I can see him round the corner ahead and the kids close behind. The sled is chattering with the fast speed, making as wide corners as they can to navigate the road. Almost to the bottom the last mile mellows out and is a gradual slope so starting to slow them down to light speed. The kids' eyes are huge, their hands are frozen to the sled bars, a permanent smile on their faces.

Bill asked, "Want to go again?"

They said, "NO!"

What an adventure for them. Bill took Tiff up a mile and let her ride down on his back as he steered the sled. What a fun day we had, no money, but lots of love...

Hornets

I know it seems rather strange to be talking about hornets in the middle of winter, but they imbed themselves in the logs and somehow find a crack or crevice to dormant themselves, then when the stove gets cooking they start to move. I can kill 30 hornets in a day in my house. They swarm the windows and you have to watch where you walk and sit. I have been stung time and time again.

The other day I rolled over to turn out the light in bed, and a hornet stung me 5 times on the chest. Well you know what that does to a chest that is already a 42 double D, I was enormous. Then after a week they started to itch, oh what a site, not a fun thing. We just learn to live with the varmints. The last three years I have been stung 23 times. Having bees year round is not what you say a plus. I told the kids that is why I'm fat because each time I get stung I swell and the swelling never goes down, it's not my fault. And then I smile but I'm beginning to believe it, I just get rounder...We're hoping that oiling the logs this year will cut down on the survival rate of the little varmints, until then bug spray has become my trusty

friend.
Winter

Winter is severe; won't Montana give us a break? The log house is our only haven. This cold weather is not good for sawyers. Everyone's only averaging 30 logs plus driving 70 miles one way.

January 1982, 20 below zero, snow miserable. Temperatures dropped, winds 60 to 70 mph all roads closed, kids stranded at school. Loggers stuck in the mountains.

The school just called they're going to try to get the kids home behind a grater, get down and pick them up when they arrive. Bill just barely got the ole wrecker running. The snow has drifted terrible as I drive down the mountain.

I wait to see the yellow bus following a snow plow pushing the snow and the mist going everywhere. The bus driver can hardly see. The kids jump out and wade through the deep snow and strong wind to the truck, now to get back up the mountain. 4-wheel drive is a must in this mess and on this mountain.

Now chop wood, bring it in and snuggle up by the fire. Winds and bad weather suppose to hit again, the storm is suppose to come from the west, not as bad as those eastern storms that circle around and hit us with a double whammy. Blew all night our drive way is no more. Bill drives ole Tessie up and down to try to find some path, drifts 4 ft deep. One of the state guys tried to plow our mountain road, no luck. He got stuck and now our road is impassable.

I get home from town and have to hike again with 4 sacks of groceries, 10 lbs of flour; gallon of milk and 2 gallons of saw oil. I call Bill from Jeanie's house. He's a bear as he didn't want me to go to town anyway. It's always later then he thinks I should be, so he tells me to have them drop me off at the bottom of the hill and walk up.

The wind is blowing, and dark is coming on when they drop me off. Bill meets me at the bottom, after hiking down to help me, and he is steaming mad.

"How in the hell are we supposed to get that up the hill?"

"Carry it, I guess," I say cheerfully."

I pick up two bags, and Bill picks up two. We leave the saw oil below in the car that can't navigate the road. If I never see another bag of groceries it will be too soon. I knew I was going to die and then I knew or was afraid I wouldn't. My lungs were burning and I could hardly get my breath but yet I was breathing as hard as I could. The cold air echoed every deep breath I took and made it swell inside and then exploded. It hurt like I can't explain. Bill's behind me. I feel as though he's pushing me up the steep hill. I can hardly pick up my legs through the knee deep snow.

"Please leave me alone," I yell at Bill. "I can make it up on my own."

My blood pressure's rising, my thighs and calves are hurting and burning; big knots in my muscles. I drop a sack it rips and I pick up half the stuff, throw my purse around my neck. Tiffany's coat through it now to make things worse my purse is making my head swell because it's cutting off all circulation. My arms feel as if they're going to fall off from the weight of those groceries.

Bill's miserable too, but he won't let on, just mad at me for having to come get me. But my moaning, heavy breathing and just plain being miserable makes him forget how terrible he feels. He just gets madder, which makes me mad. I'm almost to the house, I did lose it. I start screaming. I hit the door and dropped the groceries. I collapsed on the couch, my heart beating so hard, I couldn't even look at Bill because he made me furious. I needed to cool off, and he needed to go to bed...

Snow I'm sick of it

Snow again 6 more inches to add to the snow on the road. It's hopeless. We're really getting depressed. The fire's going every night since August and our wood pile's getting non existent. Bills job almost the same, been averaging $100 a week before expenses. He's sawing in waist high snow, driving 150 miles a day.

Tiffany brings her friend home from school to stay overnight. We have spaghetti, woke up to a mountain of snow, at least 23 inches and still snowing. We fix breakfast and look at the situation. Bill goes out skiing for awhile then comes back in.

"We better get Tasha home or else we won't get her home."

The snow was so deep that the cars that did go down the road got the snow in their engines and become stalled. So we fire up ole Tessie, no wipers, no heater; Bill, Tiffany, Tasha and I. The boys wait at home for us.

What an adventure, snow flying up over the bumper and cab. We can't see a thing, adding to the confusion, snow is blowing up through the floorboards coating all of us with a thin film of white dust. We finally make it to Drummond, drop her off get gas, milk, and eggs and homeward bound. We follow our tracks back, we're the only ones crazy enough to go on the road. The 8 miles home seemed long and cold. The road is hard to navigate and the snow's still coming down. We have to stop and sweep snow off the window so we can drive.

We get home and all of the family decides to cross country ski over to the relatives. If you ever knew how I skied you would know this is not a good idea for me. I fall down more than I stand. Half way over to my aunt's house we have to turn back, the storm is so bad. I was up to my ole self in skiing. I was on my back, belly, knees, side and any other part but my feet. I take off my skies and walk up the hill I tell the kids my skiing story when we get home and get hot chocolate in our tummies.

First ski trip

I was 19 years old and I have to say pretty cute. It was the age of fake hair, you wore falls (that was a hair piece that you put in your own hair to add to your locks, and add to your everlasting beauty). Anyway, on with the story, This was in 1967 and to be anybody you had to have skies and a ski rack. So I worked my little butt off to get me a pair of downhill skies. And of course a ski rack to put them on, so all the cute guys could see I was with the whole scene. I headed up to a ski lodge in Utah (Brighton). I heard it wasn't too hard, and some mighty fine guys skied there, plus a few of the workers were to die for. Off I went in my pink Renault with my trusty ski racks that stuck over the sides, my fall that swept down past my shoulders and my skiwear. What a fox.

How hard could skiing be? I had seen people do it on TV and in movies. Just point your skis down hill, bend your knees, and point your toes in. That should do it, besides I have poles to keep me up. I arrived in the parking lot, went over to the ticket office and bought a day pass, then strapped on my skies.

The day was beautiful, the sun glistened on the slopes, and the white snow illuminated everything, the air had a crispness about it. I knew this was going to be a day to remember. As I sidestepped over to the lift, one of the lift operators said hi, and asked if I had been there before.

I said, "No."

He said, "Well I have a break here in a half hour, come and see me after your first run, and we'll have a coke or something; get to know one another".

I smiled my innocent smile and agreed. It was working; the skies and hairpiece had done the job.

I stepped into the line of the chair, as it scooped me up. I almost fell out of the chair. I'm holding on for dear life, "okay I can do this," as I start to get light headed. The lift gets higher and I start to get comfortable. Oh what a cool thing. I start to swing my legs and look like a pro. The top of the mountain is approaching.

Little did I know that you have to watch your skies and slide them along as you dismount, which I didn't know how to do. Whap, I fall flat on my face, as my skies catch the ramp and hurl me out face first. The lift comes to a halt so other skiers behind me don't end up in a heap on top of me.

An Operator comes over to me, helps me up and says, "Didn't you see the sign to keep your tips up?"

I said, "Sorry, I wasn't looking."

I got to my feet with the guy's help. Now to get down this mountain in record time and get a hot date. I point my skies down the hill, and start to go down, it's not working like I've seen on TV. One leg goes one way, the other out of control, and what in the hell are these poles for? As I land in the snow, I try to pull myself up. Okay lean to one side, as my pole disappears, where is that cotton picking thing anyway? Okay now to push with one hand and stand up. I lay flopping in the snow, every way that you can imagine. I didn't know that you needed to lean with the hill to get up let gravity help you. A guy was watching me as I struggled to get myself in an upright position.

He comes up and says, "Do you need some help?"

He pulls me up, brushes me off, hands me my hat, ski poles, and points me down the mountain. By this time my hairpiece is sliding to one side, but I am confident that I can do this.

"Thanks," I reply. "Just a little rusty," I say.

I watch as he glides out of sight. How can this be so hard, he can do it? I fall again, and again, my legs are feeling like rubber, my face in the snow.

This time when I hear a familiar voice, "can I help you?" There he was again, he had gone down and returned on his next run, to pick me up and point me down hill again.

Then about the 4th time he said, "How did you get ahead of me on this run?"

I said, "I haven't made it down yet."

He couldn't believe it. "It's been 2 hours, are you kidding me? The end of the run is just around the bend. Are you okay or do you want me to call the ski patrol?"

"No, I can do it."

My ski pants were wet and coated with ice and water, my hair looking limp. My fall was literally falling off, longer on one side than the other. All in all let's say disgusting.

Finally, the bottom of the hill, I could see the lodge. Heaven was before me, hot chocolate, donuts anything, let alone maybe a date with a hunk. "I'm just going for it," I say as I push off and head for the bottom.

"What are these?" I ask myself as my body is flying in every direction. I think they call them moguls. The whole bottom of the run was plastered with the little molehills. And my skiing ability did not cope with the dips and grooves. I flew forward, and then back. I lay on my back as I was going light speed over these bumps that were making me go airborne every 10 feet. Then the catastrophe happened, my head flew back and my hairpiece left my body. I kept going one direction, as this black blob went another. I came to rest at the bottom of the lift, right below the ski shack, my makeup gone, or running down my face, and then a little kid about 5 swishes down holding this massive matted hairball.

"Is this yours?" he says.

I grab it and try to put it on, only to make a scene. The hair hung in my face, bobby pins sticking in every direction, as the hunk that wanted the date, looks in amazement, this can't be her. I limped to my car carrying my skies and my hair. Threw my exhausted body inside, and went home, dateless and hungry.

From now on I just play it cool, ride around with those skies on my car, and my all day pass on my coat. Well my skiing ability has not improved over the years. I still flop around in the snow like a beached whale, a lot bigger whale.

Now to ski home late at night a mile home then up hill my most dreaded part. I hate up hill to pieces... So much snow no church tomorrow, no one can get there.

Snow

Well another few days have passed, storms have come and gone. None of our vehicles will run since it dropped below zero. We had to fiddle with ole Tessie. We used propane torch heat to make the gears turn and heat the oil that was at molasses consistency.

Bill and I are both down. What are we doing in a place like this? Here we sit, poverty each day getting worse... Making under $8000 a year with a family of 5, 8 in the summer Insane... We really don't know where to turn. We've worked so hard on this house. Now we can hardly make a living. Bill's sawing in chest high snow, has to dig down 4 feet to saw down a tree then comes home bummed out. TV burned out which we really miss even if we only have 1 and half channels. Cabin fever is rising fast. The kids are on edge. I can't believe how miserable it is when they're screaming at each other. It ruins the whole atmosphere of our home. I wish I could get it across to them to **love one another**. IMPOSSIBLE! So now they're sitting in corners trying to be quiet, a new punishment. Tell you how it works, at least helps my nerves if nothing else.

Bill still a bear, sawing in the deep snow now into February. Bill and I are fighting more than usual. I don't know what's wrong with us. I'm beginning to go crazy. I wish we had everything we needed, not wanted. Just need a car that's not on it last leg, a pickup for Bill to get to work, a TV, my teeth fixed, while I need, lets include a dryer. Not so in that order but things would be handy. I wonder how I got this poor in 3 and a half short years.

WEDDING

It was my sister's wedding, and the weather's so bad I had told Bill I wasn't going. But sometimes Terrie is not good for me and when winter is getting me down; I don't think clearly ... a mistake.

Terrie was going to Utah, no matter what, so what would it hurt if I threw Tiffany in and went with her, I didn't have to drive. And then Tiff could be a flower girl, the boys could stay home and bond with Bill. The only problem is before Bill left for work, he told me not to go, but why not?

It's still snowing hard but no wind as of yet. I take a plastic bag with dress shoes, nightie, and a change of clothes for Tiffany, something for the wedding and that's about it. I knew I'd better travel light. We were going in her Le Car which isn't much bigger than a kitty car. It was a tight squeeze but off we tripped. The roads were snowy and packed until Deer Lodge then they were pretty clear in one lane, so we plugged on.

I left a note for Bill and the boys. Sometimes I can really be stupid and let others influence me, not a good thing.... I knew Bill would be upset that I left, but I under estimated him, cause he was steaming...

Well behind us the storm was raging. By afternoon the snow had reached a foot. The winds started blowing 30 to 50 mph and roads were closed. 6 ft drifts covered the roads and freeways.

Dustin is 8 and Nathan is 7. These two boys hike from the bus stop, keeping their hats and scarves covering their faces.

"I can't make it," Nathan says.

They both agree to get in the ole truck that is parked at the bottom of the hill. No heater but it keeps them from the wind. They crawl inside, and huddle together.

"We have to make it up the hill," they say. "We will freeze to death here and no one knows we're in this truck."

So they get out and push through the wind and deep snow that is blowing horizontally. There is no path or driveway for them to hike. Snow to their thighs, pushing and wading through, they finally reached the door.

They burst through and say; "Mom."

To their disappointment, there wasn't an answer; silence echoed back, they found the note. And waited for Dad to get home, they knew they would have to go out and get wood, and keep the fire going,

I can't believe how the Lord blessed us, for the boys being Montana wise, to get in the ole wrecker to get warm and then get up to the house. I look back now and see what a foolish choice I made and could have suffered grave consequences.

After the boys had been home for awhile the phone rings, Bill calls, "the M.H.P. has closed the roads they won't let anyone through. The blizzard is terrible; let me talk to your mom."

"Ah, she's gone to Utah, Dad."

"She what?" A few choice words, man he was mad.

He had to go through the road block as he explained that he has two young boys alone with no furnace, so they let him pass. His trip home was tense but he made it, breaking through 6 ft drifts, and blinding snow, trying to see through the white out conditions following the reflectors when you could see them, for 50 miles.

In the mean time Terrie and I had reached Blackfoot and the storm must have caught up with us cause our good roads just turned horrible; snow, 25 mile winds and blinding snow. The trip seemed forever and the kids were getting tired. We pulled in about 7:30 pm and Bill already had called. He was on the war path I call him back but wish I hadn't. He read me up one side then down the other. I felt terrible for leaving my boys, but I never dreamed the storm would come down with such fury.

Montana 42 below
It's cold and miserable. Bill went to work got 3 whole logs, before everything froze up. The next couple days are freezing and no change in weather. Bill calls and apologizes tells me he loves me and to get home as soon as we can.

I work on wedding things, and then hear from Bill again. Our water line's freezing. Luckie's water is frozen. The temperature's still 34 to 40 below with the wind chill, cars are not starting and kids are not going to school. Bill's trying to unthaw water and had to walk over to Luckie and Terrie in his snowshoes.

We're in Utah getting ready for the wedding. It's a whole different world there, no big storm temperatures are in the 40s, sunshine. The wedding was beautiful, the reception, gifts, cake and the girls were great, but was it worth it to have Bill so mad at me?

Trip Home

6 a.m. up but not raring, my eyes felt terrible, let alone my body. Was I ready for 7 people in that Le Car, because now Luckie was here, he flew in from Denver with one more suit case, talk about pack a car: 3 in front, 4 in back with suit cases to the ceiling, boots in our ears and sacks on our feet. Grab some toast so we don't have to stop. Now, let's go,

Oh pain, kids were really good considering we had 6 inches each. Now and then one would try to take up someone else's 6 inches which would cause a chain reaction of moving and tempers. Idaho Falls didn't come soon enough. What a relief to get out and find my legs again, cram back in, rearrange a few things, much better. Home's around the corner. Hike the hill and get dinner on for the family.

I see the kids trying to get up the hill, walking backwards, tripping through the snow drifts. Turn around and freeze, now up the hill trying to find the trail. I see them fall off the trail one time and sink out of sight. They're breathing hard, ears ready to fall off, hands frozen to their books and the wind's going right through their coats, hats and gloves.

I get hugs and loves. What a joy to be home, even if we have no TV, no food, and no money, averaging $300 a month. The kids just chose numbers to see if one or the other had to go out to get wood. Nathan lost. Moaning and groaning he tries to find a new way to get out of the job, but I just yelled and he's on his way.

Well Bill got home and said he was fed up of bucking waist deep snow and solid trees. You have to file your saw every two trees, frozen ice falling on you, saw not running, gas turning to slush cause of the cold temperatures. Hands are freezing so that you don't feel your fingers. You have to throw your saw up the hill and crawl on your hands and knees up the steep grade and dig down to the trees to cut them.

He heads for the employment office the next day. A stock boy for $3.35 hour and we have to travel 100 miles, that won't quite make it. Back to sawing tomorrow, good thing Bill's boss understands. He told him to come back if he changed his mind.

A cousin gave us an old 25 inch TV. The kids are so excited, but how do we get it up the hill? They load it on toboggan sled and pull and push this huge TV up the mountain in 3 ft of snow, it looked like a human dog sled

February – the days roll into weeks, the weather is still below zero, no work again. We made $110 for the month and we're eating lots of rice, wheat and poor man's gravy.

The weather hangs in the 20s, on the warm side, after being in the below zero double digit. The weather is like a yo yo but much warmer. All this snow is now melting and water is running down the mountain in sheets, looks like a river down our driveway. The river's over the banks because of ice jams, it's a terrible mess. Ice jams are when the river freezes solid from all the cold weather, and then gets thicker and thicker, then as it melts and gets warmer those ice chunks start breaking away and going down the river, only to get stuck together in a bend in the river, backing up the water and filling up the land surrounding the banks of the river. Sometimes the ranchers have to blast them, but so far the water has just made a mess.

Weather crazy,

One day it's thawing, next day it snows. Bill ruins my day saying, "We have to get wood." I really hate it. Gas up ole Tessie; the only kid that wants to go is Dusty. Nate and Tiff stay home to do dishes and make beds.

Up Rattler, the bottom road is mudding out around the corner and the scene changes. The road is solid ice, it glistens in the sunlight, and the wheels shine the ice more every turn they make. I'm a nervous wreck, how do we even stay on the road? Up and up past Bear Creek, new logging roads, if you don't remember which turn you made you could be lost forever.

Bill sees a tree, starts up the bank but the snow is past his waist so he finds one close to the road. It still is difficult to wade in the waist high snow. There's timber right on the road. 3 more trees the same way, hook on the tree, and pull it onto the road with old Tessie. It seemed we went 2 miles before we found a curve with a turn out area.

Now the trip down my hand's are getting sweaty, my heart's beating faster. The old wrecker should have ice skates on it. It fish tales and I panic. I know we are going out of control. Bill and Dusty laugh at nervous mom. I yell, "Gear this puppy down."

Bill heeds my advice, so I'll shut up. Finally the 2 mile marker and level ground, out of 4 wheel drive and home.

Really depressed, I'm just tired of living this way, never a change, just less and less money, two cars have given up and died on us, Terrie and Luckie are moving, I'm fat and ugly shall I go on? Now days I guess I would go to the doctor and get some anti depressants and things would get better. I have been getting headaches lately; I really don't know what's causing them, my teeth, or tension, or nerves; who knows?

Sawing Accident Again, maybe he's trying to do himself in…

Get a phone call about 10:00 am, the guy Bill works for asked what I was doing.

"Well, not much."

"Well then, could you possibly come in and pick up your husband from the hospital. He had a run in with a chain saw. His foot got in the way."

"Well, how bad is it? I say.

"Well, I'm no doctor but I think he still has a foot. Not too bad."

I have to borrow a car to run into the hospital, 50 miles, wondering how he is. Bill was sitting up waiting for me, his foot stitched and bandaged. He explains how he did it.

"I was just getting started," he says, "and the saw kicked back and zip right through my boot. 2 pair of socks and into my foot."

One thing the doctor said was it was the cleanest chain saw cut he's seen. Shows he really knew how to sharpen a saw, cut clean like a razor blade. But one thing the doctor said next time you do it, cut it a little higher in the leg, so we have more skin to work with.

Bill's off work again for a few days, no work, no money. We seem to always make it through, we just do without.

Spring and doing laundry outside again, the wind blowing, so it is a real task to hang the clothes out and hope the pins hold up to the strong gales, and they don't end up a mile down the hill.

No Hot Water
Hot water heater burned out while we were in church yesterday. I can't believe our luck, if it can go wrong it will happen to us. I don't know what's with us lately, but everything electric mechanical, etc we touch or own maybe look at, or even think about breaks. Even our trusty ole toaster has given up popping up, just lays there and smokes.

I get to learn how to quilt, like what else is there to do up here, might as well keep warm in fashion. I pick up Ruby and Margaret to go over to Phyllis's. They are 70 year old ladies, professional quilters. My fingers are so sore, pulling the needle through the stitches and batting.

I ask, "How do all of you do this, my fingers are killing me?"

Phyllis pipes up, "if you'd use a damn thimble they wouldn't get so sore."

So I put it on my finger that goes under the quilt.

"No, No, you can't do that. You have to prick that finger to know you've come through the quilt, this finger."

Phyllis says shows me how. I didn't let her know it wasn't helping. But at least I was trying. Now these ladies are cooks along with seamstresses, and it's lunchtime. I ate like a stuffed pig, oh it was sooo good. What an experience to sit at a quilt with the best, and they are! Learn the gossip, and the down right truth of how you should live, act, and when to shut your mouth.

Crazy ride home
What a crazy month. It has snowed three times this week. Tuesday night after art we walk out to 8 inches of snow in about 2 hrs. It was coming down so hard it would stick to your eyelashes.

Jeanie drove that night. Oh, if you only knew, Jean is scared to death of snowy roads and bad weather in general, and basically the worst driver you have ever seen. But when you have no car, you're glad to get a ride. Terrie, Shaun, Jean and I all load in the car. As we started down the church driveway you couldn't tell where the driveway was. The headlights made the snow look like a meteor shower. The wipers on full speed couldn't keep the snow off the windshield. The only way you knew where you were going was to look out the side window and see the weeds that bordered the road. Jean's getting more and more nervous. We keep reassuring her that she is doing fine, her breathing getting heavy, her movement radical.

"Do you want one of us to drive?" we ask.

"No," she yells, then on, 8 more miles of this. Can we stand it? The snow wasn't the problem, it was Jean. She was working into a lather. Her breath became short and jerky, her coat unsnapped, then the window down, she started panting. 4 more miles and the snow's still terrible. Jean drops me off at the bottom of my hill.

The snow pounding on my face, my shoes caked with snow, the soles were the type that attracted the wet cold snow and I could hardly stand. I stamped and kicked trying to get it off; finally the door is just ahead.

My thoughts drifted to the coyotes and how terrible it would be to be out here alone, even without my trusty purse. My mind plays tricks on me and I could hear things. I glanced around quickly only to see the serene snow bellowing down. How dumb, what would wander around in this crap any way. Thank heaven I'm home!

Jean has improved from those days, after her 3 wrecks, and driving school. She is pretty good, and we laugh at the old times.

Moving Dumb Dora off the mountain

What a day, today we change the appearance of our mountain. Gene let us use his Cat and we're going to move ole Dora off the hill. Move my poor clothesline and what ever else we can think of.

Our first project was clean up the yard. What a bunch of garbage we've gathered in 3 and a half years, trees, cans, sinks, piles of wood, paper, plastic, the ole pickup heaping with odds and ends. I'm not in the best mood.

I just can't see how Bill is going to get Dora off the mountain without her crashing and burning at the bottom. But he doesn't really care. He really despises the ole girl after living in her almost 2 years. Rocks, wood, blocks, frozen underneath her so we move what we can and he says to heck with the rest. We'll roll her over it. He scoots the Cat around the trailer and positions the big blade in front of the tongue. I direct him until the huge mass of metal is inches away from her ole blue tongue and blade of the cat. He gets a chain and winds it around the tongue and blade of the Cat.

Then with everything in motion I back up. I knew ole Dora had seen her last, the metal on her sides buckling and her middle creaking. He winds up the Cat and starts backing. Bill can't hear me moaning now yelling as Dora creaks backwards down the hill. I have to walk beside the trailer to direct Bill. He can't see past ole Dora to see where to turn. Why me?

Now here we go. The trailer and blade takes off one side of the road, and then the other. Now to the corner swing wide and hope for the best. The ole trailer bouncing over the rocks, I could just see the chain breaking and Dora running rapid down the mountain. Creaking, the trailer comes to a stop in the middle of our field. I sigh, a sigh of relief. And just shake my head.

While all this is going on we are trying to keep a dog, which is in heat, from having puppies. Not a fun thing especially when you have a Bassett hound. The constant whining and whistling through the nose just let her out to play. When we do let her outside we put kids training pants on her. They work pretty good, look terrible but who cares.

Typical Plane Trip

I talk to Luckie the other day about how lucky he is to fly all the time, and he told me his typical plane trip.

Up early, I have to hustle to the airport drag my bags in, usually the weather is rotten, brief cases, suit case. Suit bag over coat, fumble for my ticket and board the plane. Through the check line to see if I'm a convict. Buzz I get to empty my pockets, metal watches, keys, etc. now clear put everything back in up the stairs. Once I'm on the plane I find a quiet seat. Non-smoking and settle back with my scriptures.

The plane almost ready to leave, on board's a dirty greasy hippy with long stringy hair, back pack. Where does he choose to sit, right in front of me? A young girl sitting next to him cringes as he positions himself. He takes his backpack and duffle bag and crams them in the space overhead, right where my topcoat was folded neatly now it goes in a ball to the back. The stewardess tells him he can't put them there so he tries to stuff them under his seat, where my feet have to go. I say excuse me, but can't you find a better place for those. He grumbles and puts them under the seat in front of him.

Now it's breakfast time. As I'm eating his long greasy hair hangs over the seat trying to hang in my food. I lose my appetite. He tries to impress the girl next to him so orders a beer and dumps the bottle upside down in a cup. It foams out and over the rim and onto her dress. My jaws were so tight then I couldn't talk or eat or rest. He then decides to relax; most people would slowly put their seat back, not this guy, Whap! His seat goes right into my knees. I could hardly wait to get to Denver and get off this nightmare flight.

I guess there are down sides to everything, but I sure would like to try to have that kind of bad day. Oh please.

Chapter 17
Poverty and Pain

Poverty and pain

Poverty and pain – It seems like those two words go together. Poverty is part of our vocabulary now. Money what is that? The kids never complain. Only once when the boys asked me to get some underwear because theirs were too small, they had jumped from size 10 to 14, man did I feel bad. When you have no money, you also have other problems, like bad teeth, you need them fixed but of course you can't afford it, so you just take aspirin and cope.

All night with a toothache my head feeling as though it was going to fall off. I do something stupid like take someone else's drug because it worked for them, and it's a pain pill ya know. Codeine pills don't touch the pain they just make's me sick. I don't handle drugs so of course let's take some kind of narcotic on an empty stomach, because your teeth hurt too much to eat anything.

I heard you could take aspirin till your ears rang, so I just kept taking them, hoping the pain would just get bearable. My teeth were rotten, and not improving I was up to 24 aspirin in a day. I would sit on the edge of the bed at night, rock and hold my mouth with a warm tea bag. Anything has to work, till it got so bad that I had to go in to a dentist. Just pulled a name out of the phone book and prayed that he would be good. He was that and very understanding. He pulled some teeth, tried to fix others and took payments until I could afford dentures.

Dentures

The eventful day came that I had to get my upper teeth pulled. Talk about sweat, and I don't sweat much for a chubby girl. I think I left hand prints in the arms of the chair where I held on so tight. No one hates dentists more than I do.

"Let's see," he says as he pulls out the ole x-rays. "I know these teeth, there must be one broken off at the gum."

I had died a thousand deaths a few months ago and helped bury it with 20 to 30 aspirin and Tylenol. The next one is loose from nothing to lean on and air seeping in caused terrific pain. We had a short discussion and decided to start pulling my teeth for dentures. He asked if I wanted gas.

"Well I would but I get sick."

"No way," he said, as he comes at me with the needle and shoots me 5 or 6 times inside, out and around my mouth. My eyes water as the needle goes into the roof of my mouth, now just sit and let it get good and numb. Now my nose seemed as if it was huge. My nose is large as it is, but put numbing meds in and around and that baby seems as though it was expanding all over my face. It seemed every part on me was numb and my eye was feeling funny, but I still could blink so I was okay.

I have been to some dentists where they hit some nerve, and they had to put a patch on my eye and close it for me because it wouldn't blink, so this was a good thing.

I'm nervous. My knees shaking, my jaw shaking and folding my two hands so tight the fingers are going white. Oh, oh here he comes with a mask, rubber gloves, tools and I'm awake. I've got to be crazy.

I really don't know what he is doing until I hear the creaking and cracking of my teeth and the pressure on your jaw. You're hoping he knows what he's doing; a couple are really hard to pull. I knew he was going to stop half way through and tell me they can't be pulled they're too hard, the pressure was intense. Then he started to break away the top portion of my jaw, and fix the way my teeth were buck, then he stitched. I never thought he would finish them and then I was afraid he'd sew my tongue to my gum. He gives me a swab of cotton bite down, I was so scared my head is bouncing off the back of the chair

He says, "Are you ok? Do you want to sit a second here and get feeling better?"

I move my head yes and sit there. I have the assistant wipe my mouth off and go out to see Terrie, I can hardly talk. I get my composure together and can even utter a few mispronounced words. Then he takes me back and puts in my new teeth.

Okay I can do this, as I stagger down the stairs to the car, luckily I didn't drive. But everyone wanted to go shopping, because how often do we get to the big city. So I go shopping. I'm doing great. My face starts to swell, and swell, looks like I went through a war, then I get queasy, not good because with me this means THROW UP, UP CHUCK, or BUICK all not good words.

Made it home, and thought I was going to die. I lived on broth and tea for a week, which with my body couldn't hurt, was sick as a dog, etc., etc. But even though I lost many pounds, my body wouldn't let go of the little fat cellulite that terminally had a grip on my thighs, so the pounds just stuck on.

Here Bunny Bunny or where is that rotten egg?

In the midst of all this it is Easter time and the kids have to go to the school for the annual Easter egg hunt. 50 dozen eggs are in every color possible. The playground was polka dotted with yellow, blue and pink eggs. Kids from the age of 2 -9 running to gather eggs, what a battle ground. And it was all over in about 5 minutes; sacks bulging, buckets heaping, eggs trampled. Go home with more hard boiled eggs than we can eat in a year. They fill our fridge. Deviled eggs, and egg salad, no choice we have to eat eggs for every meal.

Oh now the night before Easter we get to boil more eggs and dye them. Then hide the eggs because it's our turn to be Easter Bunny. We don't have the money for chocolate eggs, so we hide real eggs, after the tradition of course of dying the things every rainbow color that you can think of. I go around the house after the kids are in bed, and hide them behind curtains, in flower pots, under couch cushions, under chairs, in drawers, every place I could find. (Now why hide them in doors because it is Montana, and it is still winter outside. Most the time we don't even have water at this time of the year, cause its still frozen solid.)

3 dozen eggs, what a chore to remember where 36 eggs are. It seems every Easter we lose a few, no matter where we look we can't find all 36. Okay it will show up. Sure enough it makes itself known, the aroma drifts through the house, you really notice it as you enter and this rotten egg smell hits your nose, and makes you gag. We have to find that Easter egg, so the hunt begins, this time with no joy, hankies cover our noses. And we miserably destroy the front room until the forgotten petrified egg oozing with froth appears, behind the big picture frame by the old wood stove, which helped to emanate the odor through the house.

What a joy to finally have money to buy wrapped candy and not worry about rotten eggs. But the whole foo faa rah was getting up in the morning to see if the ole Rabbit had grabbed their eggs, and hid them, and who could find all their eggs first. So maybe poverty isn't so bad, rotten teeth and eggs. What the heck, life is great with kids.

Eagle Review

Bill is the scout master for the boy scouts, and the boys are advancing, with his help to Eagle. Now he has to take one of the first ones to Eagle Council. This is a council of former Eagle Scouts and leaders, and they drill the new scout on all the scout laws, knots and whatever else they can think of. Pretty tough guys, you better know what you're doing.

As usual our luck follows us home from Missoula. The car makes a terrible noise and shakes. My mouth shuts and nerves get tense. Bill comes to a slow stop and checks the wheel, just as I thought wheel bearing. The car limps another 5 miles again it goes crazy; another mile to the Rock Creek exit. We pull in. My cousin Wayne is working in the garage there. They pull the car in. He and Bill look at it. The spindle is gone also. Better call Blaine the father of the scout as we need a ride home. We go over to the Rock Creek Lodge bar, the two scouts following Erin and I.
We find a phone. The two boys spot a couple video machines and a pool table. Clean us out of quarters while Erin tries to get her husband or anyone to come get us. Finally Parkers are coming. But it will be at least an hour. What a sight two scouts, a scoutmaster, and two den mothers playing pool in a bar at 10:45 at night. But what's new just making memories.

Today, Bill has just been present when his 30 and 31st Eagle was presented to the boys he helped get through, two of them being his boys… They gave him a statue of two eagles, to thank him.

Depressed again

Been really depressed, Bill too busy or to angry to listen to me. Terrie and Luckie are moving and that hasn't helped. All my life I've had one close friend, no matter where I was. We shared everything together 1st – 4th grade was always Luckie. We depended so much on each other, and still today we depend so much on one another, a special bond… and now he's leaving and I'm here.

I wish I could say what I mean, how I feel. No one understands depression until you go through it. It's terrible; it creeps up on you overtaking your whole body and mind. You don't want to do anything. My house isn't helping things. I need it fixed, like real people. Like lumber out of the front room, and bedrooms, places to put things on and on. I just want to give up. What use is it here? We just exist here. I wish I were happier here. Maybe I'd feel more like getting in shape.

if we can get on top of things then maybe we can get the house fixed up. I know I'd be a lot happier. I love a clean house and it seems impossible. I can't express what's going on in my mind. I'm so upset I feel like crying all the time. I'm angry, I'm sad, I'm? Tears flow down my face and nose, and I can't tell you why. (As I read my journal, I could tell you why I'm depressed, no dang money…. No loving, and no time, what's new?)

Girls Camp 82

I get to be a leader for a several 12 to 17 yr old girls. They want us to go on a 10 mile hike, 5 miles uphill in a wilderness area with a 60 lb pack on my over weight frame. I can just see it. Heart attack city! I guess I'd better get into shape. It isn't funny.

Boy I am out of shape! The only exercise I get is when I get up between soap operas to hit the refrigerator or cupboards. Boy Montana is Hell on figures. Everyone that has moved here has gained at least 20 lbs in one year, either boredom or a layer of fat to keep us from freezing to death. Things have to change.

What a headache for month now. I've worried whether I can do it, 10 miles with a 65 lb pack on my back, the day of reckoning is here. Helped all the girls get packed and ready to go. Tuesday morning up early, 6:30, now if you know me this is not a good time because before 7:00 I am a bear! Meet at church and off for the big adventure. 32 miles of dirt road, Fish Creek, up and up rotten road snow, I shake my head, where is my mind? Taking 10 girls up in the wilderness, hiking with packs on our backs, bummer. Finally arrived at 11:30 a.m. but most wards had already left.

Put on our packs and headed up. We had to shove more food into our packs which was an impossible feat but we did it. Pam and Kristy Little were a great help to me. My pack weighed 60 lbs. before food, gross. I strap it on and head up. Here we go, Pam, Kristy, Kim, Denise, Becky, Brenda, Julie, Billy Jo, Trixi, Tammy and me in the rear, as always. My doubts are still there. Am I going to be able to do this?

I must not look like a leader because people ask me who the leader is.

"I am."

Oh, then do this or that.

The trail started to tell the strong from the weak, and spread us far apart. My girls would turn around and wait so I wouldn't be lost forever. The day was a real test. I could tell I was out of shape, but not as bad as I thought. Up hill, down, now then forks in the road, which way do we go?

Some of the leaders that were in the front had left a message to go down the hill. So for over a mile we hike down to the bottom of this canyon then meet people coming up, tired and disgusted... We took the wrong road. That's all I need.

Sister Timothy says, "Just go straight up the mountain."(Easy for her, a day pack on her little back, and she weighs maybe 125, She looked like a mountain goat just a strutting. I'm carrying another person on my hips, let alone a backpack.)

The mountain is over grown with heavy underbrush. We have to cross big drifts of snow, walk through mud and over fallen trees. I knew if I ever stood up straight I would fall backwards, only stopping at the bottom of the canyon. Afraid and tired I grabbed for every secure thing I could to help me up the steep terrain. Girls started showing their exhaustion having to rest on fallen trees and big rocks.

"When will we ever reach the top?" I think to myself. Others are hurting as much as I. Then I see Kristy, Kim, Pam, and Denise there a little higher. I see the rest of my girls cheering me on. It made me feel so good to see all them waiting for their trusty leader, ha, ha. We're finally at the top, at least to the other road. Now to keep hiking up and up my calves ached and my shoulders felt like they were hamburger. On we go.

The girls start spreading out again and again I end up in the rear, my pack, age, and ballooned body doesn't help matters. Finally to the crest of the mountain, now down to the valley, to the lake. We were so high the clouds passed by, sometimes engulfing the girls ahead of me and then disappearing.

Now I'm hiking all alone. Trying to balance myself across the huge snowdrifts, that block the road, I could see where a few girls had lost it, and slipped, catching them several yards down the mountain. Please not me I prayed silently. Now on a lonely ledge looking over the edge, I knew if I fell I'd never be found so I hug the mountain cause my pack was getting heavier and heavier and my feet less steady.

Rounding the turn was a familiar face, Tammy or Julie was waiting for me I can't remember because by then my brain was also going numb. The lake was in view now. And when you can see the end your strength starts to leave, I knew they would have to carry me in. I struggle past the lake to camp. My girls are all there cheering me in.

"Come on Pennie, you did it!"

And I did.. I fall to the ground in relief. Here we are 5 to 6 miles back in and I can't move. Woe is me...

The rest of the day was work also. Set up tents, build fire pits, and build latrines. All of our girls up on the hill working on the pee spot. Now how do we do this you ask? Well we are going to be here for 3 to 4 days, so we need a substantial hole that we can go in and cover up, not leaving a trace. So we start digging with our fold up shovel. And most latrines have to be waist deep. So we grab our littlest girl Trixi and put her in to measure the depth. Then cut branches and lash logs together for a seat. Pole for toilet paper and hour later we're done; lets split to the lake soak our tired hot feet.

Well the lake was like a freezer, our feet burned when they touched the water. Soaking feet is not an option.

Dinner wasn't anything to look forward to. But when you have hiked that hard and far, anything sounds good. We had to cook in a # 10 can that we carried on our belt, all the way up it beat on one thigh, so of course I will have one leg that looks like it went to a spa and the other cellulite city.. Oh who am I kidding nothing helps my thighs or hips, any way on with the story...

Dehydrated applesauce, stew and biscuits wrapped around a stick. To cook over an open fire what a joy, smoke in your eyes, and dirt in your food and usually burnt. We did okay rehydrating the applesauce. We just finished eating when it started to rain. Tell the girls to secure their tents make them water proof with tarps and cover their packs.

Then the crazy leaders have us standing in a cold drizzle for a program, finally the weather convinced them that our program would have to be cut short, as the storm became more intense. I help the girls get tucked in their tents, rain pouring now, dripping off my nose. I feel soaked. Oh I pray these little girls are okay.

The night seemed to stand still as it poured on us and the wind whipped and the lightening lit the sky on fire. I stayed awake listening to how rotten Mother Nature can get (what are we doing up here?). I was really worried for the girls, their tents weren't as good as mine and I was getting soaked, I wonder how they are?

You know I'm 34 years old and really not a mountain woman. Give me a recliner, candy bar and soda and I'm fit to go for a couple of days. No I'm up here on the top of some wilderness, hoping I don't die, and wash off into the lake. I could think of 5 or 10 ladies that could hike up here better than I, but no I have sucker stamped on my forehead. Everyone thinks because Bill is mister Scoutmaster, superman for hiking and camping, Mrs. Scoutmaster is the same. Well I have news for them; this fat chick ain't even in the same league. But I'm stuck up here now and if I want to live I better figure out how I'm going to hike my huge butt out of here.

Well morning finally crept in but the rain still hadn't quit. It let up a little so it wasn't raining buckets. I got up put my wet pants and shoes on. Met at the door by 2 drowned girls, poor Julie and Becky were soaked from head to toe. I had them crawl into my tent and I said I'd start a fire. What an experience, trying to dip water out of the fire pit so I could start a flicker Good thing Bill threw some sterno in my pack. Got some kindling and twigs and put some sterno on it, Walla, Fire! Now find more wood, hike around breaking dead branches off trees, not a bad fire! Get a can boil some water for good ole hot chocolate. Get something down the girls to warm them up. All the girls up now and all soaked. Julie and Becky slept in 4 inches of water; their tent fell down in the night. Tam and Kim wet, Trix and Brenda not any better. Now 6 people are in my tent. I'm running cups of hot chocolate over to the girls. They're bummed out and me also. I'm leaving this place. I tell them we'll get home somehow. The rest of the leaders agree we are going to have to get out of there now, or we won't get out of there.

Our girls had to try to squeeze the water from their sleeping bags that now weighed 10 to 15 lbs each. I was the strongest so I helped all the yearling girls get packed back up, tents down finally the last ward to go. The hike out seemed even more intense cause it was cold and rainy. My body ached with each step my calves tied in knots and my shoulders panged in pain, why can't lakes be on the top instead of a valley? The girls all stayed by me. The faster ones hiked then waited for me, taking turns hiking with me encouraging me on. They were all laughing cause my stretch polyester elastic pants just kept getting longer and longer as I hiked, pretty soon the waist was tucked under my bra and I was walking on the knees. I kept trying to pull them up, but the heavy pack with all the little girls stuff just kept pulling on them. Each girl took her turn, what special girls.

My girls in young women are so neat. They all get along so well. By the time I reached the top of the mountain I thought I'd died three times but I did it again. I hiked out 5 miles with 70 lbs on my back. The cars were in sight. I was so tired tears welled in my eyes and my feet once more started to stumble I can't quit now I told myself, just another quarter mile. One of the girls took my pack from me, all of a sudden I felt like a feather, a wet feather but a feather. We had to squeeze in people's trucks, vans, cars to get back to the stake center. 100 hot stinky wet girls, umm umm what an aroma....

We got home, and the next day decided to go finish out girls' camp at Millers Lake 7 miles from home. Drive up take a raft, cool pop, chips hamburgers. This is the life. We completed all the camping requirements of camp. Had fun.... Fair weather camper I am.
I have gone to camp now for over 17 years, been first year leader and last year leader which I thought would do me in. But mostly I'm camp entertainment, which is trying enough. But it's me...

August 1982
The weather has returned to hot and dry. We went to MIA the other night. On the way down the hill

Dustin says, "Stop Dad. There's a rattler."

There by the mailbox was a brother of the one we had just killed, 4 ft long 8 buttons, 3 to 4 inches in diameter. We didn't have anything in the car so Bill gets the hatchet.

I said, "You're crazy."

He walks up to it and throws the hatchet like an Indian, that hatchet flew straight and strong, whack, right past the snake. Okay now what. Bill grabs a stick, and the snake starts to follow it with his head showing his fangs. He gets a big rock and hits him but it doesn't faze him. Just at that time a policeman shows up.

"What do you have?"

"A rattler! I say. "A pretty good size."

By this time the snake had moved into the long grass by the mailbox. Bill asked the policeman if he had a shotgun. The patrolman got it out of the car, put a shell in it.

Bill says, "Shoot the end of my stick and you'll hit the snake."

He says, "I'm not going down there. You take it and shoot it."

Bill shoots the thing; it cuts the snake in half so he throws it out on the highway, and cuts off its head and buries it. Now we're on to scouts, as he hands the patrolman his gun back.

Chapter 18
Something New

Suckers

The rage has hit Drummond, suckers, in every color and flavor, big balls of sugar with a stick. Moneymaking deal, Gene and Linda are opening the business. Parkers and their family have started one in their basement. You turn your suckers into a company in Missoula who distributes them all over. Well at least I can go to work. Gene's factory is in the old green building in Drummond. They're hiring a lot of church people, or whoever wants to work. By the time I heard of it, the only job available was the cook.

They have a job of breaking the molds, then wrapping and labeling the suckers, and cooking. The factory is employing 6 to 8 people. Now cooking is not my favorite thing to do. But I can do it if it will feed my family. 2 cents a sucker, each batch would make about 36 suckers, 72 cents a batch.

Blaire and I cooking, now that may be a problem, Blaire is quiet and shy, hard worker, but I don't know if he can measure any better than I can. The first thing we do is measure the syrup, and the sugar, then bring to a boil, putting in the candy thermometers and watching the hot candy bubble and boil to a certain temperature, the hardball stage. Then remove and add the many flavors. Just at the right time pour it into heavy metal molds that are lined up on cookie sheets. The heavy hot pans would stress your arms, as you had to work fast and the weight of the pans would weigh on you as the day went on.

The smell of the suckers would get on everything. My hair reeked of cinnamon, or strawberry, coconut or licorice, which would make me gag. We had to stop work, so that we could work out the bugs because we were ruining too much candy and supplies. Well they decided that maybe the cooks were the problem with the factory and production. Now how does a nice guy like Gene tell you that you stink as a cook, and the factory will fold if you cook anymore rotten suckers? My kids loved the rejects. I guess the amount was rather high compared to other factories.

Gene said, "Ah, Pennie I thought maybe you would like to wrap instead of cook, would that be possible?"

I don't know what he would have done if I would have said No.

So now I'm the mold breaker and wrapper, oh this job is sweet. The only problem is that when breaking the suckers out of the molds the sharp pieces of candy are like glass and cut your hands. 4 to 5 hours does me in, I think it is the smell.

Each day my kids would just have to hug me and say ole caramel today or watermelon. Now that one would stay for days in your clothes and hair, it was hard to clean out even with shampoo. We would bring home the rejects, those are suckers that broke, or just didn't pass inspection for color and etc. for the stores. My kids loved the bags of rejects, because they couldn't afford 50c a sucker to buy one. The factory didn't seem to work out even though they had some good cooks, Margaret Parke, and Elaine. It lasted about 6 months. There were too many companies all at one time flooding the market. Those suckers were everywhere.

Work
Bill has been working long and hard, the hours for a rancher are not fun in the summer, they are long, and then longer. He had bailed all night and then worked all day. He was really tired and he forgot to put down the stacker door. He drove under the freeway and bent it right in half. Bill was sick about it.

Saturday they fixed the stacker but the fields are too wet. It really has been raining lately in the afternoon and evenings. The days are really hot, then it clouds up and thunder showers move in. Lightning strikes everywhere as these awesome storms roll across the valley.

Ranch work is the Pitts. You never see your husband and then you see him too much because you need to help. Now this is not a fun thing, especially for me.

Grasshoppers are the worst I've seen, and I've seen it pretty bad here. Maybe the cold weather will do away with the rotten creatures. I'm tired of them crunching below my feet and the ground moving ahead of you. The lawn seems to disappear as you watch them devour everything. They are so thick that they roll in a huge mass tumbling over each other for a chance for another blade of grass. You can't imagine how thick they've been they have eaten my garden to stubble all they leave is sticks. I pray they're not this bad next year. They seem to destroy everything. They stick to your clothes and even end up in your hair, talk about sending me up the wall.

Indian summer
It has turned terribly cold for September, highs in the mid thirties, and lows in the teens. Snow is dusting the crops, I guess to do away with the stinking grasshoppers…

We're rocking our fireplace for the 3rd time. The big river rocks were way too heavy for the beams. Now we have flat rock but can't lay it cause we had to put the stove back on with tin foil to heat the house, so we could warm our derrieres. That lasted for a couple years, cause the kids threw the logs in on the thin rocks and they started to crumble. So once more we are taking apart the fireplace, and this time we are putting old bricks from the store and school in town. I think this will be the one that lasts…Because the third time is a charm, they always say.

New Years 1983
Bitter cold 30 below zero, every plant and tree is crystallized. The snow cracks and squeaks as you walk and the cold air bites hard at your nose and throat as you breathe. New years Day seemed like a heat wave at zero to 10 degrees, so Bill decides the family needs to go skiing or ice fishing at Jens.

We travel up to the lake, the snow's deep and the scenery is beautiful. The only trails in the snow are where elk, deer and coyotes have traveled to water. We inner tube down the hill a few times, I'm screaming the whole way. Snow goes up my back and afraid I'm going to fly off, I hold tight to Bill. Then after we warm up by the fire we put on our skis and head around the lake. Everyone's better than old mom. I do great on flat, but downhill I get scared and my derriere hits the snow. We go across the frozen lake, and on to the hill. Tiffany's doing great and I finally get up courage to go up, now to get down I just head for it. Fall twice, oh pain, back over the lake again and head for the car. Bill and the boys ski home 8 miles. I head back to Jens to wait for them.

January snow
The week has been a real bore, trying to get back in the grind after the holidays, still trying to lose weight. I have dropped 30 lbs with only 50 to go. My big highlight is watching the soap *Young and the Restless*, maybe I should reword that. Let's say listen or watch the fuzz. Sometimes I can make out if it is a guy or

girl, or sometimes I do have trouble with objects. It's better when the kids are home, because I send them on the hill, to turn the antenna a little to the left. No one more circle, then wire in place. This is no easy chore as you have to watch for rattlers in the summer time, and you slip and fall in the winter as you climb the steep hill to the antenna, then yell back and forth till you hit the right spot and wire it in place.

I love my kids so much. They show me so much love, never want to hurt me in any way and have so much patience with klutzy mom. Tiffany's starting to tell me girl talk; she is growing up so fast.

Coyote food

January 18th, the neighbors dropped the boys off at the highway after basketball last night. It was pitch dark and they had their little pocket flash light, but the beam only lit 2 ft in front of them. Everything was okay till they hit the gate at the bottom of the hill. Then the dark started closing in on them and the coyotes started howling. They seemed to surround the boys, Nathan 10 and Dusty 11. Their fear started to grow. Nathan started crying then screaming, hoping it would scare them off, but the howling only increased and became louder and more frequent, more seemed to join in. We were in the house.

Bill said, "Do you hear something strange?" as we opened the door we heard Nathan screaming for us.

Bill yelled to the boys to head for the light in the window, told me to go outside and turn on the car lights. Now wait a minute, why do I have to go out there and turn on car lights, when I could stand in the house, and shine the flashlight? But of course I lost and trudged out to the car. I stepped out the door with the big flashlight, just on the porch I could feel the chills go through my body. I shined the light on the mountain toward the sound then 2 eyes glistened back. Scanning the mountain I caught 2 more eyes then another. The whole mountain was covered; it seemed to sparkle with the eerie reflection. The boys running now toward me, the car lights lit the mountain and the pack froze in position surrounding the house. The howling ceased but the animals didn't move.

Nathan was shaking and breathing hard. I gave him a hug and reassured him he was safe. I clicked off the lights and this little body ran faster then it has ever run before. But the coyotes left as fast as they came. I think they thought they had an easy meal. The kids must have sounded like food and they were moving in. It was nice to have the door, with the wood latch to keep us safe. Wild animals hadn't learned to pull the rope to get in. Thank Goodness.

Smoking Slippers
Ice has been a real challenge around here; we had lots of snow and cold, now warm and bitter cold again. Now this combination makes for ice, ice on everything. It covers fence posts, trees, wire, cars; you name it ice seemed to cover it. You can hardly stand up without corks. I don't know how to explain the ice. It's unbelievable; our whole back yard is covered. The kids put on their ice skates and skate on our back lawn.

It's beautiful, everything is white, but we have to have chains in all our vehicles to drive almost anywhere that has any type of incline to it. And that is all of Montana.

Bill stayed home from church with a toothache. The kids and I ventured off to church alone down the road. It's like an ice skating rink. You can't steer the car, it follows the ruts bouncing back and forth but somehow is staying semi forward. After church it's time to trek up the hill.

The only way that we can even think about getting the car up the driveway is chain up. So the kids and I stop at the bottom to try and figure out how to put on the chains. I would rather learn than walk the cotton picking mountain, heaven forbid I might lose weight. Besides it was almost impossible, because one step forward, 2 slides back, it was horrible.

Then I saw Bill. He whistles to us to stay put and he knows he can't walk, so he grabs one of the sleds. Mistake.... He reached light speed before he hit the first corner, then the sled started bouncing. Bills eyes grew huge. He knew that his life was flashing before his eyes, as they start watering from the speed and just trying to keep his body on the sled and the sled on the road. He had never traveled that fast on a sled before. He knew if he tried to jump off he would kill himself, but he knew if he stayed on he would kill himself anyway. So he tries to slow himself down with his feet. He was wearing moccasin slippers, his toes heated up and the stitching wore away in seconds. It took all his energy to steer it through the gate. Then it happened. He flew into the sticker weeds that lined the road, going light speed. And the weeds cut him like a knife right up the side of his face. Lesson learned: Not to sled, on ice with smoking slippers…

As years came and went, we had to invent ways of getting up and down the hill, from having fun to going to church.

Chapter 19
Ranching
Moo Moo and Manure

Ranching and Calving

Today we move over to live at the Jens ranch for one week while the boss is gone to California. The cattle are starting to calf, feeding is a real chore. Take clothes and some food and then head over home 30 miles round trip to start the fire and feed Barney and the cats.

Monday wasn't my bad day, things went pretty good no calves and Bill fed the morning by himself. I fixed lunch and then helped him feed the year old calves in the corals down by the railroad tracks. I had to learn to drive the big Massey Ferguson Tractor so I could follow Bill down to the calves and feed. Pitch hay in and then go pick up the kids from school, fix dinner check every 4 hrs to see if the heifers have calved, temperatures, Cold 15 degrees and snow.

Up, have family prayer off to school and back to help Bill feed the cows, heifers, bulls and calves. I was tired and wet, manure up to my ankles. I hate that smell, even if it's cold and half frozen. Pick up kids and fix dinner and all over again. I sure am tuckered as the week goes on. I seem to be more run down. The pitching of hay and the wet mud, snow, rain and goo is working on my patience, along with kids. Upset Little's kids are fighting and everything rubbing off on one another. Oh yes we are not alone...
Popping Calves

Not used to being away from home and my wood heater. Wake up to 6 inches of snow and 22 degrees. Well it does it every time, when the weather is the most miserable, wettest, crappy, and down right ugly those heifers started popping calves.

Thursday night we watch 019 she's been in labor 3 and half hours but can't seem to get things going, shall we take it? I call Darrell, he's gone. Then I call Max, he says yes it has to be pulled. So Bill and I work on the Heifer... chains and jack ready. Bill pops the bag. (That's the bag that is now bulging from her rear end, what a pleasant sight, and she does not like it either.) The feet are huge. He reaches inside hooks up the legs as I see his arm disappear. Then the work begins.

We pull with all our might but nothing. Bill stretched out, feet propped against her seat end and pulling with all his might then both of us. So we hook up the jack, a U shaped tool that fits around the buttocks, then hooks the foot chains on to a hook and starts jacking. The legs move out slowly then the head appears. As Bill pulls, I clean its mouth out and slap the calf. The calf looks like it's a month old, it's huge. We dry her off and sigh with relief. It's almost 2:30 in the morning before we crawl into bed. We're up the next morning by 6, a big 4 hrs of sleep. Bill goes to check heifers and I take the kids to school then come back to check on Bill and the other women in our life right now.

He calls me on the radio. "Get down here, Pennie, we have another we can't pull. I need your help."

But when I get down there he tells me to get a hold of Darrell, I couldn't reach him so he tells me to get on the radio and call the vet. I call Annette Applegate to please contact the veterinarian, for us and have him come out. Reception is really bad so we hope the message got through.

We flag Uncle George down in his logging truck he comes over to help us pull the calf. The feet are huge again. This is a big calf. Just as George goes to leave and try the vet on his radio, Mark, the vet drives up. I have to go back and get 5 gallons of hot water.

He works and works on the cow, putting chains on the legs and pulling with all our might. The vet tries to get the loop over the head, but can't find it. The head is tucked backward; the vet says the calf is probably dead. But we have to get it out. We work on it for about an hour He has to cut it up inside. But the calf is so big there is no room inside to take his hand and cut it up without cutting the mother. We'll have to do a C-section.

We get ropes and tied up the cow turning her on her back, then shave her belly 2 ft by 1 ft square. Clean water, disinfectant, tools, antiseptic, drugs. He then gives her a sedative. Runs the needle of deadener down under the skin where he's going to make the incision, rubs and feels the area, then makes the incision, through one layer, then 2 more. Pulls the intestines to one side, washes out the area, and the uterus is in view, cuts open the uterus and the calf is in view. I hand him the chains to pull the calf out he puts them around the legs. Darrell and I pull hard, out it comes. Dead as the vet thought. (If it's alive you give it mouth to mouth.) Now to sew her up, she can only be on her back one hour. Sew the uterus, replace the intestines, and sew each layer separately the stitches are I mean the thread is really coarse and tough. I help him hold the needle, tools instruments, more thread. Now let her down, prop her up with hay bales, so she doesn't bloat. 2:30 pm I'm exhausted. The rest of the day I was done in, had to cook dinner and try to clean the house.

The girls pitched in; a real challenge being away from home, Saturday our last day here then home. Go and feed with Bill, he's driving the tractor this time. I drive the pick up with Kristy. We go and feed the bulls, then down to feed the calves and pitch hay. Kristy and I worked hard and laughed a lot feeding the bulls. We'd drive, stop pitch hay, drive, stop, pitch.

Long winters, and no husband, and no money are wearing on me. So depression is part of my life. The kids are fighting, and mom is yelling. We made a whole $8000 dollars last year and with a family of 5 that's hurting, but what's new? When I really get depressed I don't even write in my journal so the months roll past. Bill is still farming for Dave. I'm still trying to lose more weight, big emphases on still…
I just have to get my head on straight sometimes and think… There's no place like Home….

I feel so protected here in my log house, even if the floors are unfinished, the windows are old as the wind whistles a high sound through them. Even though we don't have money the Lord sends so many blessings to us. All we have to do is love and obey. Thank you father for the help you give us in so many ways.

Depression and Adversity

Thinking back

I was thinking the other day about the many trials and adversity that I have had in my life. First time I remember Adversity was at 6 years old.

I woke up. "Luckie, look what I have! A new cowgirl outfit' and look what's on your bed, chaps!"

We both jump up, giggling as we dress with excitement, why did we get these? Let's go ask mom. We run through the trailer, our happy voices echoing, but mom can't be found. Dad opens the door, walks in and kneels down beside us...

"Mom went away, I can't tell you why, she just left, she needs some time; know that she loves you."

"Why? Dad Why? I don't understand."

We learned to do things with out a mom. Dad tugged on my hair as he rolled my hair in rubber spoolies with ends sticking out all over and 2 little kids trying to help cook dinner. I pull on a metal cupboard door not thinking about a pan of hot grease that was on a hot plate on top of the cupboard. The door's stuck so I pull with all my might. Then all I remember is screaming as hot grease covers me. As I fall back my dress covers my face but the rest of me is covered with hot oil. My dad runs over to me strips off my clothes, and wraps me in a white sheet and takes me in the car to a small town doctor 10 miles away. That night I lay with huge blisters that covered my body. If I rolled over they would pop and ooze and the pain was unbearable. The inside of my legs was the worst. They put new bandages on my legs each day for weeks. The Lord was at my side for the burns seemed to make mom leaving not as bad. My body healed with doctor's care and a family's love.

Then I had my good friend die, my little dog. How I missed him. I knew that nothing could hurt so much, until…my mom was killed in a car wreck, when I had just turned 10.

Once more my dad tries to comfort a little girl and boy without a mom. The

Lord was once more by our side when our mom was killed by a Drunk Driver, part her fault for being in the car with him, but it doesn't take the hurt anymore away.. She was the only one killed as she flew out. Somehow we missed the bus that night that was suppose to take us to Montana to be with her for the summer, we would have arrived to find out our mom was dead. The Lord has always blessed me in my adversities having someone there to love and take care of me.

He helped me cope with a step mom that seemed to hate me; I memorized church songs while locked in a closet and really enjoyed the quiet time. Cause if I wasn't in the closet, I had to work. So I made me a comfortable spot in there. Stashed some food now and then and made my own world. She would tell me that it was closet time, and I really didn't mind, because I didn't have to do anything... and I had things in there a heart that glowed in the dark. I would slide it under the door, let the light shine on it and then bring in back inside. The white heart would glow a bright green, it seemed magic to a 10 year old.

My brother and I have a special relationship from those hard times. We always were there for one another to buoy one or the other up. Telling each other that it can't be that bad, and when we get older things would be better.

Now the house, and living in Montana, a huge adversity with blessings hidden here and there.
And the Church and Gospel in our lives, the Lord blesses us so much. As we have gotten older more trials come and you wonder how you can handle another, but you seem to get through and be stronger for it. Thanks for all my support from family and friends.

Dolls

Trying something to make money, I decide to make up a pattern and make stuffed dolls. First it was just for my daughter and Christina for Christmas, then other people liked them and asked if I would make more, and they would buy them. Well this was another answer to a real problem, like not eating. So the Pennie Pudgy Business came to be.

Terrie and I worked for months on these dolls, every color and every hair color. They had lots of hair. I cut them out, sewed them, stuffed them and then sculpted them. Terrie added the hair and painted the eyes. I made the clothes. And so it went, unless we got behind, then I wound hair, or lets say the kids wound hair, sew strips and sew on by hand. In a few months we had made over 112 dolls and still getting orders. At least I could feed the kids; I sold the dolls for 28 dollars. Cabbage Patch dolls were a real rage right then and no one could get them, so my dolls were selling like firecrackers.

I think my kids think they don't have a mother, because every time they see me little naked bodies, with no faces, surround me. Lots of yarn, stuffing, thread, what a nightmare! If that is not enough I try to have house parties also, and deliver and make any thing and everything, so besides building on the house, I am chief carpenter, painter and boss of my kid crew. Now the house has more sawdust than usual and the hours of sleep are less and less as people request more and more things. Oh what have I done? My kids hate me but pitch in to help.

Bill is working hard 7 days a week, feeding and etc. so he's in bed early. I roll in close to midnight after scratching in pages of my journal. It's the only thing that keeps me sane right now.
The Dolls are a real push right before Valentines Day, the hours we work on them seem unreal but when we get the checks it helps carry us through to another payday. Hoping that we can save some for something fun, like doors, windows, bathroom, wallpaper, microwave, maybe even cupboards. What a concept!

March, the weather is unpredictable, one day 50 degrees the next snowy and cold. The wind chills you through your clothes and freezes you to the bone. Money seems to be my downer right now, I just can't seem to make it stretch. I would just like shoes for my boys; their toes are coming out the ends. They never say anything cause they know that it won't help and that we would get them some if we had it. Food is one of the big factors, and keeping warm. Went shopping the other day and found Tiffany a pair of shoes for $2.00 a size to big but she didn't mind.

Took the boys with me to deliver dolls, the streets packed, trying to get my last minute stuff done. I called got the address and proceeded to what I thought was the place. The houses became close and the numbers didn't coincide.

"It has to be behind those houses," I say to Dusty as I point to a dark well trodden trail behind a rather worn apartment building old house.

I send Dustin with the garbage bag with the dolls inside.

He asks where 310 is. A girl peeks out shrugs her shoulders and points back of the house. The screen door is falling off and he raps on the door, no answer. A large dog is sniffing at his heel. He opens the door to see a dark hall and a door well used. He slowly goes up the passage way and knocks but no answer. He runs down, out the screen and back to Tilly

"No one home lets go mom"

"They have to be there," I say. "They said there would be someone there all day."

"Well then that's not the place. If she lives there she's poor. I can't see her getting ballerina dolls; they need a place to live…"

We leave for awhile and I try again. Nathan goes this time except he wouldn't go up the stairs or even near the dog.

"Heck with it mom. Call them."
Oops wrong address 3 blocks up and a big 2-story house, the boys wanted to strangle me.

Cupboards

Max Hollist came up this week to put in my cupboards. Some one in the branch bought them for us. I saw the cupboards for the first time a week ago. They were just the shell and I could almost realize that they were mine. It didn't sink in. Then I had to pick out Formica, a kitchen with Formica. 5 years, almost 6 with 2x4's holding up the sink. No, I take that back. One year the washer and dryer held the sink between them and a bucket underneath held the water I drained out after packing it in. How far we've come but I never dreamed this!

Monday Bill helped Max haul the cupboards over, 2 trips; I never thought he would finish bringing in cupboards and wood. It was just bottom cupboards but not having any to ones I can actually open and shut, slide this way and that, oh my I think I'm going to cry. The house was a disaster for 3 days.

The cupboards are in and ready to stain and urethane what a job.. I put in so many hours staining and varnishing, now Sunday night I sit here looking at my kitchen I can't believe it. It's beautiful, a dream come true Thanks heavenly Father for the blessings you shower on us.

May 20th 1985
School is almost over, unreal. The kids are in track and Tiffany's doing great kicking butt. Nate was doing super too until he pulled some ligament in his knee so the ole high jump went to the wayside. Dusty still keeps trying; he's getting stronger every year. His stick-to-it-ness is unreal. I'm so proud of him for never giving up, always giving it that extra push.

Garden
Today we planted or should I say started to plant ours and Bryant's garden, rows and rows of potatoes. The kids Rota tilled with our new machine and planted the potatoes a step, apart as Uncle George say. When your heel is on top put one at your toe, step on it and go on. We planted 30 lbs red and white mix. The tomatoes: 13 plants with tires around and 13 within mulched beds. 9 crock neck squash then it was to dark to see anymore. Corn tomorrow, more tomatoes, beets, onion, lettuce, carrots, zucchini, and what ever else we have to grow I hope we can handle an acre garden. Woe is us but nice this harvest. I pray it will all come up and prosper well. The kids helped really well tonight. We need their help before they head for their jobs where they make money. Well everyone's exhausted including me.

It can Snow every month of the year in Montana, So if you plant a garden just pray....

Chapter 21
The trip to Hell and Back
(World Jamboree)

What a neat opportunity to take our scouts to the World Jamboree. It was only going to be 550 miles away, so as a small scout troop we worked so we could go. We raised money doing everything that we could. As you know by now Bill and I had no money of our own, so if the boys wanted to go they would have to make some money for fuel, tents, food and what knots. We tried everything. We made homemade pretzels and orange Julius's and sold them in the parking lots, and on the sidewalk in front of stores. We washed cars, and sold Easter egg wrappers, had spaghetti and chili feeds. We finally had enough money.

12 boys and Bill as leader, no one could take off they said, so Bill volunteered me to follow in another vehicle, ours in fact. A member volunteered his big van, and we loaded all the boys, gear, and food and off to Canada... Now we thought to save money we would have dry food, and pancakes, soups, sometimes the food was sick. The kids were pretty good, but just craving a good ole hamburger or hot dog would be like a steak dinner.

We had every personality when it came to boys, some very passive and some overbearing and bullies, oh what a combination. We arrived at Glacier National Park and told all kids that they could not bring fire works into Canada so if they had any to bury them. So Bill let them out and they scattered and then tried to draw maps as to where the buried treasures would be found in a week. Then we headed over Going to the Sun Road. If you have never heard of this road it is a narrow steep winding road that winds around the glaciers, and water falls fall on the road. A narrow rock wall protects you from the huge canyon below. We stop for a rest, and of course the kids run over to the edge, and walk on the ledge.

Bill yells at them to get down, "What are you thinking? Obliviously you are not..."

We pile into the van and our little car that follows behind, but first we have to get out and push my car because every time we stop ole Fife Fiat won't go without a nudge. Boy scouts pushing with all their might. It really should have been a poster, the glaciers behind us and this steep road and little boy scouts using all their weight to get me so I could pop the clutch then off we go

Bill with the hoodlums and me with my kids and all the paraphernalia... Up up we go and then down and steep winding road, the van swaying and swerving as the curves get closer and more intense. All of a sudden I see a window fly open and spume come out. But not too far out and plasters the kids in the seats behind. The war was on, as a mass dry heaving began, and that started with gag reflex, Bill the driver.

Oh what a site as puking kids empty out of the van. The van reeks of vomit and the kids are not doing well. We stop at the bottom, get them drinks wash out their clothes in the creek the flows next to the road. Things are better so off we go again. We're almost to Canada ... Maybe we could drop them off and leave them ... a thought... Hide fireworks because we knew we couldn't take them into Canada.

Over the border and now to spend the night at a rancher's home here that one of the ranchers in Drummond knows. A huge ranch, we set up our tents down by a little pond, wrong thing to do because when the sun went down the mosquitoes came out. The clouds rolled in and it started to rain. It rained harder and harder and lightning started to strike as we lay in our tents. One strike came so close you could smell the burning air. The snap was so loud these tough boys were scared but we managed till morning. Dew settled on everything and the boys were not crazy about and powdered eggs and hash browns but hunger does strange things and they ate it, along with their tang.

Off to Banff National Park, one of the prettiest parks in Canada. . A long drive ahead, once in Banff we go to the little town, and then head for the park and get ready for a fun hike or two. When we get to our camp site, we stop to set up tents but you are not allowed to get off the pavement. Now wait a minute how are you supposed to put up tent stakes on pavement, what kind of wilderness is this? Bill was so mad, that he waited till dark. We moved in on soft ground, sunk our tent stakes and then up early before some ranger fined us. Needless to say we didn't stay another night, and headed down the road for the jamboree, we would camp along the way, and not in some publicized yuppie park. YUK!!

The Countryside was beautiful, the only draw back, was the fighting the boys did, and we had a fistfight or two per day. But once the testosterone was let loose, things got better and everyone seemed to mellow.

Now we're at the Jamboree. It was crazy, thousands of little green boy scouts. We sure couldn't spot our guys in a crowd, so we had to have a meeting place at a certain time, give them some spending money and let them go, to collect pins, and see the different exhibits from different countries. It was really interesting and fun to be there. It was an experience we knew that these boys or we would never experience again.

Now to head to Calgary stampede, but before we get there we find a park that has cement runs and little sleds that you can race down the hill. The boys had a riot going around each curve and trying not to tip over and skin themselves for life, but somehow we got them all back in the van in one piece, with only a few scrapes and abrasions. Calgary; now this was a huge city, especially for little Drummond boys and girls. The train we rode on was mega fast and the rodeo; well it was a rodeo and lot bigger than Drummond's. But once you see a bull throw a rider or a horse buck, they are all the same, whether in Calgary or Drummond.

Now to gather kids and head back to the ranch. The money was running thin, kids are tired and ready to go back find their fireworks and hit the good ole USA. I was ready for home also, having to push Fife everywhere we went became a real scene and a lot of people would join in pushing and off we would go. Let's get back to real food, no dried food for any of us for a long while. We stopped at a campground just this side of Glacier, still in Canada, that had a pool. Shaun, Scott, our boys and Tiff all would talk double Dutch. These people thought they were from some other country and the kids played along.

Double Dutch is our language like pig Latin but you are putting extra constants or vowels. I never could figure it out either, so if the kids wanted to tick me off or say something they didn't want me to know, that funny language would rear its ugly head. Thanks Terrie for giving me misery for teaching all of them that stupid garble.

Blessings (or Moulton Iron)

Back home and back to routine, or almost. The power went out during a huge rainstorm, right in the middle of cooking dinner for Bill and the boys before they went camping. So I pulled out the camp stove and finished dinner on that. I forgot that I hadn't turned off the stove, because the power was out. Knowing ole Montana the power stays out for long periods at a time. This time it had been out over 4 hours so I played a couple concentration games with Tiff. When it was almost dark we had to go get Christina and George because they were alone, so was Jean and she asked us to come over there. I drove over and visited. Then at 10:30 the lights came on, we talked a little longer and then Terrie came to pick up her kids. I decided I'd better get to the ole homestead and clean up dinner, when all of a sudden I realized that I never shut down the stove.

I put Tilly in fast gear as we bumped and bounced up the steep road to our house. The rain was still coming down and the road starting to run with water and ooze with mud. I ran to the door and pulled on our rope latch, flew in the old timber doors and could hardly see. The house was thick with smoke and our poor bird was barely chirping. I opened doors and windows after shutting off the stove. The pan that was on the burner was beet red, the gravy had cooked hard and dissolved, the spoon molded itself to the heavy black pan. I thank my Heavenly Father for blessing us so our home didn't go up in flames. I know we were blessed. Hours of elbow grease, smoke filled rooms, open windows, how easy things can happen, before you realize your life has changed. I pray God's love always protects us.

RAIN the last 3 to 4 days we've had some great showers to help the drought, they say that it's drier than most of the old timers have ever seen it, for May or anytime of the year. There is no pasture grass for the cattle to graze on in the hills, it's rather scary. This rain is a blessing that we've all prayed about.

We finished the garden this morning. I pray it will flourish cause we sure need the food.

Bad Times (have we had any good?)

The timing belt in ole Blue broke. Someone got in my purse and stole the cash out of it at church, $180.00, everything we had to live on. How could someone steal from us that hardly have anything? I guess I shouldn't have been so trusting but I thought my purse would be okay. Little do we know about some people?

Next morning Bills work dog, Scout, is missing, we looked everywhere. The kids find him by the river shot in the head and dropped off by the river. Luckie got hit by a tree. The guy next to him was skidding to close and knocked a tree over on him. He was kneeling down and it came over on his back. He thought, "I'm dead" then he thought "No get up." He is real sore but considering what he has been through, his name (Luckie) is holding for him.

The family is having a hard time getting over the loss of Scout. The money was nothing, the truck can sit, we can eat wheat and rice like we have been doing for the past 10 days. But our dog, Scout was so special to us. He'd cry when we left, wake up the kids every morning, chase cows out of the yard, go everywhere with Bill

Jeff has an accident and Grandpa's Liniment

If it isn't one thing it's twenty others. Jeff is trying to make money and learn many different things. He has a terrible accident with the chainsaw. He puts the blade into his knee. He's up in the mountains cutting logs down for the ranch when the saw slips and goes into his leg, lays it open. He screams for help,

Now if you ever heard Jeff yell you would know something is up. Bill is a ravine away from him and comes running, he knows what's wrong. If you put a novice with a chainsaw and you hear a scream it's usually not a good sign. Bill administers first aid and packs the kid down the mountain and into the vehicle, gives him a blessing and takes him to the hospital for stitches. It is 8 miles down a rough road and 30 miles on the highway to the hospital. The cut is about 8 or so inches long and huge and gapping. They try to stitch it but a chainsaw cut is rugged and jagged, and almost impossible to get a good clean mend. They do the best they can, and send him home. Jeff is miserable. After the numbness leaves and then the pain comes, and Jeff lets you know.

We have some homemade liniment that my grandfather invented for horses when they ran through barbed wire fences. It would heal them fast. Now I have had this stuff used on me all my life, so I know what it can do and how it feels, not good feeling but really works wonders. So we decided Jeff needed this liniment that was made out of white lead, turpentine, tincture, and vinegar, some kind of acid... I know it could kill you or heal you, so we poured it on him. I mean it was only 30 yrs old then. Just shake and then stand back, cause it will burn and then itch, you think you're going to go crazy. But it worked. After a week of hearing Jeff go crazy and jumping around on one leg, his knee was beginning to heal. He started to swear by the stuff. The smell was terrible, so he had to go out on the porch to pour it on, and then no one would sit by him for a day or so because he stunk so bad, it would reek of all those smells, and turn the air around you green. Nasty but it was the best. Good enough for animals, good enough for me he would say, as he poured the last of it on.

June 20th I wake up can hardly move as every joint in my body aches. I then look down and see I'm covered with little spots, from my neck to my toes. They're so thick you can hardly see between them. Terrie says it's the measles. I then find out, Jake a 5 year old has measles. Woe is me. I haven't been so sick in a long time. It's an effort to walk across the room or pick up anything. It didn't help to lie down. You sure learn to appreciate how much your health means to you. After 5 days in agony I'm feeling better today, just in time for my anniversary.

Our garden froze today, June 26th. All that work and now everything is black and droopy.

15 years ago today, I tied the knot for better or worse, what a hectic day that was. Hurry here and hurry there but yet what a neat beginning to a new life, a married lady.

Washing dishes, 3 kids, dinners, lunches, go here, go there, doctors, dentists, build houses, bury animals, shed tears, laugh a lot, move, share, think, grow wide, grow wider, grow poor, go gray. Above all Love, love husband, love kids, love grandma, love animals, love the gospel and love our home. Love is the center of everything. Bill and I share so much. We do love each other a lot even though my body is rounder and gray on the roof. Bill never fails to tell me how much he loves me. I'm a lot meaner, I think it, but don't say it enough. But I do love Bill. He is so caring, works so hard and takes super care of his little family.

My anniversary is almost over. We had steaks out on the front deck, baked potatoes, pretty tasty, not expensive steaks you know the ones people use for stew meat. One thing about it, it takes a long time to eat. But still they were steaks or hammered shoe leather, whatever you call it.

The weather is hot and miserable, no rain, temperatures in the 100 degree range day after day into July. The forests are like tinder, you can smell the pitch melting out of the trees, the fields are burning up and the river's turning into a creek. The smell of burning trees surrounds us and the sky is red with the smoke of forest fires.

August – relief comes with rain and cold, go figure. Still poor, groceries are really thin. We've gone a month on $70.00 worth of food.

Bike stolen

"Hey Mom, we are riding up Bear Gulch to look at the China diggings, okay? We are done with our work."

"Okay kids, just be careful," I say.

Dustin, Nathan and Russell are going to Bear Gulch 3 miles away. The Chinese diggings are walls of solid rock that they laid for the gold to channel the water. For miles the rock is stacked just like bricks, it is amazing to see. The kids know these roads like the back of their hands. Up and up they ride, 9 miles now and they park their bikes to walk over to the sight. They hear a truck, they are still over the side, then they hear it stop and then speed off. They run over to find that the truck has taken their bikes. They run after them with all their might and they notice the plate on the pick up is from Missoula, but the people left these young boys to fend for themselves and walk 9 miles. Loggers rescued them as they walked down the steep dusty road, tears in their eyes, Dustin cause he knew we didn't have money to replace the bike he had had since he was 7. Why do people have to steal? The pain it causes sometime is so hard.

Bassett Heaven

Barney died today September 1, 1985 and I can't believe it. I think we are living under a rotten cloud with and no silver lining. Barney has been our dog and best friend for over 11 years. It's hard to realize he's gone. He was always barking with excitement as you drive up the hill, checking out all the garbage in the area marking his territory as he went, playing catch with grapes, running into the house and locking up his legs so you couldn't budge him out. Eating every people food you could think of, his tail spinning like a propeller as he ran through the tall grass. He was king of the mountain here, out lived every dog around and then today he ate something poisonous. I hate to think that someone would hate Big Dumb. He did bug a few neighbors but most of them loved him as much as we did. He was famous in getting into things he wasn't supposed to. Sure going to miss the ole pest, what a fun dog he was, getting old, a little deaf, and lived up to his name Big Dumb. Barney loved comfort and food. Give him those two things and he was set.

Nathan buried a bone and his favorite blanket with him. Tiffany said the prayer over the site talking to her Heavenly Father telling him to watch over Barney up there and let him be happy. Tiff was the one that found Barney at the bottom of the kids trail down to Bryant's. Even when he was sick he couldn't resist making a trek to see what was happening and what was good down the hill. He's buried on the hill with Bilbo and Scout.

Thinking about Barney almost everyday thinking he is going to stick his nose through the door, or scratch on the window, hear that high-pitched wine, or his tail slapping the floor. Giving himself away that he was hiding somewhere in the house. Barney had a knack of making everyone mad at him but yet smile and love him. The time Terrie packed Luckie's lunch in a cooler and set the cooler outside to keep cool. When Luckie went to leave for the woods it was gone. Where could it be? Luckie goes without it 4:30 am.

Terrie calls me up 3 hours later. "Have you seen Luckie's lunch; you know the little cooler, up there?"

I said, "Don't be ridiculous. Barney couldn't carry that up this mountain."

Just as those words passed my lips, my eyes caught a glimpse of a red cooler out on the lawn, and Barney drooling just sitting there by it, he just couldn't get inside. That dog had packed this cooler up a steep mountain a half a mile. Remember the ice cream a few years back, and breaking open all Jim's food and eating everything but the dog food, breaking Luckie's water line in his trailer, chasing a cat, forever chasing a girl dog. Only coming when he was good and ready, dragging clothes off the line to make a bed out of. Curling up in the winter time with 3 cats covering him (built in fur coat), playing games with the cows at 5:30 in the morning, and running around Bryant's at wee hours barking just to tell them he was back when we returned from a trip, he could open the latches of the door by figuring out that he could jump up catch his paw on the string and then push on the door. Col. Barney you crazy Bassett, you're part of our lives forever we love you.

The money is so tight; we're spending less than $25.00 for groceries in 2 weeks. We eat a lot of homemade bread, beans, rice. We're living off what we have in storage. It's hard to understand when you're trying your hardest and living the Gospel that the blessings you feel you should get don't come. We get blessings, I know, just not always the way we would send them ourselves. But I guess we wouldn't grow as much. I hate to see my family go without. We had a friend give us some survival crackers that are from the 2nd world war, and we ate them' they are a mix between a saltine and a graham cracker. Oh please, the kids can't even hear the name now, without gagging. But they did help us survive, so they lived up to their name.

 One pair of pants for school, they don't even ask for anything. I love my kids, they so understand living in a house with no doors, we push ole worn out Tilly tomato everywhere, and the paint is chipping off, the seat decaying from the sun. People ask us what we are doing in Montana.

We answer, "Raising a family close to our Father in Heaven."

The weather is unreal, hard to figure out. The northern states are getting unseasonably cold weather. It's supposed to be 42 for a high in September. It was a terribly hot summer with no water so the crops were poor for the cattle. You can see why the Lord wants us to prepare for hard times ahead. The unrest in the world is crazy.

Chapter 22
Yellowstone on 100 Bucks

October Vacation to Yellowstone

The family finally takes a vacation together. We were going over to see Bill's sister Barbara in Seattle but Bill came down sick the night before we decided to leave so one day or our vacation is shot. We have 3 days left. Let's go to Yellowstone, the kids haven't been there since Tiff was 3 Dusty 6 and Nate 5. Dusty called for reservations in Yellowstone and its $32.00 a night for all of us in the Snow Lodge. How great, that lodge is fabulous. We'll splurge and go, off season rates are great.

We load up ole Tilly tomato. Kids are crammed in the back and the boys have their knees tucked up around their chins with 200 miles to travel. The weather is cold and snowy but at least the park won't be crowded. The weather didn't improve any as we neared Yellowstone real cold, below zero, icy roads. All kinds of animals are out and the kids are excited. I'm looking forward to the Lodge and a neat room, the huge stairs and massive beams.

We round the corner and Snow Lodge is a half mile ahead. I tell the kids to use their best manners, funny thing this road leads us to an old army barracks. The Old Faithful Hotel is the next block, this must be the parking. We find another road that leads over to the massive structure Old Faithful Inn. CLOSED FOR SEASON the huge sign is bolted to the doors.

"You've got to be kidding, what are we paying $32.00 a night for?"

We make a few phone calls and can't seem to get anything but recordings. The next closest lodging is in West Yellowstone 50 icy miles away.

We're tired and say; "Let's try it. It can't be that bad."

We were wrong... Our room was all the way down the hall to the right. The bathrooms for girls were down the hall turn and down another hall. Our room had a double bed and an army metal bunk bed that sagged when more then Tiff laid on it. Bill's and my bed was like a piece of cement (miserable). We started to laugh our only vacation and we're in a army barracks 9x9 room with 3 kids, one of the kids had to use the floor, we almost fought for that position. Let's go eat something like a burg and fries. There are only 2 small stores open in the park and the Snow Lodge and restaurant. We wait our turn to go in. It had tablecloths, napkins folded in shapes of birds, water in stemmed wine glasses 3 of every utensil.. The kids look at us.

"Hey Dad I don't think this is Mc Donald's."

The waiter comes up and looks at us, then hands us menus without saying a word. Bill and I swallow as the prices jump out at us. We have $100.00 to stay 3 days food, gas, lodging we just shot $32.00 things were looking slim.

"Order light," we say to the kids.

"But Dad, nothings less then 12.95 and even the potato is extra."

We finally found something in appetizers.

"Yes mam, we'll have 5 cups of soup and 2 salads. No water is just fine."

Our order arrived in a moment, small cups of clam chowder with a sprig of parsley and 2 lettuce salads. We told the kids eat S L O W… They don't know the word at least the boys don't. Then we split the salads on our soup saucers the waitress returns and asks us if we would like to order now, that we had our appetizers?

Nathan pipes up, "Boy I am stuffed."

"Me too," echoes Dusty.

"Just the check," I said. $12.50, it doesn't sound bad now but we're use to eating for a month on $30.00 dollars.

Bill tells the maitre'd, "I only grow the stuff I can't afford to eat it too."

The kids tell us there are vending machines down the hall, off we go cheese and crackers, and stale donuts what more could we want, and only a quarter. We all try to retire, fight for the bathroom with the other bimbos mostly college kids running around in their BVD's and finally in for the night. We start to laugh then almost cry ourselves to sleep. Oh pain, this isn't our waterbed.

Up early, no breakfast here, we'll drive 50 miles to West Yellowstone. We found a good local hang out with a bunch of locals shooting the breeze. We have breakfast then head for the Park again to have a full day of touring.

Buffalo
The first night we arrived in the park we walked around Old Faithful basin. It was late in the evening and dusk was coming on but we ventured on showing the kids the different geysers. About three quarters around we see buffalo feeding just ahead. Now you have to admit those things are scary and huge.

I tell Bill, "Let's get out of here."

He laughs and says, "Did you hear about the guy just a little while ago who got gored by one of these?"

That's all it took. I took off fast.

"Hurry you guys," I yelled.

Everyone was laughing.

The buffalo were interested in the grass along the walkways and started to close us off from civilization. We had to drop down a hill, over a bridge and then just around Old Faithful.

Bill is teasing me as usual and says, "You better slow down there's probably one blocking the trail as you get to Old Faithful."

No sooner had he said that then there he was, this huge bull buffalo, not 15 feet away. Needless to say my knees went weak. It wasn't funny anymore we were out there alone it was dark by now not a sole around.

"Oh Bill, what are we going to do? Buffalo are on both trails back to the lodge and ranger station. No one would find us out here till morning. Nothing will be left of us but buffalo stampede remains."

Bill said, "Pennie think about it, we can go on the ground around the buffalo, but it says stay on the sidewalk. Were not those buffalo not just walking on that earth? I don't think it is going to cave in with us."

We made a wide loop in the thin crust behind him hoping it wouldn't cave in. I figured if he crossed it I have 10 to 15 lbs leeway. Tiff and I start to run safety, just ahead. Bill and the boys are still laughing; not funny and I don't forgive them at least for 20 minutes.

The next few days of the trip are fun and rather scary at times when Bill pulls up to a buffalo eating no more than 8 ft away and tells me to take a picture. I knew he would gore Tilly tomato and my car and I would be toast.

We stayed in West Yellowstone; we found a room for $30.00 at the Thunderbird with 2 double beds, TV and shower. It was Heaven… I don't think the kids will forget their old mom running from the buffalo, eating just soup and water for dinner, earthquakes and sharing the room at the lodge. The $100.00 is gone but didn't we have fun.

Winter or spring?

The weather has decided to give us the ole January thaw, coming right on schedule. It's causing lots of black ice and dense fog. It's hard to drive, no impossible to drive. Our driveway is becoming like slush after 3 months of snow and sledding down it to make it to school, work or to get food. Sometimes it was so fast that you would lose your sled out from under you as your head is planted into a snow bank. Snow, we've had snow since November, has decided to melt but only enough to make the roads and our driveway solid ice. The car slid off the driveway. We used hot ashes from the stove and finally Tilly tomato was back on the driveway. Only to play ring a round the rosy all the way down, what a ride. I'm so glad Bill was driving and I was watching.

No one has seen a sight until you see a 200 lb. Mom wearing logging corks. But it's the only way we can get anywhere. It is so slick you don the corks and dig the spikes in the ice and walk wherever you have to go or sled, because there is no driving up and down the hill. This is the only way to get to church. Everything is flooding and our field is a lake. The kids took the canoe out after school and floated around in our alfalfa field. Drummond has a river running down Main Street, sand bags line the streets. The river's over its banks at every bend. School let out early because the road to Hall had 6 ft of water over it. I walk the mountain a lot, but don't mind as my two teenage sons are on each arm to keep me company and carry any grocery's I have. We have some neat talks as we hike through calf-deep snow, or with water streaming around our ankles. How fast children grow up and how very much I love them.

Luckie went into business this month around the 10th of March 1986 Everyone in Drummond loves him, he should make it.

Cold snow and a blizzard, then hot one-week, no coat weather, and then Katie bar the door, Ugly miserable winter again. 6 inches of snow…

Now days when it snows, we play with the grandkids.

Chapter 23
Hard Times and Good Fairies

HARD TIMES for someone else

Terrie and Luckie are having trials. Shaun rolled their Le Car 2 miles from home. He hit a big rock which hurled him off the road, that's how a teenager tells it anyway. Today I think about how we drove around in this mess of a car, crawling across from the passenger side, because the driver's side is caved in and door won't open. What a mess!

Terrie's pregnant with Heather, and sometimes we have to push to get the piece going in traffic. I'm sure people thought, oh those poor white trash, cause I know they weren't thinking, "Oh look at those rich witches." Life does go on, Terrie and Luckie ended up with another Le Car and life seemed better for awhile.

My kids are always so sweet to me, writing me letters, telling me how money doesn't matter, just our love. And Nathan's always saying, "Mom you're skin and bones, you must have anorexia."

"Every time you look in the mirror you see chubs."

"Well mom, you're not, please eat up," he says.

I smile and say; "sure you nut."

He just wants me to be happy.

Aug 7th

The weather has been pretty dry. A little windy, but today the winds are gusting pretty strong and the power goes out. Well in Montana, or at least in the Drummond area, this happens a lot so you don't think anything of it, and just light candles, or just wait for the power to come on.

Nathan runs in and says, "Mom, have you called the power company?"
I look at him and say, "NO, just because the powers out?"

"No mom, the lines are laying in the yard. The pole broke off at the ground and all the lines are down."

The crew worked from 5 till midnight to secure a new pole in a rock bed, and side hill.

Sept 9th
Bill has been off work now for 11 days. I don't know what we're going to do for money. The power, phone and who knows are yelling for money. I pray Heavenly Father opens a window or door soon.

Two weeks without any money coming in and money going out, gas, milk, lunches.

Sept 22nd
It has rained now for almost 4 weeks sometimes just a sprinkle but for the most part a down pour. The hay is rotting in the fields. Bill finds jobs here and there, surveying. It's nice to have some money come in, and Bill smiling again.

Thinking
I sit here with the house empty, except for Bill, thinking that not too far down the road this house will always be this quiet. No Nathan rocking his skateboard across the upstairs or racing through the kitchen doing a hang ten, high jumping the couches, spiked hair, pink suspenders, his funny cartoons.

Dustin is always being serious about how something works, or in the kitchen sticking his fingers in my dough, frosting, or whatever? Always curious how things work and usually ends up in trouble for seeing how it ticks, getting girls numbers, trying to decide how to drop one for another and not to hurt their feelings. The boys … Huge shoes, deep voices, lots of wash! "Chill out mom," said by Nate as I hype out over something.

Tiffany with her blanket, curling iron and stuffed animals and babies just so, night lights everywhere, Rocky Mountain jeans, big sweaters, basketball, track, our long talks over problems, hers and mine, or she not talking in the morning to anyone till she is good and ready. How much I love you three and cherish the times together always good, a little trying but always good …

The Big Hunter

Life in Montana seems to be crazy all the time, if we're not freezing in the winter, being eaten by massive mosquitoes in the summer, something has to be going wrong. Well life seems like its not improving. Living in beautiful Montana does have its drawbacks. No money, finding work at times is not easy, what work that can be found is hard work; most is out in the weather, the hard physical type. The kids move pipe, to help out. I make dolls; work at every place in town part time. Bill also tries his hand at whatever to feed the family. The kids never complain, they do write in my journal how they love me and they don't care that they don't have money, then wish they had some food to eat besides; beans and bread, poor man gravy, etc

Well Dustin decides that he needs to help so he ventures out the door and takes his rifle; he is going to bring home some meat. God gave us wild animals to eat, and by heck I'm going to find some for my mom and dad. Over the hill and up the gulch he hikes. Early in the morning the sun is barely up, the clouds are hanging low, and the fog is hanging around the mountaintops, as it does on fall days in Montana. The frost is on everything, he is wearing his bright orange hat, and vest, for his pure white hair glistens in contrast to the trees and brown brush so he keeps it well covered.

Silently he moves, trying to keep his scent downwind from the deer he is hunting. The kids have traveled these mountains daily and know the many places the deer go, as they were usually playing and come upon a herd of deer. But this time, it was not a game; he was here for a purpose. There before him is a herd of deer, moms and babies, no bucks. On he hikes, then sits down behind some brush and waits, soon a deer saunters down the draw, then another, one with a baby but one didn't seem to have a fawn. He watched for a long time, then got on his knees and prayed to Heavenly Father if this is the deer that he should shoot for food. Clear as day, the answer came to him to shoot it. He aimed his gun, and got her in his sights. Bang the sound echoed through the forest, as the deer dropped to the ground. He had done it. He goes over and prepares the deer for moving her home. Cutting out the scent sack and gutting her out, now to get her home, all alone with no tag. I can drag her and then roll her he thought. When he sees someone he quickly sits on the deer like it is a rock and waves, they drive on. Once he gets it to a safe place, he goes to Luckie's to ask for help to get a deer he shot.

"You shot a deer?" Luckie says.

"Yes, my family needs meat. So I did it. You're the only one that has a truck that can get it. Dad's not home so would you?"

Luckie goes up after dark and drags the deer into his pick up and drives it to our house, helps us skin it and hang it up to cure. We all thank Dustin, after cussing him out for leaving for the day and worrying us sick. I am thankful for such a good kid that helped the family with food.
There is nothing like deer steak, sliced thinly and cooked in bacon grease, a little flour, salt and pepper. It makes your mouth water. Fried potatoes and corn top it all off. We were feeling fat and sassy.

Northern Lights
If you have never experienced the Northern Lights, I will try to explain them to you as I saw them. I was depressed and down, money was non existent. I'm fat as always, but on with the story. I go outside to try to think and get my life back in order. Looking up in the sky at night in Montana is breath taking as you see millions of stars and planets dancing across the sky. The Milky Way and the total stillness of it all I can usually look up and relax as I see the awesome wonder before me, but tonight I couldn't believe my eyes, I'd always heard how the lights danced but my mind couldn't comprehend such a thing and then there it was before me, lights flickering and dancing over the mountain tops. Like big spotlights, they seemed to surround our house and then focused on a spot in the sky, then changing and flashing again. It lit up the whole sky in bright lights as the night sky danced and flashed before me in the stillness of the night. How could you look at such beauty and wonder if there is a God?

Poverty and Love "What in the Hell are you thinking?"

Three days before Christmas, I'm going to the store to get a few things very few. "As you kids know money is the tightest it's ever been. We have $30.00 to our name. Christmas is going to be light (feather light) this year."

"We don't care mom, we always have fun. Can we go with you?"

"Alright,"

All three kids jump in the Subaru and the wise guys are off to town.

To brief you on the past events everything has seemed to go wrong at our house, one thing after another. The fridge would heat in the freezer, the microwave blew a fuse every time you shut the door. Our well or pump is going bad so the toilet gurgles all night, the pipes pop and air comes out of the spout, then drenching you when water comes. To top it all off, the oven element sizzled to an abrupt end. That doesn't seem too drastic but we hadn't bought groceries in over a month and I had been baking bread and such to make the ole income STRETCH... 3 days before Christmas, no money for anything but we'll make it back to the store..

"Okay you kids, I have to be thrifty here. I have $30.00, $5.00 for gas so we can get home and $25.00 for groceries. Dustin, while I shop could you run across the street and pick up some key chains from the craft store, for Christmas gifts, they are 20 cents?"

"Can I please take the car?" he had just gotten his license.

"I guess but be careful."

Nathan and Dustin take off. Tiffany stays with me and helps with grocery shopping, flour, sugar, milk, eggs, a 8lb turkey that was $4.00, we were doing great... All of a sudden, Nathan comes running in.

"Mom, you won't believe it! Guess What? Dustin locked the keys in the car."

I just looked at him, "You didn't! This better not be one of your sick jokes you boys."

"It's not mom," Nathan says.

Dustin is standing sheepishly. "I did mom, it was an accident."

Now any loving mother would have said I understand son things happen, but I was a little stressed and this is the true story.

I lost control, standing in Tidyman's "Dustin you didn't! How could you be so dumb? You numb skull, idiot, you find someone to unlock that door, don't you remember we have no money?"

A man standing across the isle must have thought what a witch! "Mam, I couldn't help overhearing your dilemma, maybe you could call the police, and sometimes they open cars."

I felt like telling him to keep his long nose out of my business unless he could cough up some cash to help, but I just faked a smile and turned back around to Dustin.

"You get your butt in there and find a tow truck or wrecker then call them and tell them we have no money or only $10.00."

I put groceries away, leaving the small turkey, milk and eggs, totaling $15.00, checked out in tears and rolled the cart of groceries over to the office, where a park bench was placed by the office door. Dustin is on the phone, me on this bench, crying, groceries beside me, people looking at me like I had shop lifted and I was waiting for the cops to carry me away. Nathan hit the magazine rack.

Tiff kept saying, "Mom please stop crying, we'll make it. Everyone is looking at you."

"I don't care," I said, blubbering, "I hate poverty... What a rotten Christmas."

Dustin comes out, "Mom I've called 8 tow places or wreckers and they won't come out for under $35.00 or $40.00. This guy will for $25.00."

I said, "Dustin, read my lips. We have $10.00 tell them that."

We finally reach a tow company close by that will come over and do it for $10.00. He was just going home and he will come over and open the door. 5 minutes later Dustin comes in with the keys.

"Give me that." I grab it clinching my teeth, load our few groceries for Christmas dinner and start to drive home down the street 2 blocks I start to cry. The kids are puzzled.

"Now what's wrong mom?"

"I bought a turkey and we don't even have an oven, to cook it in."

We all started to laugh, how could we all be so dumb? They hug me, and I apologize for yelling. Then the car starts to sputter and we pull in to the gas station. Dustin and Nathan get out to put gas in the car and wash windows. Just then I hear a knock on the window.

"Mom do you have 30 cents more? I wasn't looking and the numbers just whizzed by." I reached out to cuff him, but he knew he'd better move. Everyone started digging in and under the seats and in the glove box, we tried to find what money we could, 1 nickel, 8 pennies 1 dime that's it, no more. The girl said, "Go ahead." We started home, tired, poor and laughing at our luck, and the rotten day Dustin had.

Good Fairy
Edie calls that night when I got home, telling me everything she has for Christmas, how her house is fixed, on and on and then asked me how things were? I should not have... but I told her, in tears. She wanted me to drive our Cherokee down to Idaho Falls on Christmas Eve. I told her I had no money for gas, tires, food, nothing.

Edie and Scott collected money from some of the relatives bought food, tires and an oven element. They drove all night to bring it to me for Christmas, then turned around and drove back 500 miles to get home for her kids to have Christmas, What a nut, but I do love my sister, and her giving spirit. I hope they don't have to experience some of the tough times we have. I appreciate them and the love they showed to our family. Edie was six months pregnant, and it was a real sacrifice for her to drive all that way to bring food and goodies and then turn around to make it home for Christmas for her family. All I can say is, Thanks Edie and Scott for being the good fairies that we so desperately needed.

This is a picture of my uncle George and aunt Elaine, They were heaven sent Angels to help us .. Through all Types of trials.

Chapter 24
Chimney Fire and Bats

Chim Chimney

Well it's chimney-cleaning time again. I hate fall when we have to clean the soot out of the pipes. Wood stoves are so much work. First you kill yourself getting the firewood from the mountains, then haul it home, stack it, cut it up in small 18 in. pieces. Then cover it and then get the stuff and haul it in the house. Okay now to start the fire, we are freezing.

Find paper, wrinkle up, kindling that is small cut up wood, then the logs, then the matches. Okay where did the kids put the matches, they were here yesterday. So now you hunt for the matches, so that you can have heat, now open everything up, all pipes and airways so that the flames get plenty of air Okay now… the fire is blazing and it starts to roar….

We've done it this time. We have started a chimney fire. The stove turns red and the stove is creaking, you can hear the fire deep breathing but to stop this beast before it burns my log house down. I open up the fiery furnace this is no easy task, as the door is glowing and the handle is scalding hot. Now to locate gloves that aren't wet, or don't have holes, and throw a pitcher of water in there, for it instantly turns to steam and is spouting out of the stove. My eyebrows and the hairs on my arms are singed

Okay that was not the thing to do. I send the boys up on the ladder in a snow storm to the top of the roof with a bucket of water, and told them to pour it down the pipe. This also was not a good thing as the steam came back up the pipe and spilled all over the poor kid, his jacket was crisp from the ice chunks that now encased him and the soot that collected with it. His coat is plastered with frozen water with burning embers flying from the pipe and onto the roof. We finally get it cooled down and once more we stave off the soot monster..

About a month later the fire goes out of control again. I'm at my computer class and someone gets me out of class and says the volunteer fire department has been called to a fire at my house. My heart drops how can this be? Bill's at home, he is so good… but the fire once more raised its ugly head and had a mind of its own. The pipe glowed red and no matter what he did the thing would not cool down, of course he doesn't throw cold water like I do in a hot melt down stove. He calls the fire department and men are running through my house, dragging hoses and trying to cool it down. The house was a disaster. So now we get to clean the chimney

Cleaning Chimney 101(or only the whites of my eyes)

Number one lesson to learn is never, never clean a chimney with your husband; this is a big, big No, No. It causes strain, and words that you usually don't say. Husbands and wives should not work in stressful situations together, no husbands and wives should not work together period. Because it makes stressful situations ... and Bill and I seem to always get in some kind of situation that turns to a disaster.

I always wondered why in movies, you see chimney sweeps all covered with soot, with their big brooms, and the furniture inside covered with white sheets. I thought that it was just part of Mary Poppins to have soot flying everywhere and your face blackened. WRONG!

"Okay Pennie I need your help."

Oh I dread that line (I need your help). It means I will not do it right, no matter what, and I will hear my name yelled in many different manners.

"What now Bill?"

"It is time to clean the chimney."

Bill usually uses a big chain. He crawls upon the house, drops a logging chain down and starts swirling it around as it bangs the side of the pipe, and creosote falls into the stove, leaving the pipe semi clean. This was all fine until we got a new stove and well, since the fire. Bill found out the fire department has chimney brooms that we can use, so Bill goes and gets the brooms and the adventure begins. Put the ladder upon the balcony.

"Hold this ladder while I get on the roof, can you do that?"

"Maybe," I think. (Why do we have to do this again? Bill and I get along great unless it involves him giving me instructions, which I cannot do fast enough or well enough for him.) Back to the story...

I do an extremely good job at that, as he goes up 20 to 30 ft in the air.

"Okay now go down and check the stove for any leaks, or see if the pipe is secure."

So down the stairs I go. Everything looks good. He scrubs and polishes. I can hear the creosote trickle and fall down into the stove. But this new stove is a terrible design so you have to take the stove pipe apart to clean out the chamber that you just filled up with soot. I'm trying to balance pipes as Bill unscrews the screws and gently slips the bottom pipe loose. There before me is the black soot heaped in the stove pipe opening. I turn on the trusty vacuum and start sucking.

"Just be careful," Bill says, "and do it slowly so as not to plug up the vacuum."

"Okay."

He goes outside and I start to work. Alright this is working great and the machine is working overtime on the black remains of many fires. All of a sudden I look through my glasses, boy they must be getting dirty, cause I can't see very well, not! The vacuum has clogged and I didn't notice. In the mean time everything that I have been sucking up, is shooting out the other end all over the front room. I quickly turn off the contraption. There before me is a gray shadow over everything.

A fine dust of soot lay on my rug, furniture and the air is cloudy with particles that haven't settled, or can't find a free place that isn't covered. What a mess!

Just as Bill returns, I hear "PENNIE! What are you doing?"

He helps me clean out the vacuum, and then I try to get the mess cleaned up, now to put the pipe back together. I am covered with a black layer of soot. All you can see are pitiful eyes looking out of hazed over glasses and my white sweat shirt is now a charcoal gray.

"PENNIE, I love you," he says, "only you could clean a chimney like this…" Just another adventure at Wiseacres.

Bats in the Bedroom

Rats, bats,, cats… you name it, but this was one of the freakiest things yet. I was packing to go on a trip with Terrie. When I went up stairs, turned on the light in my bedroom a black thing flew by my face and landed on the logs over the bed, there he hung… I couldn't believe my eyes, a bat! All I could think of is that movie with John Candy where he's trying to get this bat out of the cabin and it sticks to his face. Okay, I will die if he touches me. He is huge, well in my eyes he is.

I call Bill, "there's a bat in our Bedroom!"

He just ignored me, but the screams made it more real to him, as the thing went from wall to wall hanging here and there. He told me to get a baseball mitt and a towel and we would catch him and let him go.

Okay let's see how we do this. It finally ran out of wall space and landed on the floor. They walk strangely, wings folded back and kind of roll from side to side with the big wings laying on each side, big dark eyes, and little nose. I really didn't look at his teeth as we crept closer and threw the towel over him and then Bill took his gloves and a baseball mitt and cradled him in it and carried him downstairs and out the door. The bat didn't look back and flew away. We have quite a few around here, they swoop down at night when the mosquitoes and bugs are around, and they get their fill. It's amazing to see them fly and catch the mosquitoes and other bugs in the air, and Montana has their abundance of them, bugs and bats.

The bats swoop down and fly low down through my porch, they fly so fast that you can hardly see them as they target their insect victims. So we like them just not in my bedroom and sleeping hanging from a rafter, not a good plan. We had two more in the house. Bill got them out 2 days later as they were downstairs hanging from the rafters in the front room. Not what I call a good decoration, but a real conversation starter for sure.

We figured they got in when we were putting in new flooring in the kitchen and removed the old stove and the stove pipe was left open they just flew down and into the house. Or maybe they were living in there. Who knows? But we hooked it up fast…. And I really haven't been plagued with bats since. I just enjoy them from afar and sometimes a do a little neck bob as they swoop past after their dinner.

We have had magpies in the house. The door was left open and in jumped a magpie, a big bird like a crow, only what a nuisance. Cunning and quick he flew around the house, me trying to get him, and him scared so he was splattering my house with bird droppings, no matter how I tried he would dodge me. I ended up with white splatters on my shirt, then my head as I tried to get him by the neck. I opened all the doors and hoped that the stupid thing would fly outside, but to no avail. I was getting frustrated and ready to get the pellet gun, when he flew into the window and fell to the floor. I picked him up and he shook his head, and as we both went outside, he flew off no worse for wear, just a few pounds lighter from expelling himself all over my house.

Lesson 2 – don't leave doors open, creatures come in, cats, rats, bats, birds, and mosquitoes and spiders.

Sizzling summer

Summer into September almost 3 and half weeks since Bill has had some money come and in the cupboards are looking pretty bare. I sold a ballerina doll today for $28.00 and spent $27.09 on no frill groceries, eggs, soap, sugar, flour. I wonder how many people have to really buy and live on beans, rice, noodles, and pancakes.

Bill's really down about work, just working odd jobs to keep the wolf from the door, and feed the family. He's talking about moving back to Utah, but I won't budge. We have everything here and with all that we have done I not quitting now, we can do it...It's hard to live in Montana. The Bryant's are discouraged and having a hard time making ends meet also. But that's what refines a true Montana person, dig your heels in and last it out!

Here I am Chubby as ever, even splitting wood doesn't help my waistline.

I got pretty good at sawing down trees, chopping or splitting is not my forte, then chiseling I've made 3 beds with Bills help, not that has helped my waistline either, but they look pretty cool and don't cost anything when you can go up and drag down the knarly piece and make something out of it.

Chapter 25
Chubby and Wrecker Bait

Okay I'm Chubby

... Diets, now if that isn't a waste of time! Have I ever-lost weight before? Well, that is a big **yes!** It's just yes, over and over again, cause I gain it back, and gain it back. Can't figure out why I'm fat and everyone else in my family, Father, Mother, brothers, all are skinny. Then there is me, the plump well rounded sister. I go to doctors and they look at me and won't believe that I don't eat constantly. They ask me about my family, "is your mother fat? Is your father?" "NO, No" I say, they remark, "then why are you so LARGE?"(polite word for FAT!)

They accused me of closet eating. Oh please if I want to eat I don't have to eat in a closet. There are other rooms in the house, bedroom, bathroom while soaking in a hot tub, hall, pantry, who could forget the living room? Heaven with the commercial reminding you of all the things that you can make, or that you already have in your cupboards. Why would I have to eat in a closet? I don't hide what I eat it hangs all over my thighs and hips. Okay they break me down I do graze. Just now and then, you know the cookie here, diet pop to minus out the cookie, isn't that how it works?.

If you want to get rich in this world, just write a diet book, or invent some pill that will work wonders, the glamour stretcher. I don't know how many times I stretched with the big rubber band type device that you hooked to your doorknob for $9.95. You would glamour yourself into shape with Jack La-Lane or Richard Simmons, oh give me a break. Then there's Jane Fonda and the workout videos. I flitted around the front room, stair master, and just plain did myself in, but then I was so proud of myself I would reward myself with a treat. You know just one, one of this, and one of that. Yes I've tried them all, weight watchers, Tubbs, the protein drinks, the diet pills. Now there were some dandies that would help you clean your whole house, and want to go out looking for more. I had so much energy I didn't know what to do, okay keep my hands busy, solution make something to eat. Results are, I'm still Chubby.

Enough is enough

The time has come once more to go on the dreaded diet, you know the time of year when everyone says, that enough is enough, they are going to lose pounds and inches, so they make a commitment to lose weight, and exercise.. Oh how I hate that word. Or maybe all those words, diet, lose weight, exercise, commitment, where do we stop? Anyway on with the story ...

First I run off to the store and buy the blow up pants that are suppose to sweat the pounds away, vinyl blue babies, with a tube that you hook up to a pump and exercise, as you blow up your pants. You stomp and move and pretty soon you are this large, well larger than usual blue butted vinyl monster it's hard to bend, and your legs rub together making a terrible sound. You look like a blue Michelin tire man. I danced around the house; now I'm a bad smelling fat girl in a horrible outfit, but it has to work, the commercials said if you did this, I would look like... I can't believe I fell for it, so the pants go in the closet then on to the Goodwill. Now on to bigger and better things... like Jogging how adventurous...

I guess I could do what my friends did. Two sisters decided to go jogging every morning, put on their extra large sweats, because why jog if you are not extra large? Oh please... anyway these girls headed around the neighborhood of course their chunky dog ran with them his tongue hanging out and almost dragging behind them. Each day they were out there suffering and faithfully exercising, one day it's going to pay off they tell each other.

A neighbor pulls up in his car and says to them; "Hey, I have been watching you girls every morning jogging around the neighborhood."

They nodded and thought how nice for him to notice, and then he said it, the rotten, no good, varmint said: "I want to tell you how much weight your dog has lost."

Well that did it, they jogged over to the nearest grocery store got two Twinkies, one for them and one for the dog.

I'm now a Grandma, and you know fat is where it's at. Your grandkids love to push on you and hug you, they don't care if you're fat they just say, "Grandmas are supposed to be Fluffy." So I'm going to believe them, life is just to short to keep stressing and I seem to do a lot of that lately.

Stuffed Kitty

November has been unreal, below zero, 36 below in Drummond, a foot of snow, wind and more snow. Now that kind of weather will put you in the mood, I'm not sure what kind of mood, but it will put you in a mood. I had to go to town to finish getting a few things for my Thanksgiving dinner, so I left the turkey in the sink thawing in water and ventured in to the big Missoula, the "Zoo".

I stop for parts for Luckie and I get a message to get a turkey. What is Bill thinking? I have a turkey in the sink but they are only 25 cents a lb so I grab one

more for later. And head home.

When I reach home, I can't believe my eyes, there in the kitchen sink is a stripped turkey, every bit of meat is gone just the bones all hooked together laying there. It looked like some piranhas had come up the house drain and picked the poor bird clean, but no it wasn't some kind of fish. It was our hungry cats. They had reached up and hung from the string to open the latch and opened the door, then the 9 cats started to fight and squall as they devoured a 15 lb bird.. I was so mad, we hardly have any money and they eat our Thanksgiving turkey. We didn't see them for days and when we did they were not feeling well a little sluggish as their stomachs bulged from the massive amounts of food they had devoured.

Towing and House guests...

Bill has bought a Tow Truck, why not make life interesting...gee lets see he has been a logger, surveyor, rancher, sewer man for the city, custodian, mill worker for the saw mill, Alaska fisherman, and now a Tow truck owner and operator, Well here goes....

Bill is good at finding people out and about, that seem to need our help. Not that we have any money, and can add a lot to their life, but he figures we are better off then them so he offers a clean bed and hot meal, what ever I'm cooking just add more. Our first guest was a 15 year old prostitute, okay you say not a good idea with teenage boys, and yada, yada, yada... anyway on with the story, she was traveling over to eastern Montana to try to change her life, and had picked up these hitchhikers and now they wouldn't leave her alone, they were devil worshipers, Scary, in every since of the word. Bill says, she came into the shop and his heart just went out to her and her little boy. He was headed home and said you are coming with me. He called me and said prepare another plate at the table. I was making spaghetti so things stretched just fine along with homemade bread. The girl was so pretty, but the clothes that she wore yelled Prostitute. Short Levis with her bum hanging out, a tight shirt and cleavage was more than I wanted my young boys to see. But all in all you could see a neat girl inside. Well I was telling myself that anyway, it made me feel better as I subjected my kids to filthy language and a new way of life, they had not seen, in well-protected Drummond, Montana.

As we ate as a family, my kids received their first lesson on swearing, and city life. They heard words from a three year old they had never thought of saying or wanted to. The girl told us of her life in Seattle, how she had prostituted since she was 11 and then had this little boy when she was 12. She said that she had never been in a home before, that she could feel the love, and asked if we would keep her son. I asked her if she was scared going with just anyone? She said, No, why the worst thing that could happen is that I could die.

Well to me that is pretty bad. She stayed with us for 3 days; we got her new clothes, and found enough money to send her to her sister's to hopefully change her life. Eight months later I received a letter from the girl, how her life had changed because of our family. She was working as a waitress and had turned her life around. She just said Thanks ...

Our next guest was a little different. Bill also found him out on the highway. He was pulling a kayak from Idaho to get into the Missouri river so that he could kayak across the United States. He had to get out of the Columbia, and hike to the Missouri, his feet were blistered, so Bill brings him home to recoup here. He was 78 years old, gray and thin, really in good shape, friendly ole guy. We took him to different places around Drummond, the ole ghost town, and behind our house in the forest to see the beauty of our home. Then he was off with his little wagon and kayak, hiking to Helena, and the Missouri, then the Mississippi, then the Ocean to Florida... a few months later we received a post card that he had made it. And thanked his little family in Montana for helping him.

Then we had the guy from the mental hospital in Seattle, who had just escaped from there, but of course we knew nothing of this. Nate our son just felt sorry for this guy, cause he was black and sleeping in his car it was cold. But in Montana it is always cold at night whether it is July or December. So he asked if we could bring him home for the night. We fed him and offered him a bed. As we are talking to him we find out he has just escaped from a mental hospital and when things go wrong he just can't help himself and he goes whacko and starts going crazy, he almost killed someone. So here we are with an insane slasher in our house.

Bill's off towing and two young teenagers and I are in the house. We stay up till Bill gets home and then I tell him what I found out.

He rolls his eyes and then lays awake during the night listening for the crazy guy. Then all hell broke loose, as a rumble and crashing down the hall. Bill jumps up, and runs down the hall, turns on a light to find this guy standing there with the large fan at his feet.

"Gee you should move that thing, someone could kill themselves. I could have kicked that thing all night."

Bill got him settled back in his room after a bathroom break, and we tried to go to sleep. The next morning we decided we needed to send this guy down the road as quickly as possible, here a slasher knows we don't lock our doors, knows we leave keys in the car, and knows almost everything about us. Bill told him that he knew some ranchers who could use a hand haying for a day. And that would get him some money to get his car fixed and down the road.

"Oh, I can't do that, he replies that hay get stuck in my hair, and I have to Vaseline it to get it out."

So once more we put out money to get this guy on the road. I told Bill it was money well spent, like lifesaving. So off he went in the sunset and we were so grateful, then we had a talk about who we brought home next time.

Well the guests have ranged from small families, to college kids just needing a break and a warm place to stay. Bill is just a great guy and when he sees someone in need he will call me up and tell me to put another plate on the table, or fix the spare bedroom for a crowd cause he's headed that way with some cute college kids and they are welcome until their parents can come an rescue them. We have had foreign chicks stay for 3 days, from Czech. Bill called them the chicks from Czech. They were a lot of fun and seemed to make themselves quite comfortable in our home, they brought their own food, cause over in Europe they don't eat as we do. In fact they eat a lot less and healthier, they would set down with just bread and cheese, greens and fruit. And they were off for the day, we really enjoyed the girls, Bill teased them something terrible, but they just took it in stride, we fixed their car and got them on their way to Seattle where they were meeting some friends and heading on to San Francisco.

The tow truck has been our salvation, the first few years of a new company are hard, but if you can stick it out, things do get better. As I write this book and look back after 15 years in the towing business, and all the crazies, miserable weather, and high fuel prices, the good out numbers the bad. You meet too many nice people and everyone is pretty happy to see you.

Bill has won numerous awards from AAA for Outstanding service, and has won National fame with his tow trucks in Tow Times. He won first place in the nation, had a photographer fly out from Florida to photograph the truck in snow, and he got his wish, it dumped and dumped we could hardly get the picture before Bill could go to work.

Fun times and Poverty we still have on occasion, but have learned to enjoy parts of it, and put up with the rest.

(We won Top Tow Truck in Nation with this one.)

Chapter 26
Rattle, Rattle, Crash
Beep Beep

It's the pits to not own a nice car. When we were in Utah we had custom vans, sport cars, pick ups and all at the same time. But here life has changed as the big P word has come into our life, POVERTY. It has been a blessing to bring our family together, but I hate it. When you live in Drummond one thing that you have to have is a vehicle, one that you can trust and can get you down the road.

Well we had cars, and they got you down the road, but let's say not in style. There was Fife the Fiat This car was an ugly dirty lime green sort. We hauled our kids, and Jeff, Tammy, Chris, which overloaded the poor girl. Jeff never had enough room in the back seat as the 6'4 kid was all arms and legs. So he decided to stick them on the ceiling, & fix our ripped headliner, which only made it worse, so it was hanging on our heads, well we had to put a stick between the seats to hold the liner out of our eyes so we could drive. So when the Fiat hit the road we didn't shed too many tears.

We were the kind of people you see and wonder where they came from, and how they could live that way, as they watch kids pile out, broken windshields, sticks holding up the ceiling, and not doing a good job of it, as we had to constantly reposition it and swat at the sagging material in our eyes, having to push it to get it going, bald tires, smoke barreling out the back, and putting in as much oil as gas.

Tilly and 10 kids

Tilly is still going strong after a month and the bolt is hanging in there. You just make sure you fill the oil when you check the gas.

Terry was having a birthday party for Corey. They were going swimming in Deer Lodge; free swimming. Jeanie is supposed to drive but isn't home, so Terrie has 16 kids to take swimming and how does she do it in 1 car. Well now days you couldn't take 16 kids plus 2 drivers. You would need 2 nine passenger vans, or 3 6 passenger cars, which wouldn't work because you need an extra person to drive the third car. So now that makes 19. Well nineteen won't fit in 3 cars so you need a forth car to fit everyone in. But now you don't have 4 drivers, so you recruit more people, which makes for more hassle.

Well back to the story. We didn't have that problem because who knew that you couldn't shove as many as could fit in a Volkswagen. So I had 10; 3 in front 5 in back and 2 in the back window compartment. Off we went, all having a good time. Swimming was fun, and then Chinese fire drills in the rest area. We stopped at the A & W and ordered 18 ice-cream cones between the two cars. The girl almost fainted.

Cars were meant to haul people, and I used Tilly for that. I was the Cub Scout den mother and had 14 boys. Well I took those boys everywhere in Tilly. We went to the mountains to pan gold, hike, dig up trees and plant them in our yards, pinecone hunting, whatever. Tilly would take me and the boys. And those little boys just knew that car had a secret button.

had one. He just laughed and so did I. On the dash was a little button that had a B on this red light. You would push it to see if brakes were okay and it would light up. Well I told the boys that it was the booster button, and only worked down hill if they pushed it. Before I could finish, one of the boys would push that button and I would step on the gas and say I couldn't stop. They would laugh and jump up and down kids heads popping left and right, me going crazy. What a good time we had in that little red car. 15 years later one of the boys that I hauled around asked me about that button and said he believed that car had that Booster button for years, and wondered where I got such a neat car, because no one else had one.

We did everything in that car, taught every kid to drive as well as the neighbor and cousins. The ole girl just kept going, hardly a heater, and when the heater did work the kids shoes would start melting. The floorboards were rotted through and she went down the road with a bump and a grind. She did it all, up in the mountains with the cub scouts hunting for trees to plant, or gold panning.. Always a challenge but no problem if we didn't have enough cars, we just made do.   We did Chinese fire dills in the rest areas or parking lots, what a hoot, as half the neighbor hood would climb out and run around the car and then pile back in. I wouldn't let them do it at the stoplights like I used to do; for one thing there isn't a stop light in Drummond. I loved that little car. It seemed to always get us through the worst of times and the best of times

Today I have grand children and I have taught them about the super buttons, my little Spencer will always ask me, Nana push the Super button, we need to go fast. I have a new VW now but can't fit the kids in it so I take the Durango with a lot more power, and kids still giggle and have fun and have a new super button..

Tilly dies

I guess we knew this day would come. Bill's saw not running again, another day of no pay, that is what logging is all about, if you can't get to the mountains, have a saw and fuel. No work, no pay, no food.

Head for Missoula to drop off saw and go around town doing errands. Let's look at cars. See if we can find a deal but no luck. We went to every car lot in Missoula I guess. Tilly got huffy or mad cause after we picked up the saw and started home the ole oil light comes on. Bill stops out by Clinton one quart, glug, glug down on the road again, light on again. She went through a quart in two miles, Tilly's croaking. I felt so bad. We call Terrie to see if she can come get us. Bill and I get a paper to read the want ads. No luck, fight a little and then wait. Terrie came finally. We borrow her old car ole blue; we'll have to fix Tilly but when? We pray that somehow we can find a car in our price range. Now what would that be a pedal car? Next morning Bill's off to work, we get a call from Luckie that he has found us a '73 fiat for $975.00 so we go to the bank and beg for a loan. Now days we call the bank, and say do you want to loan us money for this interest rate, or shall we take our business elsewhere. The ball is in our court.

But then we had to sign our life away. If not to a bank, to one of those financial agencies who are more than happy to loan you money at 32% they grow fat on the poor. Bill and I had learned about the loan sharks, from our early years and taking out loans to pay loans, and never seeming to pay off the existing loan. Hating to answer the phone knowing it was a bill collector. That is why we were so poor now, cause we decided to live on what we made. If it wasn't in our pocket we didn't spend it. Loan sharks are the only option if you don't have a banker that takes pity on you and trusts that you will pay him, after you put up your home, car, toaster, stereo, beds the only thing they didn't want was the kids.

Bill and I sit at the bank, we try to look presentable wear our best clothes or something close to that, curl the ole hair, and act on our best behavior. You feel like scum, I hate to beg for money! Them having to know our life history, why we needed this and why we couldn't get this. Then promise your life, and then wait for days as it goes to a committee, if that isn't a joke. As the bank executives sit around a big table and play poker with your finances and life. After all the sore feelings we got the loan. We did have a nice guy who trusted us, and I have to thank him for that. I think we would have gone off the deep end. And now we had to finagle enough money to get a bus ticket to Billings to go get our car sight unseen.

Luckie gets me at 4:15 am to drive me to the bus in Bozeman. Snow all over, big flakes floating down, as I walk out of the door and the head lights of the car reflect off the white like feathers in the air, they're so big I even caught some on my eyelashes. The roads were hazardous; slush piled on the road, grabs your wheel and tries to throw you down for the count. I'm glad Luckie was driving in that mess, a real rush to try to get me to the bus on time. I have to be in Bozeman 140 miles away by 8:00 with 2 passes to cross. We had our old brother sister talks and the time flew as we discussed our problems and worries, our future and feelings. We make the bus with 15 minutes to spare. I sit on the bus and feel out of place. I remember I have been on a mountain in Montana for years now, had a headache, and didn't know if it was from tension or starvation, hard to say. I find a kicked around aspirin in my purse, been rubbed around so long it had a shine to it. No water, try to work up some water in my throat so it wouldn't lodge in my throat. Here goes nothing, not bad for a beginner, as it hits my dangling thing in my throat, and I start gagging, okay this is cute, as all the people turn to look, at the person dying in the middle of the bus. Then I turn and smile.

Bus trip from Hell

Come to think of it, have you ever ridden on a bus? What an experience, especially a long trip. I got to do the trip from Ogden, Utah to Butte. Bill could not come and get me when my ride back home from Utah fell through so he said a bus is the next option... Oh Hanna, this bus had every personality that you could think of. The lovers in the back, the bearded sweaty guys, and the fat motherly type, different nationalities and of course it had to be crowded and I had to hold Tiffany because I didn't have money to buy an extra ticket. A 500 mile bus trip takes 650 miles because they stop at every cow town and on every back road.

When we reached Pocatello there were all kinds of police cars surrounding the place, and a guy with a gun is waiting for our bus. He wants the woman that's sitting by me, or course. She starts to scream when she sees him through the window and he goes crazy hammering on the door, and wanting her out of there. The police finally get him under control, and I calm the lady next to me, then she starts crying cause they are hurting him. She was mad and so got on the bus to leave him. He raced the bus with his car and beat it and was going to do himself in if she didn't come back. She got off the bus to be with him and I had a free seat by me. Oh boy, Tiff has a seat. 4 yr olds are hard to hold that long, let alone their skinny butt bones will make your legs go numb. We go on down the road 40 more miles. Once more the police board the bus as they are looking for someone, sure enough they find him, a drunk in the back harassing people. Drunks are not allowed to be on public transportation. So he had to leave until he was sober. When more off this bus, by Butte Tiff and I will be alone. NO such luck but we did get to Butte. Bill was waiting and we gave him a great big hug, and made him swear that he would never make me ride a bus again. Of course most bus rides are not like that one, just Pennie Luck. You know me by now.

Just get me back to good ole Drummond, the home of the Bull shippers..

Chapter 27
Bad Smells

Cat Fishing

One more thing goes wrong with this house, and I think I'm going crazy… no I already have we have already come to that conclusion. How do you Cat fish in Montana? There is no Catfish; well we did it, amazing you say. We had a cat named GG short for Garbage Gut. She was always digging in the garbage, as you drove up the drive way and crested the hill, her head would pop out of the burning barrel, covered in soot and licking her paws. Well cats really never stayed around very long, because of the coyotes, mountain lions, and dogs, kids, cold miserable weather to add to the confusion. Anyway GG was pretty good at hiding, but the winter was one of those 3 dog night ones, and GG would crawl up in the rafters to keep warm, we never thought any thing of it, till pretty soon we didn't see GG anymore sticking her head out of the garbage can.

Then spring came and an aroma that you can't explain exploded through the house. Oh, NO. Did that cat die in the rafters Bill? What a stupid question as the air in the house was green, for months we sprayed disinfectants on the logs trying to cut the horrific smell, in the cool of the evenings it wasn't bad, but as the sun heated the attic up, so did the decaying body, oh we could hardly stand it, as summer neared and the temperatures soared the smell over took everything, you couldn't function with a dead cat over your head.

"I can't stand it any longer," Bill says, as he put on some boots, gloves, rain gear pants.

"What are you doing," I said to him.

"I'm going Cat fishing…"

He got Nathan's old World War II gas mask, and a long pole that he taped on to a vacuum tube, then he taped on a hook to that and went up the ladder. First he reversed the vacuum and blew lime in the rafter hole hoping that would cut the smell that was emanating through the house. Then he switched the hose, and started sucking, and dragging. My sister's sister in-law was up in Montana for a visit and came over just as Bill was on the ladder.

She looked at him and asked, "What are you doing?"

"Cat fishing," he replied.

"What," she asked again.

"CAT FISHING! "What's that?"

Just stick your nose down in that hose and take a deep breath."

Trisha picked up the hose and took a whiff, "oh my goodness." Her face turned green and she started to gag and puke.

"Now you know about Cat fishing in Montana," Bill said, as he scraped the remains out and they fell to the ground piece by piece.

Trisha never forgave Bill for that one, but she really hasn't returned either. 10 years later on a hot summer day and you're upstairs, you get just a hint of GG, so out come the air fresheners, Lysol and disinfectants, maybe it's just me but better safe then stinky...

Broken knee...

Today I broke my knee. I went to the school to bring some papers into the office. It had been snowing for the past week, so the roads were slick and snow packed with ice underneath the fresh fallen snow. I got out of my car and started into the school. As I came closer to the sidewalk at the high school my foot slipped and gave out from under me. My knee went one way and I went the other. Then I lay there not knowing what to do. The place I fell could not be seen from any of the windows, so I lay there. Okay here I am in the snow and I can't move. My knee felt as though it had been ripped away from my body. I decided I needed to get out of the gutter before someone thinks I'm a large snowy boulder. So I tried to drag myself to the sidewalk, with no avail. Then the cooks came out of the building and started down the stairs at the other end of the school, they waved at me. Okay maybe they will notice that I'm not supposed to be down here.

"Are you okay Pennie?"

"No, I think I broke my knee."

They call the ambulance, but it's volunteer so I sit out in a snowstorm as the volunteers, gather from around the valley. I try to convince them that I really don't need an ambulance just get a car. I can get in and drive to the doctor or whatever. Please this is not life threatening... I don't know if it was lack of something to do, or it was standard to pick an injured person from the ground and transport them to the ER... Now I think you have to know how I am built which is rather chubby... I have lets say food storage in my body that rather stores below my knee in a bump. Two little ambulance attendants try to lift me into the ambulance. No deal, they can't budge me.

I scoot myself over and winch myself into the back of the emergency vehicle. As I lay there, they start to ice my leg, not where my knee no longer is, but the fat deposit below.

"Oh dear," they say as I move the ice pack.

"You can't move that you are all swollen."

"No, I am not, that is my leg."

"No dear you are delirious your leg is all swollen and deformed."

"Look lady, see this leg, it looks just like that leg,"

"Oh my, did you break both legs?"

"No, I have fat storage in both legs. Just Ice my knee!"

Now they want to remove my shoes.

"Don't do it," I say, "You will be sorry, my shoes are not leather and I have no socks therefore my feet stink."

Would they listen? No! They take off my shoes. Oh for Pete's sake, I can't even stand the odor.

They said, "You aren't kidding" as they all start talking through their noses and holding their breath.

The air inside the ambulance is now green, it is snowing heavy now and the ambulance is crawling to the ER, really guys I will be fine. Just let me out of here. They have me strapped to a gurney and I knew the doors were going to fly open and I would be sailing down the road any minute. Once at the hospital they have to get me out of the ambulance, I was amazed the bed just kicks some kind of legs that pop down and I slide out easily and they roll me into the hospital, stinky feet and all. Shoes tied up in a plastic bag with dangerous written on them.

    Well I broke my knee, or should I say damaged it good. I had ripped the which-ma-call-it tendons, that held it all together, and it was laying to the back and side. By the time I got help it had decided to move back in place. But it wouldn't stay there, so they worked on me and then sent me home to re coop for a couple months. What a job to get back in to the house when your knee is falling off, and there is over 8 inches of snow. It's a good thing the 4x4 was running, good ole Subaru.

    After a month or so, I had to return to the doctor for a check up, and he had me wear shorts, oh what a treat. Anyway he looked at my big legs and felt them up one side and then the calf.

    "Do you hike?"

    "Does this body look like I hike," I say.

    "You have the most muscled legs I've seen in a long time."

    "Well thanks, but I think it's from getting up and hitting the kitchen 2 - 3 times an hour."

Chapter 28
Cover Your Eyes

My Bathing Suit adventure

I have just been through the torture and humiliation known as buying a bathing suit to fit this fat oversized body. When I was a younger the bathing suits for woman let's say for the mature figure, were boned, trussed and reinforced not so much sewn as engineered. They were built to hold back uplift and dazzle. Your chest looked like two torpedoes ready to fire weapons of war, and could harm anyone who happened to be to close and you turned around quick, you could slice them down. Bill told my friend Launa to help me find a swim suit. I dreaded it. The last suit I had was the one described above, but the torpedoes were to small for the bombs that were on my chest now, and I was carrying too much cargo in my belly and underside that the elastic had given away under stress.

I reluctantly went shopping, and Launa didn't give up, here try this one and this one, they all looked like, ya know, the fat lady's suit on the beach you always see.

"Okay just give it here, I'll buy it."

"No you try it on," says Launa.

I go into the dreaded dressing room, ya know, the one with three mirrors so you can see all ugly sides of you. Well today's stretch fabrics are designed for the model type girl with a figure chipped from marble, the mature woman has a choice, she can either front up the maternity department and try on a floral costume with a skirt coming away looking like a hippopotamus who escaped from Disney's *Fantasia,* or try on the fashionable rubber band, where the suit becomes part of your body, showing every ripple, only in shark skin, or vibrant colors. I noticed the extraordinary tensile strength of the stretch material, the Lycra used in bathing suits was developed by NASA. This material could launch small rockets from a slingshot, which gives the added bonus that if you manage to actually lever your self into one you are protected from shark attacks. The reason is that any shark taking a swipe at your passing midriff would immediately suffer whiplash. I fought my way into the bathing suit, dancing around the room knocking into walls as I hurled my body in different contortions to get the suit on, but as I twanged the last shoulder strap in place, I gasped in horror-my one bosom had disappeared! I found one bosom cowering under my left armpit. It took a while to find the other at last I located it flattened beside my bellybutton. Then the sales girl that always sticks her head in at the moment that you're at your best, bending over with your derriere pointing at the door.

"Are you okay she asks?"

"Do I look all right? Yes fine," trying to hold my cool, as I am sweating now because this rubber band is now cutting off circulation to all parts of my body and making my head swell, not a pretty site.

Okay I'm sick, here were my boobs spread across my chest like a speed bump. The suit fit all right, but unfortunately as I looked behind, my behind was not in the rubber band, but it looked like that product Gak, I oozed out rebelliously from top to bottom. I just wanted to puke. Okay I tried a cream crinkled one that made me look like a lump of masking tape, and a floral job that gave the appearance of walking window box. I tried on a bright pink one with such high cut legs I thought I would have to wax my eyebrows to wear it. Then the black one, you know the color that makes you look thin. This number made my midriff look as if I was wearing a life saving inner tube under my suit.

Launa found me this striped job with longer shorts, now if they could only be long pants. I tried on the suit with the so called boxer shorts, well the front is rather covered in stripes that muted my huge speed bump chest and came down to a V to try and make my waist look thin, no small, okay smaller than my chest, oh whatever, then the shorts that billowed around my thighs. Okay after masking tape, rubber bands, and getting sick in the dressing room this is it. I have a bathing suit that I hope the drawer wears more than me.

I guess I could go on and on about my life in Montana, but the last scary thing was the wild fires that came so close to our home. Is this the End?

Chapter 29
Is this the End?

Wild Fire..

I sit here and ponder what is going to happen to my home, we've worked so hard for 22 years of struggling and doing without. On August 7 a fire started in the mountains 20 miles away. A truck got over in some tall grass and the catalytic converter set the grass a blaze. Before anyone could get anything done the fire had spread to two thousand acres in a couple hours. The land is parched. A dry spring and sparse winter has made the woods tinder dry. They say that even the sun shining through a broken piece of glass can start a fire that no one can control.

I watched the fire burn, and though it was tragic and I hated for the mountains to be on fire, it really never affected me. But the fire increased and the winds picked up so the retardant bombers couldn't fly, and the helicopters dumping water can't keep up with the trees exploding into flames, shooting flames hundreds of feet into the air. As the days and nights went by, the sky became black with smoke, your nose burned and the wind carried it toward our home. It lay over the valley as a grim reminder that it was a dry and unfruitful summer. The river is a trickle, never have we seen it so low. And the mountain sides are brown with no feed for the cattle to graze on for the summer. A few days later it had traveled over 15 miles and is now coming toward my home. They closed off our road to our home. And brought in men from all over, but the most harm it seems is they are fighting fire with fire, and on a usual year that might work, but this year, it is plain crazy. They start a back fire and it got out of control. Now you can travel for 20 miles and see the whole mountainside on fire as far as you can see. The fire can jump a 4-lane highway. The smoke's so thick that you can't breathe, the sky is a brown red and engulfs everything and it's almost eerie. How did this happen to our beautiful country?

Neighbors are calling and offering their horse trailers to move our stuff from the house as the fire creeps ever closer to us, only a couple ridges over. The Helicopters are working furiously all hours, as they sweep down and scoop water out of the Clark Fork River or they use the huge helicopters that have the tanks in the belly. They hover over the water just feet from touching as the large vacuum hose sits in the water and sucks up hundreds of gallons, the trees lay over from the strong winds, the water swirling around spraying everything within a hundred yard radius. They take off over my head as the water that is caught in the hose sprays everything underneath it. I watch them fly over the fire and dump, and return again. I am so worried, for my home has no insurance on it, because we live to far from a fire station, it's log, we have a volunteer fire department. Wood stove, we had a shingle roof, but then put a green metal roof, but still insurance companies turn us down. So I sit here wondering if all our hard work and our whole life are going up in smoke. What do you save? Pictures, genealogy, grandma's antiques, crafts, and things you love. I just don't know.

Loggers are put to work making fire lines, only to almost get caught in the wild fire and it engulfs their machinery as they try to stop the monster from burning everything in sight. Our friends had to jump and run, to save their own life, as the fire turned and came back on them. Thousands of dollars of equipment charred, but at least no lives this time.

I received a letter **If you have to Evacuate**. It stated: We wouldn't be asking you to do this if we didn't have to, so please help us by being prepared.

If this is your preliminary notice, then you have some time to:
1. Get your sprinklers set up in your yard and on the roof if necessary
2. Load your irreplaceable items in your car or pick-up so you are ready to leave quickly.
3. Load other items in your car that you will need for however long you could be in a shelter or with friends and family
4. Move domestic animals and their food to a safe location.

When you get order to leave:

5. Close and lock your windows and doors and take down your curtains. If possible put plywood over the windows.
6. If you have a propane tank, turn off the gas at the tank.
7. Turn off electrical appliances except for refrigerator and freezer.
8. Remove all flammable materials from the home, garage, shop, barn, etc.
9. Tie a white cloth to the front door as you leave.
10. Leave ladder to the roof against the house.
11. Turn on sprinkler system.

The fire fighters really concentrate on the homes. They have people that will help you get what you can, and then try to save your home from the danger that lies ahead, if the fire reaches you they spray a fire retardant, that's made from the stuff they fill disposable diapers with, and then they said they seal the moisture in with a shaving cream mixture. I was praying that my log house was not going to need this. Ranchers brought over pumper trucks and parked them in our yard. If the fire burned the power lines our water would be nonexistent and then so would our home. So our good neighbors and friends rallied and helped us where they could.

Calls come in everyday, some for encouragement, others to say that they heard that we were going to be evacuated, that the fire was not going to miss us, so be prepared, and pack up what you know you can't replace. Just like I said before, where do you start, do my memories end here? What is more important or what do I want to burn?

I watch the cloud of smoke that seeps through the windows and doors; everything smells like we have been in a campfire. I can't explain my emotions, my house, my home, and my life.... I just wait and water, we clear everything around the house and we keep everything wet, burning embers fall through the air and land on the house and deck, everything is covered with a gray ash, house, cars, land, flowers, you name it.

Our grandchildren come and help water. We have to keep Nana and big Grandpa's house safe. Everything is covered with water, especially the grandkids and us. Not knowing what or when is hard. Is our life in this home going to end here?

The helicopter pictured below flew for weeks over the mountains around us and dropped a thousand gallons at a time on the fire. Then flew back to the river, and filled his tanks, they worked for 3 weeks of doing this, the sound of these huge helicopters whipping the air, became part of our life. They worked 16 hrs a day. Joseph and Melanie were in awe of how big this helicopter was, as I drove them down the road and close to the fire to see this huge monster. What does a 3 and 4 year old think of all this? Melanie was outside and felt the wind come up, dropped to her knees and asked Heavenly Father to please stop the wind because when it blows it makes the fire come closer to Nana's house, and we don't want it to burn up..

One day in tears, I told my daughter, Tiffany, I didn't want my home to burn and she said, "Mom, Heavenly Father turned the fires and saved the logging equipment, what makes you think he wouldn't save your home? Especially after all you've been through to live here and never give up? Just have Faith!"

We were so thankful that we had the helicopters here and the river so close that they could get water from, to help slow the fire from peaking over the mountain, and destroying our home. The fire almost contained has moved back in

the mountains behind us. I thank my Heavenly Father for saving my home, as he turned the fire, and subdued the winds. Moisture has come to parched Montana and surrounding states. Rain has been a great gift from God. A blessing from Heaven showered down on the good people of Montana,
 Thank you dear Father in Heaven.

Afterward

Well I guess I'm about done telling you about building a house in Montana, and the trials we faced. Today I think things would be easier, the winters are not as bad.

Either we are used to them or the volcano changed the weather. Money has helped make life easier, and kids are married and now we have grandkids.

Dustin has a wife and 4 kids and has reached his lifetime goal as a Pediatrician. I'm so proud that he didn't give up; he stuck to his dream and worked to get it.

Nathan is a School teacher here in Drummond, teaches Spanish and Technology and is currently working on his Master's degree. I admire my kids for doing what they could to get through school and make something of themselves. Nathan has a wife and 3 kids.

Tiffany, went to College and played College ball, to help her get her degree, and then married a hometown Rancher. She is a hard worker helping her husband on their ranch, and has 4 little ranch hands to chase cows and fix irrigation ditches.

I marvel at how far my 3 kids have come. And their determination, I think having a hard life has taught them compassion, and hard work.

Bill and I are still in our home we built and love every log and crack, it's still not finished, the upstairs still leaves something to be desired, but the cats keep the mice down now, and we just enjoy the 11 grand kids.

This is just a short portion of our life. But just a word to the **wise,** If you build a house, **finish it before you move in, and make sure you have water, toilet, and a good rain proof roof...** And **don't build on a mountain** unless you **love to see the beauty of Montana.**

Printed in the United States
26667LVS00001B/37-42